IMAGE AND IDENTITY
The Making and Re-making of Scotland
Through the Ages

edited by
DAUVIT BROUN, R. J. FINLAY AND MICHAEL LYNCH

JOHN DONALD PUBLISHERS LTD
EDINBURGH

British Library Cataloguing in Publication Data
A catalogue record for this book is available from the
British Library.

Printed and bound in Great Britain by
Bell & Bain Ltd, Glasgow

Contents

Contributors

Dauvit Broun
Dept. of Scottish History, University of Glasgow

Ewen A. Cameron
Dept. of Scottish History, University of Edinburgh

Helen Corr
Dept. of Sociology, University of Strathclyde

Edward J. Cowan
Professor of Scottish History, University of Glasgow

Carol Edington
Dept. of Scottish History, University of St Andrews

Richard J. Finlay
Research Centre in Scottish History, University of Strathclyde

Michael Lynch
Professor of Scottish History, University of Edinburgh

Catriona M. M. Macdonald
Dept. of History, Caledonian University

Graeme Morton
Dept. of Social and Economic History, University of Edinburgh

Fiona Watson
Dept. of History, University of Stirling

John R. Young
Research Centre in Scottish History, University of Strathclyde

INTRODUCTION

Scottish Identity and the Historian

Dauvit Broun, Michael Lynch & Richard Finlay

A history of Scotland which focuses on Scottish identity, rather than on the more traditional concerns of Scotland's institutional and political development, is faced with a particular challenge. Instead of dealing with Scotland as a single concrete entity, such as a kingdom, it is necessary to confront a variety of Scotlands thrown up by the different ways in which images of Scotland and Scottishness have been created and recreated in the past. At times this variety has resulted in ambiguity, if not open conflict, in what Scotland and being Scottish was understood to mean to Scots themselves. National identity is not a static phenomenon. It changes and reinvents itself. Consequently, Scotland and Scottishness have meant different things to different people at different times. It is the purpose of this volume to examine some of the varieties of Scottishness and Scotlands which have existed throughout the ages.

In many ways, the middle ages are the crucible in which Scottish identity was forged. Dauvit Broun argues that the idea of Scotland as a single country corresponding to the realm of the king of Scots, and of the Scots as all the kingdom's inhabitants, may only have taken root during the thirteenth century. It is too easy to use the gift of hindsight to gloss over the complexities which were experienced by contemporaries. The Wars of Independence have entered into Scottish folklore as the nation's finest hour. Yet, as Fiona Watson points out, there was no single patriotic path in this period. Although Bruce went on to emerge as the nation's saviour, this was not necessarily apparent to contemporaries. History remembers the victors, but King Robert's actions were, in the context of their own time, highly controversial. The simplistic notion that the Scottish aristocracy were a fractious bunch who were only out for themselves is standard historical fare. Yet, viewed from the perspective that the Bruce's actions were violent and unconstitutional at a time when it was not known what the final outcome would be, the hesitancy and confusion of Bruce's opponents becomes more understandable.

Ideas are central to identity. As Ted Cowan shows, the Declaration of Arbroath was a complex mixture of history, rhetoric and politics. Scottish history was reworked to provide the template for the justification of the Wars of Independence. For many, ideological warfare was just as important as combat in the field as it provided the justification for action. The ideas to sustain and vindicate the cause of Scottish freedom and the Bruce kingship were a crucial element in defining the nation and were ones which resonated throughout Scottish history. Armed with ideological justification, the kingdom needed soldiers to defend such ideals. As Carol Edington points out, the influence of chivalric ideals in Scotland could be married to the military needs of the nation, although a knight's quest for personal honour did not always square with the patriotic cause. With the ever present danger of English aggression, Scotland needed heroic defenders and much endeavour went into building up the cult of the Scottish patriot. It was an amalgam of the ideological and the practical. The cult provided inspiration and example which contemporaries were urged to emulate.

As the Covenanting Wars of the seventeenth century clearly demonstrated, religion and nationalism were an explosive mixture. But, as Michael Lynch argues, the Reformation in Scotland was a protracted process and the reinvention of Scotland in its Presbyterian garb took much longer than conventional wisdom allows. Indeed, the Scotland of John Knox took several generations to mature and the period was marked by a profusion of competing claims, all of whom claimed to be the true heirs of the nation's inheritance. Nor was this unique to Scotland and a comparison with other European countries shows that the Scots were just one of the many nations who claimed to be God's chosen people. Institutions were not only part of the state apparatus, they often provided an important focal point for the expression of national identity. As John Young points out, the Scottish parliament has been much neglected by historians, most of whom have castigated it for its weakness. According to new research, however, this is not the case and one of the key features of the parliament's development in the period after 1603 was its growing power. This is borne out by comparing it to other European institutions and it was one of the principal reasons for its demise in 1707.

The eighteenth century marks a period of transition in Scottish national identity. Whereas many of the definitions and ideas of Scotland were confined to the political elite, the socio-economic forces which swept Scotland in this period meant that the opinions and ideas of more and more Scots become more audible to the historian. Yet, as Richard Finlay points out, the period is marked by a variety of often competing Scottish identities and the emergence of the British state as a complicating factor in the equation. Again problems of hindsight abound and while Britain grew into a national concept, this was not necessarily apparent to contemporaries at the time who were bound up more with their own difficulties in trying to adapt Scottish identity to a rapidly changing society. Conventional wisdom over what is and what is not nationalism is challenged by Graeme Morton who explores Scottish civil society in the nineteenth century. Crude expectations that Scotland should have risen up and broken the shackles of English domination are dismissed and Morton illustrates how nineteenth century Scots had a very clear idea of themselves without resorting to the extremities of nationalist insurrection. In short, the Union did not necessarily compromise Scottish national identity.

The modern era, because of the availability of sources, enables the complexities of identity to be further examined. As Ewen Cameron shows, the Highlanders of the nineteenth century had their own sense of historical identity which they used in pursuit of political objectives. Catriona MacDonald demonstrates, local identity is of great importance in defining how people perceive themselves. Indeed, the power of the locality is central to the ebb and flow of politics in this period. Finally, Helen Corr demonstrates the unusual combination of gender and national identity. While much of the construction of national identity was geared towards men, the Scottish education system promoted a gender identity for women which did not work to their benefit. The belief that the Scottish education system was egalitarian can not be sustained because it deliberately treated women as unequal.

Readers may wonder why there is no specific chapter on the twentieth century. In part this is due to a lack of space, but more importantly, it was decided that as the century draws to an end readers may like to ponder for themselves what it means to be Scottish. After all, this is your century and it is your identity!

CHAPTER ONE

Defining Scotland and the Scots Before the Wars of Independence[1]

Dauvit Broun

However strange past images of Scotland and the Scots may seem to today's eyes, some basic features have remained recognisable for centuries. In particular, the idea that Scotland is defined territorially by the geographical limits of the kingdom, and the notion that the Scots are the people of Scotland, appear so obvious that they barely seem to justify comment. Before the mid-thirteenth century, however, even these fundamentals would not have been familiar. For those living within the kingdom's bounds at that time 'Scotland' and 'Scots' usually meant something quite different. To make matters even more confusing from a modern viewpoint, there was no agreement—even among the literate few—about where they thought Scotland was. The most dramatic illustration of this is that it was possible in 1214 for someone to refer to 'Scotland' as limited to the area north of the Forth and south of Moray,[2] but for someone else in 1216 to write unambiguously of 'Scotland' as including Galloway in the south-west and the Merse in the extreme south-east.[3]

It might seem tempting to dismiss such variation as something awkward, rather like the miriad unstandardised weights and measures of the pre-industrial age, which need only concern the specialist. This would be a mistake. If contemporary definitions of 'Scotland' and 'Scots' are taken into account it is possible to gain new perspectives on Scotland's early development, as well as achieve a more general appreciation of how even such basic terms can be flexible and adaptable.

It must be admitted that defining Scotland and the Scots hardly seems to be much of a problem according to the generally established contours of how Scotland first took shape in this period. From the beginning, we are told, there were Scots (originating from Ireland) who settled in Argyll around the year 500 AD as a branch of the Ulster kingdom of Dál Riata. Around the year 843 Cinaed mac Alpin ('Kenneth I'), king of Dál Riata, became king of the Picts and so formed the kingdom of Scotland by uniting Picts and Scots. Scotland's kings are therefore numbered from Cinaed (Kenneth) onwards. In the process the Scots overwhelmed the Picts, who subsequently vanished. The kingdom expanded southwards, taking Edinburgh in the reign of Illulb mac Constantin (954-62), and incorporating 'Strathclyde' after its last king died (probably) in 1018. The Scottish king at that time, Mael Coluim mac Cinaeda ('Malcolm

II') (1005-34), therefore, sometimes vies with Cinaed mac Alpin as the first king of a 'united' Scotland.[4] Throughout such an account 'Scotland' is defined as the Scotland of today, progressively 'unified' first of all when 'Kenneth I' overran the Picts and (allegedly) began to rule most of Scotland, and then finally when his successors gained control over what remained of mainland Scotland. The Scots, in turn, are ultimately the people whose kings conquered the Picts and expanded their realm into southern Scotland. Bede referred to them (while they were still confined to Argyll) as *Scoti*, so any quibble about the matter would apparently seem unnecessary. In short, Scotland is seen first-and-foremost as a concrete reality—the medieval kingdom and, ultimately, the present-day country.

No-one would deny that the early development of the Scottish kingdom is a fundamental part of Scottish history. There is an important distinction to be made, however, between the kingdom on the one hand and, on the other hand, the 'Scotland' understood by contemporaries before the wars of independence. As noted already, it was possible for someone nearly two-hundred years after 1018 to see 'Scotland' as only part of the area ruled by the king of Scots. If contemporaries did not automatically equate 'Scotland' with the kingdom, it must be asked whether by doing so ourselves we may be losing sight of an important aspect of Scotland's history in this period. Moreover, giving insufficient weight to contemporary definitions can lead to distortion. The use of 'Scots' by modern historians to refer both to the kingdom's inhabitants in the time of Wallace as well as the people from Argyll who (we are told) overwhelmed the Picts, threatens to obscure how the meaning of *Scoti* changed fundamentally in this period, and actually meant 'Irish/Gaels' in Bede's day. Indeed, 'Scots' as a general term for the kingdom's inhabitants does not appear to have gained universal acceptance in written sources until the late thirteenth century.[5] Neither does the generally accepted view of Scotland's origins do justice to the insistence of contemporary record that the Picts were the people of the kingdom for at least a generation after 'Kenneth I'.[6] Because the usual outline of Scotland's early history is not sensitive to how people in the Scottish kingdom at the time defined themselves and defined Scotland territorially, it actually fails to address the early development of 'Scotland'—as distinct from the kingdom. It therefore risks giving insufficient attention to a significant dimension of Scotland's formative period as a society. The question of how contemporaries in the Scottish kingdom defined 'Scotland' and 'Scots' in this period can not, however, be given a simple answer, and this essay will not attempt to cover all aspects of the subject. Also, the issue of how the kingdom itself was identified will not be discussed fully. It may be noted, however, that in charters from the 1160s onwards the entire realm of David I's successors was increasingly referred to as 'kingdom of Scots' or 'kingdom of Scotland',[7] which brings us back to the question of how 'Scotland' and 'Scots' were defined in this period.

Everyone who studies Scottish history in the twelfth and early thirteenth centuries is accustomed to referring to the country north of the Forth as 'Scotia'. This is justified by an abundance of contemporary references. Before the mid-thirteenth century, however, *Scotia* could be understood as the area north of the Forth, south of Moray and east of the central highlands. A topographical description of Scotland (dating to sometime between 1202 and 1214) referred to the mountain-range running north from Ben Lomond and Breadalbane as 'the mountains which divide *Scotia* from Argyll';[8] a charter of David I relating to Urquhart Priory addressed the 'worthy men of Moray and *Scotia*';[9] and, in a section of *Gesta Annalia* (attributed to John of Fordun) which probably reflected the words of a contemporary source, William I is described as returning 'from Moray to *Scotia*' in 1214.[10] *Scotia* was not always the preferred term in Latin; another term, *Albania*, is also found in writings of the twelfth and thirteenth centuries.[11] *Albania* was simply a Latinised version of Gaelic *Alba*, 'Scotland'. It is noteworthy, therefore, that *Alba* itself was once applied to the area between the Forth, Moray and the central highlands.[12]

Now, Gaelic *Alba* and Latin *Scotia*, if used today, would normally be translated 'Scotland'. There has been an unwillingness, however, to translate them so unless they referred to an area more or less equivalent to modern Scotland. Instead, the *Scotia* (or *Alba*) of the twelfth century tends to be called simply 'Scotia' or 'Alba'—no doubt with the aim of avoiding confusion. In writing about this period in English a distinction has therefore been drawn which reserves 'Scotland' for what is recognisable in today's terms as Scotland. Such a distinction, however, is impossible in medieval Latin or in Gaelic (the native language of the great majority of medieval Scots before the wars of independence): *Alba*, of course, is the only term available in Gaelic, and *Scotia* (or *Albania*) is all that is available in Latin. The best way to reflect contemporary terminology, therefore, would be to translate *Alba* or *Scotia/Albania* as 'Scotland', even if it denoted only part of what is now Scotland. In this way it would be easier to appreciate that, from the perspective of contemporary usage, 'Scotland' already existed as a territorial term before it was redefined during the course of the thirteenth century to include most of modern Scotland.

It would be too simple, however, to say that 'Scotland' meant one thing before the early thirteenth century, and then changed into something else. It is important to emphasise that before this change occurred there was, in fact, a striking variety in what 'Scotland' could mean. The region between the Forth,

Moray and the central highlands was only the most restricted definition of 'Scotland': indeed, in the contemporary 'Scottish' section of the Holyrood chronicle (1150-89) it is possible that 'Scotland' was used in a rather general way which included the area south of the Forth.[13] Such variation in meaning is even apparent in a single text. In the topographical tract referred to earlier (datable to 1202x1214), 'Scotland' is described in detail as either the entire mainland north of the Forth and Clyde (though not Caithness), or the mainland north of the Forth, but not including either Argyll or the Lennox.[14]

This is not to say that the variety was endless. For most of the period before the wars of independence there were, however, at least two 'Scotlands': a 'lesser Scotland' (the area between the Forth, Moray and the central highlands) and a 'greater Scotland', which imprecisely included most of the mainland north of the Rivers Forth and Clyde. The equation of 'Scotland' with the whole area ruled by the king of Scots was, at best, only embryonic before the thirteenth century. Although no specific examples of the idea of 'lesser Scotland' can be cited later than 1214, it may be noted that chroniclers at Melrose, in a passage relating to Scoto-Norwegian diplomacy of 1265, referred to the Hebrides as 'the tiny islands lying around the full kingdom (*ampla regio*) of the Scots'.[15] This equation of mainland Scotland with the kingdom at it fullest extent seems to echo the idea of 'greater Scotland' as distinct from 'lesser Scotland'.

The most difficult of these 'Scotlands' to grasp is doubtless 'lesser Scotland'. How could it happen that 'Scotland' once referred to an area approximately only a quarter of the landmass of Scotland today? The most likely answer is that this was probably the original extent of 'Scotland' when this term was first coined in Gaelic as *Alba*. This sits uneasily with the long-accepted view that *Alba* simply denoted the kingdom created as a consequence of a 'union between Picts and 'Scots' under Cinaed mac Alpin *ca* 843. In the only sources likely to reflect contemporary usage, however, it was not until 900 that *Alba* replaced 'Pictland'.[16] Two texts, moreover, suggest that one way in which *Alba* was understood in the tenth and eleventh centuries was as equivalent to 'Pictland'. The Scottish chronicle in the Poppleton manuscript, which may have originally been compiled during the reign of Illulb mac Constantin (954-62), presents Cinaed mac Alpin and his successors as rulers of Pictland;[17] and a Gaelic stanza on Cruithne's seven sons, which may probably be dated to some time before the mid-eleventh century, uses *Alba* for the territory of the Picts.[18] If it was possible to conceive of *Alba* as Pictland by another name, then it may be wondered whether the switch from 'Pictland' to *Alba ca* 900 may have signified first-and-foremost a recasting of the Pictish kingship shorn of its Pictish ethnic label.

If the new-fangled 'kings of *Alba*' in the tenth century saw themselves as kings of Pictland by another name, however, this would have been little more than a fiction as far as the Scandinavian-controlled north was concerned, or Moray whose rulers appear to have regarded themselves as kings in their own right.[19] In reality, therefore, it is likely that kings of *Alba* consistently controlled only the area between the Forth, Moray and the central highlands—in other words, 'lesser Scotland'. The application of 'Scotland' to this area suggests, therefore, that what I have termed 'lesser Scotland' may be recognised as 'Scotland proper'—the original core of the kingdom of *Alba*, 'Scotland', in the tenth century. From the beginning, however, there were probably two 'Scotlands': 'Scotland proper', where the kings' rule was well established, and a 'greater Scotland' over which they might have hoped to rule, and only partially and sporadically achieved a loose overlordship.[20] This may not be the whole story, however. It is striking how these two 'Scotlands' seem for centuries to have been unaffected by the successful expansion of the kingdom's territory southwards after the mid-tenth century.

The way in which contemporary perceptions of 'Scotland' developed before the wars of independence, therefore, can offer a different outline for Scotland's early history than that given by concentrating on the kingdom itself. Scotland 'begins' *ca* 900, rather than *ca* 843; but it only becomes something close to its modern meaning in the thirteenth century, rather than the early eleventh. Scotland's early history can be seen to revolve around two critical periods of change *ca* 900 and the thirteenth century—when, it may be assumed, a combination of political and social factors led those (at least) who had some stake in the kingdom to experience society in a decisively novel way. Once this is recognised, work can begin on identifying what underlying political and social forces may have been involved.[21] An appreciation of contemporary definitions of 'Scotland' can assist our understanding of Scottish history up to the thirteenth century in other ways. For instance, 'Scotland proper' may be seen as the historic core of the kingdom whose allegiance David I and his successors could be most confident of keeping, introducing knights and new monastic foundations more gradually than in other areas under their direct control while leaving much of the top rank of society undisturbed. Certainly, the kings' relationship with 'Scotland proper' was quite different from other Gaelic areas such as Moray and the north, Argyll, the Isles, and Galloway, which were forcibly brought more firmly under royal control. It makes more sense to see risings in these areas in the twelfth and early thirteenth centuries as attempts to resist the dominance of kings of Scots than as part of a general Gaelic reaction to the introduction of foreign personnel and influence.[22]

As might be expected, contemporaries generally indentified Scots as the inhabitants of 'Scotland'—which meant that Scots could be viewed as the natives of either 'Scotland proper' or 'greater Scotland', as defined above. 'Scots' in either of these senses was used (for example) by chroniclers at Melrose (in the eastern borders) describing events of 1216 and 1235.[23] It is striking, however, that when a Melrose chronicler (writing as late as 1285x91) recorded the successful negotiations with Norway in 1265-6 conducted by a fellow monk of Melrose, Reginald of Roxburgh, he was happy to regard him as a Scot, although (judging by his name) Reginald presumably originated from near Melrose many miles south of the Forth.[24] This may be taken to indicate that, at some stage in the second half of the thirteenth century, all the kingdom's inhabitants identified themselves as 'Scots' regardless of where they originated from in the kingdom or whether they were of native or immigrant stock. It would appear from the Chronicle of Melrose, therefore, that although monks at Melrose began to consider their own area (and Galloway) as part of 'Scotland' from 1216, it was another fifty years or more before they also regarded themselves as 'Scots'.[25]

If we turn back to *ca* 900 we find that at the same time as 'Scotland' (Gaelic *Alba*) first comes to view as a replacement for 'Pictland', so also the Gaelic for 'Scots'—*Albanaig* or *fir Alban* (literally 'inhabitants/men of *Alba*')—first appears in contemporary record in 918, replacing 'Picts' who are last mention in these sources in 875.[26] Presumably the Gaelic-speakers of 'Scotland proper' in the tenth century were the first people to think of themselves as 'Scots' in any way ancestral to today's sense, although it was not until the thirteenth century that people saw themselves as 'Scots' in something closely resembling modern usage.

'Scots' before the thirteenth century, therefore, is as difficult a term to the modern mind as 'Scotland' in the same period. Moreover, it is surely rather misleading to talk in English of the 'Scots' before the tenth century. As noted before, modern references to 'Scots' in Argyll up to the ninth century appear to follow contemporary writers (for example, Bede) who described them as *Scoti*. In fact, however, *Scoti* in this period was applied regularly to the Irish as well. Bede and other early-medieval writers understood *Scoti* to mean 'Gaels/Irish'—the inhabitants of Ireland as well as colonies in Britain such as Argyll. Now, the Gaelic speakers in the tenth century who first saw themselves as *Albanaig*, 'Scots', made a clear distinction in their own language between being *Goídil*, 'Gaels/Irish', and *Albanaig*. Here, then, is an example of where contemporary usage can offer a welcome release from the unnecessary muddle caused if *Scoti* in a Scottish context is translated 'Scots' willy-nilly. It would be easier, as well as more accurate, to refer to 'Gaels' or 'Irish' when this is what was meant at the time, and reserve 'Scots' for the inhabitants of the 'Scotlands' which came into being *ca* 900.

The first Scots (according to this definition), as Gaelic speakers, identified themselves ethnically as Gaels, and doubtless placed themselves alongside other Gaelic peoples such as *Fir Muman* (Munstermen), *Lagin* (Leinstermen) or *Ulaid* (Ulstermen) who also formed territorially coherent groups on a scale comparable to 'Scotland proper'. Moreover, according to the tenth-century edition of *Senchus fer nAlban*, 'History of the Men of Scotland', they continued to look upon themselves as settlers from Ireland.[27] Not only were they (or, at the very least, their *literati*) conscious of being one people with their fellow Gaelic-speakers in Ireland, but they also looked to Ireland as their ancestral home. This corresponded with cultural and historical reality: literate Gaels wrote and recited essentially the same kind of Gaelic from Munster to Buchan, and Ireland was, in fact, where Scotland's Gaelic culture originated from. If all this is taken together, it can hardly be denied that in English 'Gaels' can just as well be termed 'Irish'—for this was no more or less than how Scots (or at least those who were men of letters) in this period conceived of their ethnicity.

Now, it might be expected that this identification with Ireland and the Irish would have died out fairly soon among the upper echelons of society in 'Scotland proper' once Gaelic lost favour and status in the twelfth and thirteenth centuries. From what I have been able to find out about accounts of Scottish origins written in the thirteenth century, however, this was not the case.[28] On the contrary, not only did accounts of Scottish origins continue to repeat the umbilical link with Ireland, but there were two accounts—one certainly and the other probably written in the thirteenth century—which actively sought to make the Irish connection more emphatic. One restructured its source to make Ireland the divinely-ordained homeland of the *Scoti*; the other climaxed with the colonisation of Ireland as their sure and perpetual home. Another account identified the Stone of Scone with Tara and the kingship of Ireland. None of these accounts can be attributed convincingly to a scholarly Gael: indeed, they display a striking ignorance of Irish historical learning which suggests that their authors can have had no direct literary contact with Gaelic Ireland. Taken together, these accounts imply that Gaelic—or, rather, Irish—identity retained its vitality in thirteenth-century Scotland even among *literati* who had lost any meaningful contact with the Gaelic culture once shared from Buchan to Bantry Bay. In particular, it appears that the view of Ireland as their homeland was not simply repeated passively, but could be actively promoted. As far as our understanding of the Latin term *Scoti* is concerned, therefore, this seems bewildering to us only if 'Scots' and 'Irish' are deemed to be mutually exclusive: in fact, *Scoti* when applied in this period to the inhabitants of 'Scotland' seems simply to have reflected a continuing Irish identity.[29]

It is not, in fact, until the wars of independence that an account of Scottish origins can be found which makes Scotland, not Ireland, the Scottish homeland. In Baldred Bisset's *Pleading* (1301) the eponymous Scota actually arrives in Scotland itself, and Ireland becomes no more than a stop for reinforcements on the way.[30] The equally abbreviated sketch of Scottish origins in the Declaration of Arbroath (1320) goes further still, and fails to mention Ireland at all.[31] A more extensive text is a verse-history of the Scots from origins to conquest in 1296, written sometime between 1296 and 1306:[32] this stated that the ancient ancestors of the Scots only assumed the name 'Scots' once they arrived in Scotland from Ireland. It appears, then, that the idea of the Scots as a wholly individual and distinct people on a par with the Irish, English or Welsh was not articulated until the wars of independence.

This would not have been possible, however, without the decisive appearance by the mid-thirteenth century of a simple and self-contained Scottish identity as a country and a people defined by the kingdom itself. It is often judiciously observed that the kingdom of David I and his successors was a hybrid realm.[33] Not only did it include a variety of ethnic groups—English, Flemings, French, Gaels, and Welsh (from the old kingdom of 'Strathclyde')—but it also encompassed a diversity of regions, such as Lothian, Galloway, Argyll, Moray, and 'Scotland proper' itself, a number of which were ruled by their own kings during David I's reign. The question of how or when this hybrid realm gelled into a single country and people which withstood catastrophe and conquest during the wars of independence necessarily involves a consideration of the kingdom's institutional and political development—but this alone will not provide a satisfactory answer. A crucial consideration must also be the way the kingdom and its people were conceived by the kingdom's inhabitants themselves. This would include an idea such as the 'community of the realm' which came to prominence during the crisis following Alexander III's death;[34] the history of saints' cults (notably of St Andrew and St Margaret) should also be taken into account. At its most fundamental, however, it means addressing the issue of how Scots themselves defined 'Scotland' and 'Scots', which shows when the idea prevailed of a country and people corresponding to the kingdom, and from what this idea developed.[35]

Such an approach serves to emphasise the key point that Scotland and the Scots are, first-and-foremost, images which have been adapted and recreated according to the experiences and aspirations of the society to which they related. It would not be a surprise, moreover, if a more detailed examination of what Scotland signified in this period revealed that different aspects were emphasised by different groups. Certainly, Fiona Watson has shown how the assumptions about Scotland which motivated those who fought in the first war of independence did not always coincide.[36] It is important, therefore, not only to trace how contemporaries defined Scotland and the Scots, but to ask who identified with which image.

It is extremely difficult to address this issue in the source-starved middle ages, however. All that can usually be said is that there is often only direct evidence for those whose writings survive who (regardless of whether they were a secular clerk or a cloistered cleric) are likely to reflect views current among at least a significant group of society's movers and shakers. A clean and consistent view is not usually apparent, as we have seen with regard to different ideas of Scotland's territorial extent.

It is even more difficult to gauge how the average 'person in the field' defined Scotland and Scots in this period. This is not entirely impossible, however. There are place-names which mention an *Albanach*—a 'Scot'—outside the bounds of 'Scotland proper'. In Argyll, for instance, there is *Beinn an Albannaich*, 'hill of the Scot', and the mountain *Stob Coir' an Albanaich*, '*stob* of the corrie of the Scot'.[37] Presumably such names were coined by people 'on the ground' who considered a Scot to be unusual: if they had thought of themselves as Scots, then it would hardly have been sensible for them to distinguish a feature of their landscape in this way. Moreover, there is other place-name evidence which suggests that the idea of 'Scotland proper' was generally well known by those outside its bounds. W. J. Watson has noted, for instance, how two rivers in Breadalbane called *Lòchá* are distinguished from each other by one, flowing east, being called *Lòchá Albanaich*, 'Scottish *Lòchá*', while the other, flowing west, is called *Lòchá Urchaidh*, 'the *Lòchá* of Orchy' (after the locality where it is found).[38] These Gaelic place-names show that the people of the area (who presumably coined them) did not consider themselves part of 'Scotland'.

It is striking, indeed, how the evidence for what I have called 'Scotland proper' is predominantly found in incidental references and place-names, while 'greater Scotland' appears in learned texts (such as the topographical account written 1202x1214). It is conceivable, therefore, that the sense of a 'greater Scotland' was predominantly learned and literary, though it probably also served a political function as a justification for claims to rule all the territory north of the Firths of Forth and Clyde.

Be this as it may, the study of contemporary perceptions of Scotland and the Scots serves to emphasise that the emergence of Scotland in this period is not simply about the creation and expansion of a kingdom, but is also the history of an idea which people have engaged with, recreated and adapted. This, in turn, offers a new dimension to our understanding of Scotland's early development, and points to critical periods of changing perceptions which, it may be surmised, reflect important shifts in how the more significant groups among Scotland's inhabitants experienced being part of its society. Not only does Scotland in this way seem a much more malleable and responsive phenomenon than it would be if regarded chiefly as a concrete entity like a kingdom; it becomes the property of people's identity rather than the object of kings and governments. As a result, the existence of more than one 'Scotland' before the thirteenth century can be seen as only one example of how Scotland can at any given time mean different things to different people, or even different things to the same people.

NOTES

[1] This is an almost completely rewritten version of a paper with this title which appeared in the pre-circulated (and unpublished) proceedings of the Association of Scottish Historical Studies conference *Nationalism and Identity: The Search for Scotland*, organised by Ewen Cameron and Fiona Watson, held at St Andrews on April 6-7, 1994.

[2] *Johannis de Fordun Chronica Gentis Scotorum*, ed. W. F. Skene, 2 vols (Edinburgh, 1871-2) [hereafter *Chron. Fordun*], i, 279, describing how William I in 1214 *de Moravia rediit in Scocia, de Scocia vero profectus in Laudoniam*, 'returned to Scotland from Moray, then went into Lothian'.

[3] *The Chronicle of Melrose from the Cottoniam Manuscript, Faustina B ix in the British Museum: a complete and full-size facsimile in collotype*, with intro. by Alan Orr Anderson and Marjorie Ogilvie Anderson, and index by William Croft Dickinson (London, 1936) [hereafter *Chron. Melrose*], [62], described towns in the Merse as 'in the southern part of Scotland' when King John of England wasted them in 1216; at [64], Galloway is described as 'in the western part of Scotland' in an account of a supernatural event witnessed there in 1216.

[4] Michael Lynch, *Scotland: A New History* (London, 1991), 49. Another view is that Scotland began when the kingdom expanded south of the Forth under King Illulb: A. A. M. Duncan, 'The making of the kingdom', in *Why Scottish History Matters?*, ed. R. Mitchison (Edinburgh, 1991), 7: see also the same author's, 'The kingdom of the Scots', in *The Making of Britain: The Dark Ages*, ed. L. M. Smith (London, 1984), 135.

[5] see below, p. 9.

[6] see below, p. 9.

[7] G. W. S. Barrow, *The Anglo-Norman Era in Scottish History* (Oxford, 1980), 153-4, where it is pointed out that another phrase which was used increasingly in this period was 'kingdom of the king of Scots' (or 'land of the king of Scots'): presumably 'kingdom of Scots' (or 'of Scotland') functioned as shorter forms of this more cumbersome phrase.

[8] *montes qui dividunt Scociam ab Arregai<t>hel*: M. O. Anderson, *Kings and Kingship in Early Scotland* (2nd edn, Edinburgh, 1980), 241-3 (at 241). The tract

(known as *De situ Albanie*) is translated in A. O. Anderson, *Early Sources of Scottish History A.D. 500-1286*, 2 vols (Edinburgh, 1922) [hereafter *ESSH*], i, cxv-cxviii. Marjorie Anderson (*Kings and Kingship*, 140) argues for a date of composition between 1165 and 1184: for the dating between 1202 and 1214, see Molly Miller, 'Matriliny by treaty: the Pictish foundation-legend', in *Ireland in Medieval Europe: studies in memory of Kathleen Hughes*, edd. D. Whitelock, R. McKitterick and D. N. Dumville (Cambridge, 1982), 138.

[9]Archibald C. Lawrie, *Early Scottish Charters prior to A.D. 1153* (Glasgow, 1905), no.110: see also *Regesta Regum Scottorum* vol.i, *The Acts of Malcolm IV*, ed. G. W. S. Barrow (Edinburgh, 1960), 43.

[10]See n. 2, above. For the use of contemporary material in *Gesta Annalia* relating to other royal events in 1214, see W. W. Scott, 'Fordun's description of the inauguration of Alexander II', *SHR*, 50 (1971), 200.

[11]E.g. the account of Alexander III's inauguration in *Chron. Fordun*, i, 294-5, written no later than 1249. *Albania* was also the title of the dukedom (usually rendered in English 'Albany') bestowed on Robert, second son of Robert II, in 1398: the use of *Albania* here is usually regarded as an antiquarian revival; see *Scotichronicon by Walter Bower in Latin and English*, gen ed. D. E. R. Watt, 9 vols (Aberdeen/Edinburgh, 1987-) [hereafter *Chron. Bower* (Watt)], viii, 154 (at l.45); Stephen Boardman, *The Early Stewart Kings: Robert II and Robert III 1371-1406* (East Linton, 1996), 193 n.107.

[12]W. J. Watson, *The History of the Celtic Place-Names of Scotland* (Edinburgh, 1926), 12-13.

[13]*A Scottish Chronicle known as the Chronicle of Holyrood*, ed. Marjorie Ogilvie Anderson with some additional notes by Alan Orr Anderson (Scottish History Soc., Edinburgh, 1938) [hereafter *Chron. Holyrood*], 161-2: *Mclxxvii* [read *Mclxxvi*], *Vivianus cardinalis venit Scotiam, et visitavit Hiberniam. Mclxxviii°* [read *Mclxxvii°*], *de Hibernia rediit Vivianus Scotiam, et concilium tenuit apud Castellum Puellarum...*, '1176: Cardinal Vivian came to Scotland and visited Ireland. 1177: Cardinal Vivian returned from Ireland and held a council at Edinburgh Castle'. The chronicle becomes a contemporary Scottish source from 1150, kept at Holyrood until sometime between 1171 and 1186 (probably 1186), and subsequently at Coupar Angus until 1189 (see discussion at 35-9). Another possible example of this more general usage is in *Carmen de morte Sumerledi*, ('Song on the death of Somerled', written soon after the defeat and death of Somerled, king of Argyll, at the battle of Renfrew in 1164), in which Kentigern, patron saint of Glasgow, is implicitly regarded as a 'Scottish saint' when it says that Bishop Herbert began to rail against the Scottish saints (*sancti Scotticani*) and reproach the blessed Kentigern because his prayers appeared at first to be going unanswered: see *ESSH*, ii, 256 for translation, and *Chron. Fordun*, i, 449 for text.

[14]For the tract (called *De situ Albanie*) see n.8, above.

[15]*Chron. Melrose*, [128]: *cum minutis insulis circumiacentibus ample regioni Scoctorum*. Earlier in the sentence the chronicler explains that Mann 'was once called a kingdom', *olim regio vocabatur*, which shows that *regio* here means

'kingdom'. The Chronicle of Melrose is the principal contemporary Scottish source from 1171 to 1263 (see *Chron. Melrose*, xi). This later section, however, was not written into the chronicle until 1285x1291 (ibid., xvi-xvii), although where it is part of a year-by-year sequence (as in this case) it may have been composed from contemporary notes.

[16]See most recently Dauvit Broun, 'The origin of Scottish identity', *Nations, Nationalism and Patriotism in the European Past*, edd. Claus Bjørn, Alexander Grant & Keith J. Stringer (Copenhagen, 1994), 35-55, at 40-5.

[17]Dauvit Broun, 'The birth of Scottish History', *SHR*, 76 (1997), 5-6.

[18]Broun, 'Origin of Scottish identity', 50-1.

[19]See next note.

[20]The most successful king before David I in extending his rule beyond 'Scotland proper' may, therefore, have been Mac Bethad mac Findlaích (Macbeth) (1040-57), who was already ruler of Moray before he became king of 'Scotland'. The ruler of Moray's description as a *mormaer* probably merely reflected the king of Scotland's point of view: the rulers of Moray themselves doubtless preferred the title *rí*, 'king'. The most recent detailed discussion is Seán Duffy, 'Ireland and the Irish Sea Region, 1014-1318', unpublished Ph.D. thesis (Trinity College, Dublin, 1993), 21-2: see also D. P. Kirby, 'Moray prior to c.1100', in *An Historical Atlas of Scotland c.400-c.1600*, edd. Peter McNeill and Ranald Nicholson (St Andrews, 1975), 20-1. A different and more speculative approach has been taken by Benjamin T. Hudson, *Kings of Celtic Scotland* (Westport CT, 1994), 150-2, who argued that the rulers of 'Scotland' and Moray were two Dál Riata royal kindreds competing for an overkingship, 'one supreme king of Scots', which he envisaged stretching 'from the North Channel to the North Sea' (61).

[21]A possible social context for the new identity *ca* 900 is discussed in Dauvit Broun, 'The origin of Scottish identity in its European context', in *Scotland in Dark Age Europe*, ed. B. E. Crawford (St Andrews, 1994), 21-31: for a contrary view see Patrick Wormald, 'The emergence of the *regnum Scottorum*: a Carolingian hegemony?', in *Scotland in Dark Age Britain*, ed. B. E. Crawford (St Andrews, 1996), 131-60.

[22]As in R. Andrew McDonald and Scott A. McLean, 'Somerled of Argyll: a new look at old problems', *SHR*, 71 (1992), 3-22.

[23]*Chron. Melrose*, [63], [84], discussed in Dauvit Broun, 'Anglo-French acculturation and the Irish element in Scottish identity', *Britain and Ireland 900-1300*, ed. Brendan Smith (Cambridge, forthcoming). Another probable example is *Chron. Holyrood*, 151, which records how on Sept. 23 1168 three named individuals *fraude Scottorum interfecti sunt*, 'were killed by the deceit of the Scots' (see also comment at 37).

[24]'...none out of the sons of the Scots has ever been able to accomplish this mission except for the aforesaid monk [Reginald of Roxburgh]': *Chron. Melrose*, [129]. For the date when this was written into the chronicle, see n.16, above. In a tract on Simon de Montfort written into the chronicle at the same time (1285x1291) (but, again, concerning events of the mid-1260s) the thoroughly 'Anglo-Norman' Guy

de Balliol is described as 'by nation a Scot' (*nacione Scotus*): *Chron. Melrose*, [131].

[25]Royal scribes *ca* 1180 abandoned the practice in charters of addressing the king's subjects as ethnic groups (see *Regesta Regum Scottorum*, vol.ii: *The Acts of William I*, ed. G. W. S. Barrow with collaboration of W. W. Scott (Edinburgh, 1971), 77); this followed a similar change in practice at this time by royal scribes in England. As Professor Duncan has pointed out to me, this does not mean that French, English, Gallovidians and Welsh (in what had been the kingdom of Strathclyde) were now regarded as *Scoti*.

[26]Broun, 'Origin of Scottish identity', 44-5.

[27]John Bannerman, *Studies in the History of Dalriada* (Edinburgh, 1974), 41; 118-19 for comment.

[28]For what follows, see David E. Brown, 'The Scottish Origin-legend before Fordun', unpublished Ph.D. dissertation (University of Edinburgh, 1988), 28-183 (and, in a much revised form, in my forthcoming *The Irish Identity of the Kingdom of the Scots, ca 950-ca 1300*). R. James Goldstein, *The Matter of Scotland: Historical Narrative in Medieval Scotland* (Lincoln, Nabraska, 1993), 104-32, takes a different view, but see my review in *Nottingham Medieval Studies*, 39 (1995), 205-7. For a different reconstruction of this material (which only impinges slightly on what follows), see *Chron. Bower* (Watt), i, xxiii-xxx. This material is also discussed in Broun, 'Anglo-French acculturation'.

[29]If *Scoti* is taken in isolation, however, it is difficult to know whether Irish/Gaels is intended, or only those in 'Scotland'. The title *rex Scottorum* is a case in point: Seán Duffy ('Ireland and the Irish Sea Province', 27) has argued that kings of Scots in the twelfth century may, indeed, have seen themselves as the leading king in Gaeldom (in effect 'king of the Irish').

[30]*Chron. Bower* (Watt), vi, 182-3.

[31]Sir James Fergusson, *The Declaration of Arbroath* (Edinburgh, 1970), 9.

[32]It can be identified as the earlier core of an historical poem attached by Walter Bower to his *Scotichronicon*. A new edition and discussion of this text (hitherto known as *Chronicon Rhythmicum*) will appear in under the title *Liber Extravagans* in *Chron. Bower* (Watt), vol. ix.

[33]For instance, in Duncan, 'Kingdom of the Scots', 136.

[34]See for instance G. W. S. Barrow, *Kingship and Unity: Scotland 1000-1306* (London, 1981), 124-9.

[35]This point has been consistently emphasised by A. A. M. Duncan: see his 'Kingdom of the Scots', 144; 'The making of the kingdom', 13; 'The Making of Scotland', in *Who are the Scots?*, ed. G. Menzies (London, 1971), 138, and W. C. Dickinson, *Scotland from Earliest Times to 1603*, revised by A. A. M. Duncan (Oxford, 1977), 33.

[36]See 00-00, below.

[37]*Beinn an Albannaich* is the south flank of Ben Resipol in Sunart (Ian A. Fraser, 'The place-names of Argyll: an historical perspective', *Transactions of the Gaelic*

Society of Inverness, 54 (1984-6), 188); *Stob Coir' an Albannaich* is in the ridge of Munros on the south side of Glen Etive.
[38]Watson, *History of Celtic Place-Names*, 12.

CHAPTER TWO

The Enigmatic Lion: Scotland, Kingship and National Identity in the Wars of Independence

Fiona Watson

Introduction

National identity is understood in modern times as the sense of a common past and future pertaining to a nation, despite the diverse inherited experiences of the individuals within it. This 'modern' conception of national identity also tends to assume that the political and geographical boundaries encompassing the nation are the same, despite the likelihood that such boundaries might have moved about in the past. In other words, a single (though not necessarily homogenous) political nation must be contained entirely within clearly defined national borders. Such a definition of identity has already been shown by Dauvit Broun to have come into existence in Scotland only in the thirteenth century. He also convincingly postulates that the periods in history when 'Scottish' identity can be detected as having experienced a dramatic change are associated (though not exclusively) with advances in kingship and government.[1] Thus, almost from the beginning of its 'modern' history, a distinctive 'Scottish' identity has been profoundly influenced by the experiences, perceptions and aspirations of those who ran the country and, more particularly, of the ruling dynasty itself. This should come as no real surprise when one considers the nature of pre-democratic societies, which took it for granted that the elites knew best. This is not meant to imply that royal/elite conceptions of identity were *necessarily* at odds with those of the vast majority of the population, whose thoughts will remain, but for a few tantalising glimpses, forever hidden. Even our own democratically elected governments can present images of the state which large numbers of its citizens do not identify with and we must always be careful to find out who exactly is responsible for propagating any particular image of identity and, most importantly, why.

Thirteenth-century Scottish identity

The thirteenth-century kings of Scots, in a period of comparative peace, were engaged in doing what medieval kings (perhaps, indeed, governments generally) found so instinctive; consolidating and expanding their authority. This had, of course, been an ongoing process but they were now able to reap the fruits of many of the policies of their predecessors. The last challenge to the throne was snuffed out brutally in 1230 and Galloway finally accepted the full implications of royal control in 1236. Even the more thorny, militarily absorbing and potentially dangerous question of the long-standing Scottish claim to the northern counties of England was given up for good in 1237, which allowed energy and resources to be channelled into the development of an increasingly cohesive kingdom. It also made for expansion, culminating in 1266 with the forced transference of the (admittedly nominal) allegiance of the petty kings and lords of the north-west highlands and islands from the king of Norway to the king of Scots. This ended the long-standing security threat to western Scotland by bringing the northern half of the Irish Sea under the control of the Scottish government (in theory at least).

The creation of this kingdom, which is at last recognisably 'Scotland' to the modern observer,[2] was not an inevitable historical process as there is nothing inevitable about the emergence of any kingdom, nor its continued existence. However, the instinct of the crown, as a healthy political animal, was to continue to underline its position as intrinsic to the future well-being of the kingdom as a whole. This served to maintain the political status quo, as expected by both the secular and ecclesiastical elites, and to maximise the authority of the crown as the heart, not only of the political system, but of the nation itself.

The growing desire on the part of the kings of Scots to cash in on contemporary theories of divine grace,[3] an undeniably effective way to advance and sublimate an irrefutable claim to rule, was exemplified by the (ultimately successful) requests for papal canonisation of the mother of the dynasty, Margaret, wife of Malcolm III Canmore, and by the initially unsuccessful attempts to have the right of crowning and anointing added to the ceremony of inauguration of new kings which was an overt symbol of divine sanction.[4] This last aspect is an important one in that the blessing of the holy spirit made no difference to the *actual* power wielded by the king, but it was important in elevating ultimately the *perceived* power of the crown. This, it was presumably hoped, would have an effect on the reality of that authority. Perhaps more importantly, however, it would also have given an ecclesiastical justification to the notion of independent Scottish sovereignty in the face of the continued airing of the overlordship question by English kings and the English church.

Another, less savoury, element of the drive for enhanced authority was the way in which the crown sought to bring under firm control areas which had only recently accepted even its nominal jurisdiction. Historians must be aware of the dangers of unconsciously maintaining a centralist bias when dealing with those, such as the inhabitants of the recently defunct kingdom of the Isles, who were extremely uneasy about the development of 'Scotland' and its government. As Robin Frame suggests: 'the regions in the west and north [of Scotland] that remained to be integrated had regal traditions that the spareness of the evidence, and the concentration of historians on the eventual victors, may lead us to underestimate. ... it is unhelpful to seek a simple answer to the question whether they were within, or outside, a Scottish polity'.[5]

Ironically, King John Balliol's only real achievement almost certainly contributed to west Highland antipathy towards royal government.[6] The creation of the sheriffdoms of Skye, Lorne and Kintyre in 1293 has been described as the product of 'sensible, constructive thinking'.[7] It certainly is, if you consider that political and cultural assimilation is both inevitable and good, and that the central royal government had a duty to seek the creation of the modern 'ideal' Scotland. The crown obviously thought so, but, of course, it would. Balliol's policy depended largely on the co-operation of Alexander Macdougall of Argyll, who was to be given almost vice-regal powers in the north-west. The support of a major player in any 'difficult' area was a vital step towards integration, but the immediate consequence (and one which the crown might well have desired to achieve) was destabilisation, even a localised civil war, as other important members of that community fought to maintain their own positions. Only once the area had been 'softened up' by internal strife could the long-term aim of solving 'the difficult problem of governing the Hebrides and the mainland country west of Drumalban and the Great Glen' be achieved.[8]

Admittedly, this process had begun long before King John ascended the throne. The other two sheriffs, the earl of Ross and James the Steward, had already taken advantage of the possibility of western expansion to become well-established players in the area; their new offices effectively confirmed the existing balance of power. However, Professor Barrow's comparison of King John's ordinance for the western Highlands with Edward I's Statute of Rhuddlan of 1284, which provided similar administrative units for Wales, is a revealing one as shades of imperialism can be detected in both policies.[9] John may well have been making the most of political reality 'on the ground', given the intense interest in the north-west currently exhibited by a number of mainland magnates; but the Crown was also used to exploiting such territorial ambitions to extend its own power. Despite his historical reputation, it can certainly be argued that Balliol had much in common with his predecessors on the throne. He had every sympathy with the process of centralisation which he had inherited, and this was essential to the growth of a national identity.[10]

In essence, therefore, the kings of Scots had much to gain from the development of a national identity and could also do much to promote their central position within the kingdom. It should also be underlined that this process was already underway before the outbreak of war with England, and was in keeping with developments elsewhere in western Europe.[11] This is not meant to suggest that the crown created this sense of identity out of nothing, nor that it was engaged in a deliberate policy; rather, I would like to postulate that the institution which brought about an increasing political coherence to Scotland was therefore also the main impetus behind the transformation of the looser notions of 'Scottishness' described by Dr. Broun into the form of 'national' identity evident in the thirteenth century.[12] However, the concerted efforts of successive English kings to absorb Scotland into their kingdom, together, equally importantly, with the effects of the usurpation of the Scottish throne by Robert Bruce, transformed that burgeoning Scottish identity into something far more concrete and enduring.

Scottish identity in the immediate pre-war period

Given that Scottish identity today revolves to such a large extent on not being English, it is necessary to point out that, during the period prior to the death of Alexander III, the relationship between Scotland and England was extremely close. The secular elites in both countries shared the exclusive cultural values of chivalry and were separated from lesser mortals in a French-speaking brotherhood;[13] they were served, both administratively and spiritually, by clerics, members of the universal church, who were themselves distinguished from the rest through their use of Latin. Many members of the thirteenth-century English and Scottish aristocracy up to and including the kings themselves were related to each other by marriage and, while marriage by no means guaranteed close relations, it at least engendered familiarity. Alexander III's first wife had been Margaret, sister of Edward I; King John was married to the daughter of John, earl of Surrey, one of England's senior noblemen and, ironically, the victor of Dunbar in 1296. The list is endless and would serve as an interesting study in itself. The whole question of cross-border landholding was also one which affected large sections of Scottish and English society, and not just those at the very top. In other words, Anglo-Scottish elite society was integrated to a considerable degree, though this by no means implies that Scottish society was in the process of wholesale anglicisation.[14] The question facing Scotland's leaders in the late 1280s, having reluctantly accepted as queen the young Margaret, grand-daughter of Alexander III,[15] was the desirability or otherwise of her marriage with the future king of England; would it make that much difference?

Initially, the Scottish political community regarded such a marriage positively. The Treaty of Birgham of 1290[16] certainly stipulated most explicitly that Scotland's independent governmental, judicial and ecclesiastical systems would remain intact; but there could have been no doubt in anyone's mind that the marriage presaged a union of the crowns of England and Scotland. This was the preferred solution. The identity of both kingdoms would be preserved, and there would be no need to choose between them. It was also not the first time that such a proposal had been mooted. King Alexander himself contemplated a marriage between the Maid and a member of his brother-in-law Edward I's family as early as 1284.[17] Such a union seems to have been viewed as a natural extension of the close relationship already enjoyed by both countries and an acceptable solution to the problem at hand.[18] It was not the fault of the Scottish political community that Edward I would ultimately begin the transformation of the generally co-operative familiarity of the thirteenth century into a fundamentally hostile relationship.

The death of the Maid in September 1290 was nonetheless a worst-case scenario all round. The holding of a court to choose the next king of Scots gave Edward I an unprecedented opportunity to interfere in the future of the northern kingdom, though it is unhelpful to speculate on exactly when he decided to believe his own Arthurian mythology and create a Britain of his own design. It must be said that although Edward was one of a long line of English kings to push the claim of suzerainty on Scotland, he was the first to make a consistent attempt to put full feudal theory into practice.[19] This attitude was not just reserved for the Scots. The Welsh, the French, the Gascons, and even Edward's own political community were learning painfully that 'familiarity with royal rights could be an additional weapon in the hands of a ruler who combined an authoritarian outlook with political competence'.[20] Conflicts of this sort (Edward was himself, as Duke of Aquitaine, similarly engaged with his feudal superior, the king of France) were perhaps unavoidable as national consciousness came to be defined more rigidly by political borders. Feudal law was never intended to cope with touchy royal egos and equally touchy national identities.

Although he doubtless believed fervently in enforcing his royal rights as stringently as possible, Edward's actions undoubtedly served to stiffen the backbone of the Scottish political community and to persuade them that Scotland's sovereign rights, as invested in King John, were worth fighting for. The Scots also, most significantly, reacted to Balliol's inability to stand up to Edward by separating the person of the king from his office, removing him from effective power in 1295 due to his 'incapacity'.[21] This was the first, but not the last time, that such a drastic step would be taken in medieval Scotland. It was not, however, an attack on the crown: the chief movers in this palace revolution were without doubt the Comyns, Scotland's most important political family, who were closely allied to the king. An independent Scotland was totally dependent on the continuance of Balliol's kingship; any alternative was unthinkable, both in terms of legality and because of the continuing danger of civil war. It did not matter that at least one important component of the community of the realm, the Bruce family, maintained the opposite view. The majority, including those, such as James the Steward and Earl Donald of Mar, who had supported Bruce's claim to the throne during the Great Cause, regarded the question of the succession as permanently settled. However, the increasing assertiveness required of the community of the realm at the same time as the monarchy was effectively eclipsed must have resulted in an unconscious shift in the balance of their mutual relationship.

The phrases 'community of the realm' and 'political community' have been used to describe collectively those members of Scottish society who were entitled to play an active role in national matters; in other words to speak for the nation as a whole. Medieval society accepted that a varying number of 'good men' represented the community at large, usually by virtue of their status rather than any form of election. Such a role was regarded as part of the responsibility of being a member of the elites. The phrase *communitas regni* (community of the realm) was not used in Scotland until after the death of Alexander III,[22] and was presumably employed because the Scots wished to communicate with Edward I in terms with which he was familiar. This does not mean, however, that it came into being then. The Scottish political community is usually described as conservative, presumably because it made little or no attempt to curtail the activities of their kings, unlike in England. Indeed, it often proved singularly unable to render its combined reluctance effective on the monarch, failing in 1284, for example, to prevent Alexander III from settling the succession on his grand-daughter in the first place.[23] There is a danger of overstating this, however. Medieval Scotland was divided into regions which still maintained highly individual identities, however much most of them had been integrated into the kingdom. The magnates who held sway over these regions were thus at least as concerned about maintaining networks with neighbouring lords against others, as they were about creating a cohesive aristocratic identity centred on the court.[24] It is likely, therefore, that the king could divide and rule on national issues which were really not that many, so long as he left regional politics to those whose business it really was.

With the outbreak of war in 1296, the reaction of the political community was swift and more than usually united. With the exception of the Bruce family and some of their adherents who were already in Edward's service, the Scottish nobility rallied to the defence of their country. Unfortunately this resulted in their sound defeat at Dunbar. The psychological impact of this defeat, which handed Scotland to King Edward on a plate, can no doubt be exaggerated; suffice to say that the bubble of confidence surrounding the Scottish government since it took over from King John was well and truly pricked. It was the job of the nobility (not to mention the king) to protect the kingdom; they had clearly failed in that duty. Nevertheless, although the following months saw large numbers of Scottish nobles transported to English prisons, and the drop in confidence translated into a desire for such a disaster not to be repeated, most still had very little time for the occupying regime. Those who were released in 1297 to serve King Edward initially appear to have behaved either with duplicity (if you want to be charitable) or with cowardice (if you do not) towards renewed outbreaks of the war led by Andrew Moray and William Wallace; nevertheless, one English chronicler who had no doubt about where their natural loyalties lay, remarked that '... even though the lords themselves were present with the [English] king in body, at heart they were on the opposite side'.[25]

Problems of war and identity

The more the mind is turned towards assessing and defining Scottish identity during the wars with England, the more it becomes obvious that such a task is littered with as many pitfalls and obstacles as the field at Bannockburn. Perhaps because the period is so firmly fixed, in both the popular and academic mind, as a major milestone in the route towards a cohesive sense of the national self, it is all the harder to try to establish what that meant at any given stage on the way, rather than what it has subsequently come to mean. Much of the problem derives from the fact that there are very few contemporary Scottish sources, of whatever bias, to guide the search, and even fewer that can be regarded as 'unofficial'. This has given many historians free rein to make assumptions about the attitudes of medieval Scots which, at best, owe too much to medieval government propaganda and, at worst, are inspired to an unhelpful degree by modern political beliefs.[26] The reader is thus often provided with more insight into the writers' views on contemporary Scotland than into the hearts and minds of Scots of 700 years ago.

Given the key role played by the kings of Scots in the development and assertion of 'national' identity during the period prior to the war, it might be presumed that the deposition and what proved to be permanent exile of King John by Edward I in 1296 would have dealt a severe blow to the national cause. The careful symbolism involved in the deposition of the Scottish king, together with the removal of the more tangible symbols of Scottish kingship and identity, the Stone of Destiny and the Black Rood of St Margaret, was both deliberate and methodical. Scotland's independence, and with it the kingdom's distinctive identity, were now no more. However, the Scottish elites were able, despite their military failure in 1296 and the serious political differences among them, to act effectively in defence of crown and country from 1298 onwards.[27] They did so without the actual presence of the king in whose name they fought and who could not be separated from, indeed was absolutely synonymous with, the future of his kingdom. But they could not do so indefinitely and, after eight years of war, succumbed again to English rule primarily because of the failure of their king to return.[28] In other words, contemporary conceptions of identity were not sufficient to justify the continuation of a war purely to maintain the independence of the *kingdom*, rather than the restoration of the *king*.

In the longer term, however, the seizure of King John's throne by Robert Bruce, earl of Carrick, restored in dramatic and violent fashion the inextricable link between the very existence of the kingdom and the person of its king. In addition, Bruce's comprehensive propaganda campaign, designed to rewrite the history of his seizure of the throne, did much to update and consolidate the official royal version of Scotland's identity on rather different terms than those of the halcyon days of peace. Unfortunately it is very easy for historians to accept this official view since modern opinion tends to regard choosing the struggle for an independent Scotland as the only 'right' option. By so doing, however, we simplify and even misunderstand the complex social and political environment of the period. This is, of course, exactly what King Robert intended should happen!

Equally, the term 'Scottish' is a misleading description of the cause espoused by Robert Bruce in the immediate aftermath of his seizure of the throne, because a very large section of the Scottish political community (and many of their followers) perceived that their *duty* was to fight against him. It is difficult for modern observers to accept that the existence of medieval Scotland was so dependent, in the minds of its leaders, on the maintenance of a *legitimate* kingship. This meant that the Scottish nobility, who depended for their position on the same principles of loyalty as they in turn owed to the crown, could not be expected to attack the very social order which sustained them by replacing an absent king.[29]

There were also very good practical reasons for preferring the absorption of Scotland by England to the task of finding a new king. As had become evident almost from the moment of Alexander III's death, any choice made by the Scots themselves would have provoked a civil war. The only winner of such a war would have been King Edward, but without the concessions wrung out of him for submission in 1303.[30] Both general concepts of medieval government and identity, and the evidence of actual behaviour, suggest that the ideal of an independent Scotland *above all else* was a secondary consideration to the principles of acceptable kingship: for a number of years after February 1306, most Scots[31] preferred to live under an English king rather than accept a murderous Scottish usurper. When assessing concepts of identity and their development during the wars with England, it is vitally important to remember that other legitimate priorities might well have been of greater concern at any given time; the effects of ameliorating a prolonged and seemingly endless war on the land and its people was doubtless one of those priorities in 1303.

It is also important not to gloss over the fact that one of the main problems facing the political community was the internal divisions within it. On two occasions, once in 1299 and again in the following year, English spies provided news of unseemly scuffles breaking out between the leaders of the Scottish administration and their adherents.[32] There can be little doubt that, before 1300 at least, such incidents were connected with the continuing power-struggle between Bruce and Balliol, now transformed into a competition between Comyn of Badenoch and Robert Bruce, earl of Carrick. However, it would be disingenuous at the very least to shrug off references to the predominant role played by the Comyns as a mere sub-plot to both Balliol and Bruce's kingship.

The Comyn lords of Badenoch were the most powerful baronial family in Scotland and one English commentator made what was perhaps an easy mistake in assuming that its head must have been an earl.[33] They were the senior branch of the family, despite the fact that the head of the second branch was indeed an earl (Buchan).[34] Comyn domination of the political scene throughout the later thirteenth century was due in no small measure to the extent of their landholdings, which stretched across the north-east of Scotland down through the Great Glen to Inverlochy, and also included considerable estates in Galloway and other parts of the south-west.[35] At almost every significant moment during this period, both before and after the outbreak of war, either John Comyn of Badenoch (father and son) or John, earl of Buchan, or a combination of the three, played a leading role. The degree of co-operation between the two branches of the family,[36] together with an extended network of allies, ensured that they had a '... natural -- one might say, a prescriptive -- right to leadership of the community of the realm'.[37] Buchan appears to have viewed himself as something of a military man, leading the Scottish army in 1296, again in 1300 and 1301, and probably on other undocumented occasions. Unfortunately for the Scots, the earl was not a particularly successful general, though it is perhaps understandable, given Comyn dominance of the political community, that no-one seems to have pointed this out.

Despite their considerable landholdings and obvious interest elsewhere in Scotland, the main Comyn powerbase in the north-east became even more important after 1296, for the very simple reason that that area was comparatively unaffected by the prosecution of the war. Despite the frustrating lack of evidence, it is clear that a Scottish administration, based largely in Aberdeen, was able to operate reasonably normally there between 1297 and 1303. Naturally the Comyns and their allies took part in the war in the south and were leading members of the regime claiming to govern Scotland as a whole. However, there is clear evidence that this government encompassed two kinds of administration, one designed for war and the other for peace.

Control of the north-east was certainly vital to the prosecution of the war, and the maintenance of links with Europe was just one element of this. We know that Scottish ships were able to run the gauntlet of the blockade imposed by England,[38] and English control of Edinburgh and Berwick must have heightened the importance of Aberdeen and other north-eastern ports in bringing in supplies of military equipment and other necessities, as well as conveying emissaries to foreign courts from Norway to Rome.

Yet 'normal' government was perhaps of greater importance to those actually living in the area, either as a welcome relief or a resented intrusion. In 1300, Buchan was able to hold a justiciar's court in Aberdeen; the sheriff of Aberdeen was John, earl of Atholl, an ardent Bruce supporter, perhaps indicating that a normal peacetime cross-section of interests prevailed in the government of the area.[39] Even more significantly, a number of court-cases heard by King Edward during the English resettlement of Scotland after 1303 indicates that Comyn of Badenoch, as Guardian, had been able to prosecute successfully two pro-English landowners in the area, one of whom was the earl of Strathearn.[40] Comyn's ability to hold courts and, most importantly, to execute the judgements of these courts, speaks volumes about the success of his regime. Most interestingly, he appears to have acted without any reference to his co-Guardians,[41] all of which suggests that his government in the north-east was the most effective of all the regimes operating at the time, including the one run in the name of Edward I.

However, Professor Barrow asserts that after 1300 'the Comyn leadership of the national cause ... would no longer be accepted without challenge and discontent'. This is justified by the fact that Sir John Soules took over as Guardian at King John's express behest, apparently causing Comyn of Badenoch to demit the Guardianship for almost two years.[42] Dr. Norman Reid postulates, alternatively, that Comyn remained in office but in a subsidiary position to Soules, representing the Community, rather than the Crown directly.[43] The court-case evidence certainly seems to tie in better with this last interpretation, although if Comyn continued as guardian this perhaps reflects as much on the power of his family as on the wishes of the community. There can be no doubt that Soules must have had the support of the Comyns, however neutral a position he occupied in Scottish politics;[44] equally, John Comyn's behaviour throughout the period does not suggest that he would willingly have laid down the guardianship unless his family's power had been eclipsed. There is no evidence that this was the case. It may be, however, that he confined his activities after 1301 to administering the north-east, leaving Soules, and indeed Buchan, to carry on the war in the south-west.[45]

None of these arguments can be proved conclusively. However, an examination of John Comyn's administration ultimately highlights the difficult state of affairs experienced by the country as a whole. As the war dragged on, the impasse threatened an inexorable fragmentation of society due to the lack of an overall national administration.[46] Political theory thus surely became of far less importance than hard facts: justice was only being administered over parts of the country by any one regime, and the collection of rents and other dues, essential to the prosecution of the war and a sign of an established administration, was also possible only in particular areas. This aspect of the war provides an important insight into public opinion after six years of conflict. The rush to litigate in King Edward's courts from 1303 onwards by Scots of a comparatively broad social spectrum indicates that there was much sympathy with their Guardian's decision to submit to the only man who could govern the country as a whole. Enough was enough.

The existence of a comparatively normal government in the north-east also provides evidence for another important aspect of Scottish identity, namely contemporary views about the very nature of 'Scotland' itself. As Dr. Broun shows, 'Scotland proper' had, until the thirteenth century, been regarded as that area lying 'between the Forth, Moray and Drumalban', a huge chunk in the centre of the country. The heart of the kingdom was not, therefore, centred historically on Edinburgh or even Glasgow but beyond the Forth. Though Edinburgh was clearly an important administrative centre throughout the thirteenth century, and Roxburgh and Berwick were also significant, the kings of Scots preferred to reside in Stirling and Forfar.[47] This association with 'Scotland proper', together with the fact that the dominant political power-house operated in and around this area, gave the north-east a considerable degree of confidence in acting as the heart of a condensed Scotland largely free from English control. The collapse of Scottish resistance from 1303 onwards, the first time that Scotland north of the Forth had experienced the full impact of war since 1297, indicates that historians should take care to remember that 'Scotland' was more than just the English-dominated war-zone in the south.[48]

Change for better or worse?
The community of the realm had, up until 1303, worked impressively well by fielding armies with regularity and conducting an equally important diplomatic

offensive throughout the courts of Europe. As noted above, the final decision to submit in 1304 was not taken lightly. The expectation that King John would return in 1302 had not materialised and many became unsure as to what they were fighting for. Although some, most notably Sir William Wallace and Sir Simon Fraser, did intend to fight on, the majority decided that they wished to get on with the business of living, perhaps in order to fight another day.

Five months after Edward I finally set out his blueprint for the future government of Scotland (September 1305), Robert Bruce earl of Carrick murdered John Comyn of Badenoch and seized the throne. The impact of these actions can only be fully understood, I believe, if the picture of Scotland since the death of Alexander III described above is taken into account. Professor Barrow has stated that, despite Comyn's undeniable political right to lead the community of the realm, 'he was an almost total failure'.[49] Such a conclusion is only possible if activities taking place in what we would now regard as the heart of Scotland, the central belt, alone are considered. Other evidence clearly suggests that John Comyn, together with the earl of Buchan as justiciar of Scotland, had considerable success in government.

Our understanding of what happened next also very much hinges on interpretations of the nature of the community of the realm. The view taken here is that Scotland's natural leaders were able to provide an adequate response to the interregnum and the early stages of the war. However, the protracted nature of the conflict, and its subsequent renewal after Bruce's *coup-d'etat*, produced an unprecedented set of circumstances which many concluded were unacceptable. The events of February/March 1306 were profoundly shocking, and not just to the ageing King Edward. *We* know that Robert Bruce would ultimately prove to be one of the most esteemed medieval kings of Scots. Contemporaries did not. It has been argued that 'patriotism and the cause of King John Balliol' were not the same.[50] I would suggest that, for most of the political community, it *had* to be the same. Both political theory and political circumstance made it so. By murdering the head of Scotland's most important family and denying the right of the Balliol dynasty to the Scottish throne, Bruce split the community of the realm apart. Political theory and practice to date were quite unable to deal with this situation. Most of the country's natural leaders were eventually 'persuaded' of the 'legitimacy' of his actions not because of a genuine belief in the 'rightness' of his cause, but rather as a result of the judicious application of brute force, together with exemplary skills of diplomacy and propaganda. Bruce then became the *pragmatic* choice, as Balliol had once been.

Initially, however, the nation as a whole voted with its feet: though the new king did gather together some support, most who joined him were either already closely linked with the Bruce family or had their own grievances to prompt them.[51] Some, such as Robert Wishart, bishop of Glasgow, and perhaps Simon Fraser, were convinced of the necessity of accepting extreme measures for the sake of the country. It is quite untenable to suggest that the community of the realm had evolved by 1306 into those whose concern *above all else* was to maintain Scottish independence, and, by implication, comprised only those who found it possible to ditch King John and support King Robert. The community of the realm in 1306 was what it had always been: the country's great and good whose primary aim was to maintain the status quo as far as possible. The murder of Comyn naturally meant that his family and many of its associates had to join King Edward against Bruce. It was unthinkable that they should not do so, but, as with the previous adherence of the Bruce family to the English, it could be argued that, however important they were, the Comyns did not represent the entire community. Bruce's seizure of the throne, however, also set against him Balliol's allies, as well as a tide of important public opinion which we have every reason to believe was genuinely revolted by his actions. As earl of Carrick, Bruce had not managed to persuade the community to retain him as Guardian; why did he think that it would be any more enthusiastic about him becoming king?

Interestingly, he does appear to have been able to gain the support of reasonable numbers of 'middling men'. Lack of evidence usually precludes historians from saying very much about this stratum of society during the middle ages; the wars with England, perhaps because they created a period of disruption and crisis, afford us a glimpse of their activities. It would appear that this group, in common with their peers elsewhere in Europe, did not always regard their interests as being concomitant with those of the nobility.[52] King Edward had himself sought to dislodge them from their lords by suggesting that he would champion their interests. In 1301 English officials were ordered specifically to admit the middle men to his peace. This was, of course, mere policy. The point here is that Edward considered it worthwhile to target them, probably because he had reason to believe that they had had enough of the war. It should thus be clear that this section of society's support for Bruce does not necessarily imply that they were any more patriotic than the higher nobility (as King Edward's interest in them illustrates); rather, they were less concerned with the issue of legitimacy which was serving to hamstring the country's natural leaders.

On the other hand, even John Barbour, who wrote the first Scottish account of the wars eulogising the hero king, admits that Bruce was rejected as leader by the country at large, and even by the 'small folk' who had shown their mettle with William Wallace:

> He durst nocht to the planis ga
> For all the comounis went him fra
> Tha for thar lif war full fane
> To pas to the Inglis pes agane.[53]

Barbour is, of course, asserting that fear made them unwilling to fight for the new king, but this had not stopped them in 1297, despite a similar density of English garrisons and the humiliations of 1296.

The fact that Bruce succeeded (and it was touch-and-go for many months)[54] attests more to his own tenacity, ruthlessness and ability than in the willingness of the Scottish nation to follow him. He became king in more than name only when he had conquered Scotland from other Scots, not the English. This civil war created devastation in the north-east in general, and Buchan in particular, from which it took a long time to recover; the political impact on the area caused by the expulsion of the Comyns could be felt for much of the century.[55]

Bruce's success also resulted from the deliberate exploitation of the growing sense of aggressive patriotism sown during these years of war. King Robert did much to define and redefine Scottish identity but the biggest change, as explored by Carol Edington, was the development of a Scottish martial identity which contrasted dramatically with the complete lack of interest shown in developing Scotland's military potential in the previous century.[56]

Indeed, the activities of the officials in Bruce's chancery, employed in the task of justifying the events of 1306 both to important public opinion of the time and to posterity, are one of the most important aspects of the reign. Scottish propaganda efforts throughout the war employed an extremely sophisticated arsenal of appeals to contemporary ideals and prejudices ranging, as Dr. Edington shows, through a whole spectrum of religious and chivalric allusions. The greatest of these appeals, the Declaration of Arbroath of 1320, was by no means an isolated attempt to rewrite history. As far as King Robert was concerned, that had begun in 1309 with the Declaration of the Clergy. The difference between 1309 and 1320 was, however, the dropping of King John from any part in the proceedings in the later document; the English were now the only enemy and Scotland stood proudly united behind their king. Alas, only months later Bruce faced rebellion from many of the 'signatories' of the Declaration, perhaps galled by the obvious discrepancy between the version of events portrayed there and their own memories.[57] In the end, it is not surprising that Bruce, in justifying his right to sit on the throne, relied most heavily on his military achievement His expulsion of the English and his own enemies, particularly as a result of Bannockburn, was the real reason that he still sat on his throne.

However, there was a potentially revolutionary ideal contained within the Declaration of Arbroath, namely that King Robert or his descendants could be kicked off the Scottish throne if they ever sold out to the English. This has been taken latterly to justify the modern myth of popular sovereignty from an early period in Scotland. Such a notion would have been greeted with complete incomprehension by Bruce, not to mention his Stewart descendants; the passage was intended to underline the real justification for Bruce's kingship - success against the English. Nevertheless, its inclusion indicates a fundamental shift in attitude towards Scottish identity (see chapter four). The clerics who constructed the document, at least, could conceive of laying emphasis on the right of the *kingdom* and its people to independence, rather than the right of a particular dynasty to rule. It would be impossible to detect any change in Scottish government or the attitudes of its kings as a result of this extraordinary statement; nevertheless it surely indicates that, for some, the identity of the Scottish people now depended fundamentally on the independence of the kingdom of Scotland. This was a new form of identity which, whatever modern historians might say,[58] is testimony to the existence of a nationalism which looks uncannily like the modern version, albeit without the emphasis on rights of citizenship.[59]

Equally, there is evidence that the wars with England were perceived, at the time, as the product of a mass, rather than an elite, effort. For example, the institution of serfdom, common throughout western Europe, died out comparatively early (mid-fourteenth century) in Scotland,[60] perhaps for the same reason that significant social change resulted from the First World War: it is difficult to justify certain, more glaring, inequalities applied to those who have been prepared to fight and die for their country. King Robert I was instrumental in this process, not because he was himself interested in promoting anything remotely resembling democracy (it could not have occurred to him to do so), but because the loss of support from the community of the realm, as described above, ensured that he had to cultivate the adherance of other sections of society. Having succeeded in gaining acceptance as king by such means, Bruce had seized the initiative back from the community of the realm. It is arguable that his success provided a powerful legacy for the crown throughout the following centuries: although a number of succeeding kings did undoubtedly fail to maintain their position (and, on occasions, their lives) in the face of opposition from the community of the realm, it is undeniable that the dynasty itself remained remarkably inviolate.[61] Part of the reason for this may lie with a deep-seated belief, deliberately fostered by Bruce and later underlined by the Balliol association with Edward III,[62] that any threat to the new dynasty would challenge Scotland's very independence.

Conclusion

The wars with England were naturally of crucial importance in developing a very distinct Scottish identity. However, the thirteenth century had already witnessed a considerable change in that identity, as kingship and government became more sophisticated and pervasive. After the outbreak of war and the exile of the Scottish king, the continuing independence of the country was clearly important to those men on whom Scottish government devolved; they successfully organised military resistance and the administration of large parts of the country, particularly the north-east. However, as the war threatened to drag on indefinitely, and Balliol made no sign of returning, the will to continue dwindled away throughout Scottish society.

The murder of the leader of the Scottish resistance to Edward I, John Comyn of Badenoch, by Robert Bruce, and the latter's subsequent seizure of the throne, threw the political community into turmoil. Most could not accept Bruce's actions and either actively opposed him or did nothing. If Edward I had lived longer it is highly unlikely that the country could have survived both an English attack and a bitter civil war and there would be little cause to write this article. However, the genius of Robert Bruce lay in his ability to adapt to any given situation, military, diplomatic or administrative, and turn it to his own advantage. His legacy has been the redefinition of Scottish identity in a number of significant ways. Firstly, the independence of the country became firmly rooted as a paramount concern in the hearts and minds of Scottish people, almost certainly at all social levels.[63] A more rigid definition of what it meant to be Scottish, particularly among the elites who had been at home in a more British context before 1296 (they could now no longer hold lands under the English king), was a by-product of the focus on nationhood and independence provoked by the war. Secondly, and equally importantly, the role of the crown as the mainstay of the country's independence did much to overhaul not only the identity of the monarchy, but that of Scotland itself.

However, for the historian this is by no means the whole story; it is merely the official version, the one that Robert Bruce wanted us to accept wholeheartedly. If we set as an inviolable standard the ideal of an independent Scotland, then we will be forced to judge behaviour consistently by that imposed criterion; we are in grave danger, therefore, of misjudging the principles which were most important to the individuals or groups forced to make decisions in this difficult period. Supporting Robert Bruce was by no means the obvious 'right' choice for good Scotsmen and women, particularly in the early years of his reign, and historians must stop presuming that it should have been. We should also think twice about the effects of too rigid a definition of 'the national interest', especially when we remember the 'herschip' of Buchan and the execution of Sir David Brechin, a distinguished knight who nevertheless decided not to inform the king of a conspiracy against him in 1320 -- perhaps because he too had sympathy with the view that Bruce was taking the rewriting of history too far. As Robin Frame notes, the truly astonishing thing about the history of this period 'is the impudent success of the Bruce and Stewart dynasties in seizing the national past for themselves'.[64] Historians should think twice about assuming that 'national' identity is by definition an overriding and unifying theme in any period; we must seek, instead, to understand the complexity of the reactions to situations which have hitherto been regarded as clearcut. The crown was the overwhelming proponent and beneficiary of the redefinitions of identity in this period; by concentrating on its official view we are therefore likely to ignore a variety of Scottish identities formed from very different interpretations of events. If these other viewpoints are accepted as equally valid, however, a vastly richer vision of 'Scotland' -- past, present and future -- will surely emerge.

NOTES

[1] See above, pp. 4-17.

[2] Orkney and Shetland belonged to the Norwegian Crown until 1468/9.

[3] See, for example, M. Barber, *The Two Cities: Medieval Europe 1050-1320* (Routledge, 1994), 277.

[4] A.A.M. Duncan, *Scotland: The Making of the Kingdom* (Mercat Press, 1992), 453, 558; 553-4. Both the request for canonisation and of coronation were addressed to the pope, though the latter was not granted until 1329.

[5] R. Frame, *The Political Development of the British Isles, 1100-1400*, (Oxford, 1990), 103.

[6] It must be remembered that no-one anticipated that King John's reign would end only three years later with defeat and English occupation. His government should therefore be regarded at this point as a continuation from Alexander III, rather than as a prelude to the inevitable outbreak of war.

[7] G.W.S. Barrow, *Robert Bruce* (3rd edn., Edinburgh, 1988), 55.

[8] *ibid.*

[9] *ibid.*, 55-6.

[10] Though Scotland is regarded as one of the more uncentralised medieval kingdoms in western Europe, in comparison to England and France, it should be recognised that the activities of the crown for a number of centuries before 1300 had most certainly brought about a degree of centralisation.

[11] A. Black, *Political Thought in Europe, 1250-1450* (C.U.P., 1992), 108-13.

[12] See above, pp. 4-17.

[13] Though Gaelic and/or Scots/English must also have been spoken by most of the Scottish nobility.

[14] It should be noted that, earlier in the century, five leaders of the opposition to King John of England, which culminated in the Magna Carta, were Scottish landowners, and three of them were closely related to the king, Alexander II [See K. Stringer, 'Periphery and Core in Thirteenth-Century Scotland: Alan son of Roland, Lord of Galloway and Constable of Scotland', in A. Grant and K. Stringer (eds.), *Medieval Scotland: Crown, Lordship and Community* (Edinburgh, 1993), 88-9.

[15] Medieval kingdoms were not well adjusted to accepting queens as sovereigns; the civil war in England, precipitated by the accession of the Empress Matilda, was not much of an example to follow. However, in Scotland's case, accepting the Maid of Norway as queen was the best way to avoid civil war between the two main rival male claimants to the throne.

[16] This treaty arranged for Margaret's marriage to Edward of Caernarvon, heir to Edward I of England.

[17] R. Nicholson, *Scotland, The Later Middle Ages* (Edinburgh, 1974), 30.

[18] Historians are far from agreed on this point, however: Ranald Nicholson asserts that the marriage 'must have caused some heart-searching among responsible Scots' [*Scotland, The Later Middle Ages*, 31]; Professor Barrow, on the other hand, describes

the atmosphere at the time as 'hopeful, even joyful' [*Robert Bruce*, 28]. We should be careful not to employ hindsight to these events.

[19] Henry II had certainly been in a prime position to push a more defined version of overlordship on the Scots following the capture of the Scottish king, William the Lion, during a raid south of the border in 1174. William was forced to buy his freedom with an unequivocal acceptance of England's superior position vis-à-vis Scotland; unusually this also involved the garrisoning of Berwick, Edinburgh and Stirling with English troops as a guarantee of future good behaviour. However, Henry was clearly not that interested in Scotland, except in terms of the maintenance of a peaceful border, and, as Professor Duncan notes, 'these cords can scarcely have proved as irksome to King William as he had feared' [Duncan, *Scotland*, 230-1].

[20] Frame, *Political Developments*, 102. Edward was an improvement, from the English crown's point of view, on his predecessors, John and Henry III, who, though sporting an autocratic outlook, were not so blessed with political ability.

[21] Barrow, *Bruce*, 63-5.

[22] Nicholson, *Scotland, The Later Middle Ages*, 26. The phrase was already very firmly fixed within English political consciousness. See Barrow, *Bruce*, 16, for an eloquent description of the Scottish community of the realm.

[23] Duncan, *Scotland, The Making of the Kingdom*, 612.

[24] This point is being postulated here primarily on the evidence provided by the fourteenth and fifteenth centuries [See, for example, M. Brown, 'Scotland Tamed', *Innes Review*, 45 (1994) and S. Boardman, *The Early Stewart Kings: Robert II and Robert III*, (Tuckwell Press, 1996)], especially xv-xvi. It is an issue that needs serious consideration in terms of thirteenth century evidence.

[25] *The Chronicle of Walter of Guisborough*, ed. H. Rothwell (Camden Soc., 1957), 299. See F. Watson, *Edward I in Scotland, 1296-1305*, unpublished Ph.D. thesis (Glasgow, 1991), 56-8 for a discussion of the Scottish nobility in this period.

[26] Andrew Fisher's biography of William Wallace, although by far the best account, provides a good example of the tendency to transport twentieth-century belief-systems into the past, provoking judgements which are not justifiable in the context of the period in which the events occurred. This particularly relates to Fisher's attitude towards the Scottish nobility and their role in prosecuting the war against England. I will say nothing about the plethora of books on the same subject which have arrived on the bookshelves post-Braveheart.

[27] William Wallace's guardianship from 1297-1298 did not represent the combined will of the Scottish elites but came about solely through the unexpected military success at Stirling Bridge. Though members of the political community may have covertly supported Sir William during his guardianship, they did not come out openly and en masse against Edward I until after Wallace's defeat at Falkirk, when political power transferred back to its more traditional holders.

[28] See F. Watson, *Edward I in Scotland, 1296-1305*, Chapter Fifteen, for a full discussion of the submission of the Scots in 1304. The reasons prompting these submissions are not solely the result of Balliol's failure to return home and certainly involve the diplomatic isolation experienced by the Scots from 1302 onwards when they were deserted by both of their key allies, Philip IV of France and Pope Boniface VIII [See F. Watson, 'Settling the Stalemate: Edward I's peace in Scotland, 1303-5', in *Thirteenth Century England VI*, eds. M. Prestwich, R.Britnell & R. Frame (Woodbridge, 1997), 132-3].

[29] It should also be noted that, as suggested above [p.19], King John might well have proved an effective king if there had been no war with England.

[30] See F. Watson, 'Settling the Stalemate', 133-7.

[31] That is, the members of the Scottish elites for whom evidence exists.

[32] *National Manuscripts of Scotland*, ii, no.viii; *Calendar of Documents relating to Scotland* [*C.D.S.*] v, ed. G. Simpson and J. Galbraith (Edinburgh, 1986), no.220; G.O. Sayles, 'The Guardians of Scotland and a Parliament at Rutherglen in 1300', *S.H.R.*, xxiv, 246-50. William Wallace resigned/was fired from the guardianship before December 1298, to be replaced by John Comyn of Badenoch and Robert Bruce, earl of Carrick. These two were joined (to keep the peace) by Bishop Lamberton of St. Andrews the following year. Bruce was himself ousted and replaced by Sir Ingram d'Umfraville, a Comyn supporter, in 1300 and all three Guardians supposedly demitted office in favour of King John's nominee, Sir John de Soules in 1301 [see below, p.26] Finally, Sir John Comyn of Badenoch became sole guardian in 1303.

[33] *Guisborough*, p.297.

[34] Barrow, *Bruce*, 49; 336, n.46; Duncan, *Scotland from the Earliest Times*, 152, n.2. The Comyns of Kilbride - the third branch of the family - certainly played their part in the wars, but they are of much less significance than the Comyns of Badenoch and Buchan during this period.

[35] See A. Young's articles on the Comyns: 'Noble Families and Political Factions in the Reign of Alexander III', in *Scotland in the Reign of Alexander III, 1249-1286*, ed. N. Reid (Edinburgh, 1990), 1-31; 'The Political Role of Walter Comyn, earl of Menteith', in *Nobility of Medieval Scotland*, ed. K. Stringer (Edinburgh, 1985), 131-149; 'Buchan in the thirteenth century' in *Medieval Scotland: Crown, Lordship and Community*, eds. A. Grant and K. Stringer, (Edinburgh, 1993), 174-202.

[36] This closeness should not be taken for granted when one considers relations between the Red and Black Douglases 150 years later.

[37] Barrow, *Bruce*, 145.

[38] Barrow, *Bruce*, 93-4.

[39] *Arbroath Liber*, i, no.231.

[40] *C.D.S.*, ii, ed. J. Bain (Edinburgh, 1882) no.1592; *Memoranda de Parliamento, 1305*, ed. F.W. Maitland, Rolls Series, (London, 1893), no.296.

[41] The cases are undated but probably took place between 1300 and 1303; the bishop of St. Andrews, Sir Ingram d'Umfraville and even Sir John de Soules were all Guardians at some point during that period.

[42] Barrow, *Bruce*, 114-5.

[43] N.Reid, 'The kingless kingdom: the Scottish guardianship of 1286-1306', *Scottish Historical Review*, lxi (1982), 105-29.

[44] Nicholson, *Scotland, The Later Middle Ages*, 62-3.

[45] F. Watson, *Edward I in Scotland*, 171-3.

[46] This impasse was reached as early as 1298 when, despite significant gains made by the English in southern Scotland after that date, it was not clear that either side could actually win the war.

[47] F. Watson, 'The expression of power in a medieval kingdom: thirteenth-century Scottish castles', in A.I. Macinnes (ed.), *Scottish Power-centres* (forthcoming).

[48] F. Watson, *Edward I in Scotland*, 227-9, 232-3.

[49] Barrow, *Bruce*, 145.

[50] Barrow, 'Lothian in the first war of independence', 169.

[51] Barrow, *Bruce*, 154-60.

[52] During the barons' wars of the 1250s in England, for example, the 'middling people' [*mediocris populi*] entirely rejected Louis IX's arbitration which decided, naturally enough, in favour of King Henry III. The higher nobility, becoming sequeamish about continued rebellion against the Crown, were prepared to accept it. [S. Reynolds, *Kingdoms and Communities in Western Europe, 900-1300*, (Oxford, 1984), 272].

[53] M.P. McDiarmid & J.A.C. Stevenson (eds.), *Barbour's Bruce*, vol. ii, Scottish Text Society, (Edinburgh, 1980), p.42.

[54] The fact that Bruce was forced to flee to the west highlands, which had taken little interest in the war to date, and subsequently (probably) to Ireland implies that he risked capture in the rest of Scotland, including his own earldom.

[55] Nicholson, *Scotland, The Later Middle Ages*, 78; S. Boardman, *The Early Stewart Kings*, 12-13.

[56] See below, pp 69-81. This theme, like so many for the thirteenth century, requires greater investigation. It revolves around issues of 'feudal' tenure (or rather the limited extent of knight service) and the dependency on ancient military organisation (an indication of the lack of a need to modernise), as well as the design of Scottish castles, most of which ignored contemporary defensive improvements, presumably, again, because they were unnecessary.

[57] Noblemen did not, of course, actually write their names but attached their seals instead. See A.A.M. Duncan for the most recent interpretation of the de Soules conspiracy ['War of the Scots, 1306-23', *T.R.H.S.*, 6th Series, 2 (1992),129-131].

[58] Most modern historians and sociologists deny the existence of nationalism prior to the French Revolution [see for example, E. Hobsbawm, *Nations and Nationalism since*

1780, 2nd ed. (C.U.P., 1992), 47, 77; E. Gellner, *Nations and Nationalism*, (Blackwell, 1983), 18].

[59] But let us not forget that the nationalism espoused by the French Republic brought about the shelving of the introduction of equal *female* rights of citizenship in the national interest [See, for example, Lynn Hunt, *The French Revolution and Human Rights. A Brief Documentary History*, (Boston, 1996), 119-131].

[60] A. Grant, *Independence and Nationhood*, (Arnold, 1984), 66-7.

[61] Although the Bruce dynasty did not last beyond 1371, the Stewarts undoubtedly capitalised on their relationship with the first King Robert.

[62] See R. Nicholson, *Edward III and the Scots*, (Edinburgh, 1965) for the relationship between Edward Balliol, King John's son, and Edward III.

[63] This cannot, of course, be asserted conclusively since the opinions of the average Scot are not directly ascertainable.

[64] Frame, *The Political Development of the British Isles*, 194.

CHAPTER THREE

Identity, Freedom and the Declaration of Arbroath

Edward J. Cowan

> It is a great pity that we do not know exactly the history of this brave man; for at the time when he lived, everyone was so busy fighting, that there was no person to write down the history of what took place, and afterwards, when there was more leisure for composition, the truths that were collected were greatly mingled with falsehood.

> Sir Walter Scott *Tales of a Grandfather*

Identity, like History, is subject to change according to the preoccupations of the moment and the perspectives created by posterity. As Walter Bower noted in his masterly fifteenth century *Scotichronicon* in response to the calamities which befell Scotland in the last decade of the thirteenth century, 'the state of affairs both in the past and now is not permanent'.[1] If we now know that writings from the period are much more voluminous than Scott realised they are far from being as plentiful as we would like (whether the 'brave man' in question is Wallace or Bruce) while falsehoods, rooted in the propaganda traded by Scots and English in the controversy over Edward I's claims of overlordship, have continued to circulate. What is reasonably certain is that in the three decades between 1290 and 1320 a new sense of Scottish identity and nationhood was refined and articulated. It will be argued that Scottish thinkers of the period not only attempted to resolve their own political philosophies in response to the unprecedented contingencies which potentially threatened the very existence of their kingdom and nation, but that they also contributed towards ideas of constitutionalism which would ultimately feed into the mainstream of British, European, and eventually American, political thought. Since political ideas will be considered as practical, realistic mechanisms rather than as dusty scholastic or academic abstractions, such ideas can tell us much about how the people of the time perceived themselves and the nature of the societies to which they belonged. As such, some of what are argued to be near-revolutionary developments, not only in a Scottish but also in a European context, were to confer aspects of identity upon the Scottish people which survive to the present day. Novel responses during the Wars of Independence coalesced around the concept of freedom or *libertas* but the question of to whom the defence of liberty should be entrusted would stimulate a profound and far-reaching debate arising out of the peculiar, indeed unique, historical circumstances of the time.

It is now well established that an historiographical battle royal between Scotland and England took place in the last decade of the thirteenth century so important, so central and so diagnostic, that it would be rehearsed again and again in tedious detail during the next two centuries and beyond. In a sense battle was joined on 8 March 1291 when Edward I ordered the abbot of Evesham 'to examine his chronicles, and send without delay, under seal, everything that he finds touching in any way our realm and the rule of Scotland'.[2] The Scots' immediate response, to be reiterated many times in subsequent years, as will be more fully explored below, was to retaliate with their own version of the past and present history of Anglo-Scottish relations, culminating in the well known *processus* of Master Baldred Bisset in 1301. Ideas developed in the course of these exchanges were part of a continuum which can be traced through the Declaration of the Clergy in 1309 and the Irish Remonstrance, or 'letter' of 1317, to the supreme articulation of Scottish nationhood and constitutionalism known as the Declaration of Arbroath. It will be argued that the lofty concepts enshrined in that document represent the culmination of a process which was, of itself, a response to a combination of historical circumstances which threatened Scotland's survival as an independent kingdom. As such its importance can hardly be exaggerated and with it this investigation will begin.

It should be stressed, in common with other commentators, that the Declaration of Arbroath was a letter addressed to Pope John XXII by individually named nobles, barons, freeholders, and the 'community of the realm of Scotland'. As mentioned in 'the deeds and books of the ancients', the Scottish nation had a distinguished history, originating in the vicinity of the Black Sea, whence they wandered through the Mediterranean to the Straits of Gibraltar for a lengthy sojourn in Spain. Through the clever device of parallelism - mention of twelve hundred years after the Israelites crossed the Red Sea - the Scots were identified as a chosen people[3] who arrived in Scotland to defeat Britons and Picts while fighting off Scandinavian and English attacks, the Romans being tactfully omitted. 'As the historians of old times bear witness' the Scottish nation had held its possessions 'free of all servitude ever since', under the custodianship of one hundred and thirteen kings 'the line unbroken by a single foreigner'. Even though the Scots existed 'at the uttermost ends of the earth', they were singled out among the first for salvation through the medium of saint Andrew, the first-called of all the disciples.

This favoured people was protected by successive popes as a 'special charge' of Andrew (not, be it noted, of Peter, as the Scottish apologists had argued in the 1290s when they exploited their status as a 'special daughter of the see of Rome' against Edward I's claims), living in freedom and peace until the king of the English arrived in the guise of a friend to despoil them as an enemy.

God intervened to release his people through the medium of Robert Bruce, 'another Maccabeus or Joshua'. The next section which has fascinated posterity and which is often regarded (wrongly) as the climax of the document, deserves to be quoted in full:

> Divine providence, the succession to his right according to our laws and customs which we shall maintain to the death, and the due consent and assent of us all, have made him our prince and king. We are bound to him for the maintaining of our freedom both by his right and merits, as to him by whom salvation has been wrought unto our people, and by him, come what may, we mean to stand. Yet if he should give up what he has begun, seeking to make us or our kingdom subject to the king of England or the English, we would strive at once to drive him out as our enemy and a subverter of his own right and ours, and we would make some other man who was able to defend us our king. For as long as a hundred of us remain alive, we will never on any conditions be subjected to the lordship of the English. For we fight not for glory nor riches nor honours, but for freedom alone, which no good man gives up except with his life.

Yet the main business of the letter is still to come. The Pope is urged to 'admonish and exhort' the English king (Edward II) 'to leave in peace us Scots, who live in this poor little Scotland, beyond which there is no dwelling place at all, and who desire nothing but our own'. They are willing to concede whatever is required for peace - 'due regard having been paid to our standing'. They are deeply concerned that local wars distract from the larger concern of the Crusades in which the Scots would gladly participate if peace were their's. If the Pope pays too much heed to the tales of the English, and will not credit Scottish sincerity, future slaughters and calamities will be laid at his door. They undertake to obey the Pope and they entrust their cause to God, 'firmly trusting that he will inspire courage in us and bring our enemies to nothing'. Wishing the Pope holiness, health and long life. 6 April 1320.[4]

'Can anything conceivably be said about a document apparently so well known in Scotland as the Declaration of Arbroath?' asked Grant Simpson in 1977.[5] He answered resoundingly in the affirmative by proceeding to expertly untangle the relationship between surviving copies, or drafts, of the document in a critique of Sir James Fergusson's version of 1970.[6] However, although Lord Cooper, in 1949, had commended the re-reading of the text - 'judge for yourselves whether it does not deserve on its merits to be ranked as one of the masterpieces of political rhetoric of all time'[7] - Scottish historians with their apparent deep-seated antipathy towards the history of ideas, not to mention their fixation upon the empirical approach, have been reluctant to more profoundly probe the meaning of the document. Since, fortunately, there are honourable exceptions a brief review of the historiography of the document may be in order.

In 1947 J.R. Philip noted that the freedom passage derived from Sallust's *Bellum Catalinae*.[8] Two years later Lord Cooper pointed out that the Declaration contained at least nine quotations from the *Vulgate* and he waxed eloquent over the author's use of the papal *cursus*, indicating certain stylistic and contextual similarities in other documents emanating from the chancery of Robert Bruce. Geoffrey Barrow's absorbing study of the latter (published in 1965 and revised in 1976 and 1988) attempted to demonstrate - contentiously in the view of some of his critics - that the *communitas regni Scotie* denoted,

> the totality of the king's free subjects, but also something more than this; it meant the political entity in which they and the king were comprehended. It was in fact the nearest approach to the later concept of a nation or national state that was possible in an age when . . . a kingdom was first and foremost, a feudal entity, the fief . . . of its king.[9]

He suggested that the Declaration was to be seen as a practical counterpart to Marsiglio of Padua's *Defensor Pacis* of 1324, though upon that notion he did not elaborate. Meanwhile Ranald Nicholson had discovered the Irish Remonstrance of 1317 which was uncannily reminiscent in tone, content and composition to the Arbroath letter and which 'may have been the work of King Robert's propaganda department' since his brother Edward had, by that date, contrived to have himself recognised as High King of Ireland.[10]

The six hundred and fiftieth anniversary generated further scholarly interest, matched by the Post Office which produced a commemorative stamp and by the Nationalists who planned an eternal flame at Arbroath, but not by the Government which refused to declare 6 April a school holiday though one had been granted for *Magna Carta* in 1965. In his Historical Association pamphlet Archie Duncan soberly reminded us all that the Declaration 'is a petition to the Pope that he should write to Edward II to leave the Scots in peace'. He agreed with Barrow that it probably owed something to Edward I's letter to the Pope in 1301 which had 'maintained a similar fiction of baronial intransigence if the king should give way'. He found another antecedent in the letter of 1317 sent by Scottish magnates to papal legates, purporting 'to make the king appear the servant of his people's will and so to justify stiff necked behaviour unbecoming or unnatural in so true a servant of the church'.[11] Grant Simpson greatly expands on this theme distinguishing 'something of a European tradition of baronial letters to the papacy', citing examples from Philip Augustus (1205), King John (1212), Henry III, Edward I, the Irish Baronage (1212 and 1317) as well as a letter from Alexander II and some of the Scottish magnates in 1237.[12]

Ranald Nicholson in his massive treatment of Later Medieval Scotland believed that Barrow had mistaken 'an emotive appeal abounding in hyperbole for a workaday constitutional treatise. The Declaration presents instead a few important ideas in cogent and sonorous phrases; and the field from which these ideas are drawn is not *legalitas* but *humanitas*'. However, markedly more nationalist than he was in 1965, Professor Nicholson added: 'Simply because it is based on an assumption of universal human qualities the Declaration . . . is the most impressive manifesto of nationalism that medieval Europe produced'.[13] Professor Barrow returned to the fray in 1978 to demonstrate that the Declaration's author drew his inspiration from several different *loci* in the *Bellum Catalinae*. The actual quotation from Sallust which Philip (and the Rev. James Bulloch in the *Times Literary Supplement* June 1945) distinguished as the source of Arbroath's inspiration reads, 'But we seek neither dominion nor wealth, for the sake of which all wars and strife among humans are occasioned, but freedom, which no honest man gives up but with his life'. Barrow persuasively suggests that the Arbroath author must have had in mind the speech of Cataline: 'Behold, before your eyes that very freedom for which you have so often yearned, and along with it riches, honour and glory'.[14] He also draws some helpful parallels between the Declaration and the books of the *Maccabees* which seems appropriate since Bruce was explicitly described as another Maccabeus. It is of some interest, therefore, that in 1301 Scottish envoys at the papal court compared Edward I to Antiochus, defiler of the Temple at Jerusalem in 169 B.C., an action which led to the Maccabean revolt. Edward, they alleged, not only inflicted atrocities upon the Scottish kingdom but 'like Antiochus he defiled despotically with sacrilegious recklessness (its) church with abominations of numerous kinds'.[15]

Professor Duncan published a second article on 'the palladium of Scottish nationality' in which he minutely scrutinised the surviving Scottish copy, known as Tyn after Tyninghame, the estate in East Lothian belonging to the earls of Haddington whither it had been taken by the first earl for private study in 1612.[16] He showed that the creation of the Declaration required considerable mobilisation of effort being conceived at a large council held at Newbattle in March 1320, drafted around 6 April at Arbroath abbey, and sent off in May; the April date may have been retained to pacify the Pope who had summoned Bruce and four bishops to appear at the curia on 1 May to explain the Scottish infringement of the papal truce. 'A full-scale governmental effort with all the stops pulled out' was Barrow's response to Duncan's findings, adding that in tone and language the Declaration 'is very different from that of any normal royal letter or administrative document; its content is strongly academic, even didactic'.[17] In the most recent, and at time of writing the fullest, discussion of the document R. James Goldstein has sensibly observed that 'this important monument in the national mythology is clearly far more than a work of medieval propaganda'.[18]

The question to be pondered is the meaning of 'freedom' in the period under review. It may, of course, be reasonably objected that the answer is equally elusive if it is posed of the 1990s or, for that matter, any other historical period, anywhere on the planet. It is a truism that freedom means different things to different people at different times and in different circumstances but modern dictionary definitions, we may think, are not all that far removed from medieval usage. It is of note that freedom is an Old English word whereas liberty appears to be a late medieval acquisition. The *Oxford English Dictionary* suggests 'exemption from slavery,' - that is freedom from being unfree - personal liberty. Individual freedom and state freedom are similar, the latter being defined as 'exemption from arbitrary control,' or independence, though admittedly state and individual freedom may not always be compatible but rather antithetical. It is striking how central the theme of freedom is to Scottish historiography, a precious, and at times a slim, thread linking the centuries. It has thus always appeared dramatically satisfying that Tacitus should have introduced the metaphor, at the very dawn of Scottish history, into the mouth of Calgacus when 'the last men on earth, the last of the free', faced the brutality of Rome at Mons Graupius.

> Robbery, butchery, rapine the liars call Empire; they create a desolation and call it peace . . . let us, then, uncorrupted, unconquered as we are, ready to fight for freedom but never to

repent failure, prove at the first clash of arms what heroes Caledonia has been holding in reserve.[19]

Seventeen hundred years later Robert Burns would echo Tacitus in the anthem inspired by Bannockburn and sung to the air *Hey tutti taitie*, traditionally believed to have been played at the battle.[20] Tacitus was not to be rediscovered until the late fifteenth century but there can be little doubt that the Scottish obsession with freedom was born in the struggles against Edward I.

Professor Barrow has usefully collected references to construct 'a pedigree of the notion of freedom and liberty as used or applied in medieval Scotland'.[21] The earliest examples occur in an ecclesiastical context during the long reign of William I, a period so crucial in the secular domain to Edward I's propagandist claims of English overlordship. The problem is that these first occurrences figure in the correspondence of an Italian pope, Alexander III and an English chronicler, Roger of Howden. The first native reference appears in the *Chronicle of Melrose* reporting the Quitclaim of Canterbury by which William restored the 'dignities, liberties and honours' which he had so dismally surrendered at Falaise in 1174; 'thus, God willing, he worthily and honourably removed the heavy yoke of domination and servitude from the kingdom of the Scots'.[22] The crucial Treaty of Birgham which anticipated the marriage between Margaret the Maid of Norway and the future Edward II, and thus an inevitable dynastic union of the kingdoms, preserved Scottish 'rights, laws, liberties and customs' and stated that 'the realm of Scotland shall remain separate, divided off and free in itself without subjection from the realm of England, as has been the case down to the present time',[23] though apparently no-one felt the need to include a reciprocal clause safeguarding England's rights!

Bishop Robert Wishart of Glasgow had helped draft the treaty. When, in May 1291, Edward sought recognition of his superiority over Scotland, Wishart responded that the kingdom of Scotland 'from long ago was free to the extent that it owed tribute, or homage, to no-one save God alone and his agent on earth', echoing Alexander III's famous disclaimer when performing homage for his English estates in 1278.[24] In support, the good bishop quoted a prophecy of Gildas. Wishart's speech, as reconstructed by Barrow utilising a Scottish brief recently discovered in Spain, argued that a kingless nation could not subject itself to another. To Edward's challenge to prove that he was not Scotland's rightful suzerain, Wishart retorted that Scotland's laws denied his premise. His sentiments were, in part, echoed in the letter sent to Edward in the name of the community of the realm of Scotland broadly stating that the Scots could not speak for their absent king.[25]

There is some reference to freedom in the 'Instructions' sent to Scottish representatives at the papal court, then based at Agnani, in 1301. Edward I was said to have attacked Scotland 'when vacant, headless, rent in pieces, widowed as it were of rule by its own king' so unjustly disturbing 'the previous state of Scotland's ancient freedom'. He had ignored papal arguments about the liberty of Scotland in favour of citations from the legendary history of Britain, Brutus *et al.*, but the envoys were insistent that he could not legitimately 'make connections between the conditions of Britons long ago and his very recent acts of oppression in the present day'. Furthermore:

> the kingdom of Scotland . . . has always been completely free as regards the king of England by virtue of the common law (under which an equal does not have authority over an equal, and a king is not subject to a king or a kingdom to a kingdom, just as a consul is not subject to a consul or a praetor to a praetor) and both from time immemorial, and also now, it has always been in possession of this kind of freedom.

The document goes on to condemn the king's 'unproven fictions about an obsolete distant past'. The sophistication of argument, the confidence with which common law is invoked and bogus history dismissed, in these protestations, is both admirable and noteworthy. It has long been known that the arguments were co-ordinated by Master Baldred Bisset, canon lawyer and luminary of Bologna, a man who clearly had no doubts about his identity; nor did his colleagues; nor could their listeners have failed to understand that the pleadings they heard emanated from something more than the mouths of renegade Englishmen or feudal rebels. People who could so effectively manipulate history and common law in the advocacy of a special kind of freedom undoubtedly knew who they were and from where they were coming:

> . . . from time immemorial the kingdom of Scotland has rejoiced in every kind of liberty, and has a prescriptive right to liberty with support in this from the common law . . . And it is certain that just as the kingdom of Scotland has recently been shown to have been free when its last king died (i.e. Alexander III 1286), so it is presumed to have been free from antiquity if we make an assumption from the recent past and apply it to the more remote past before then, just as the laws dictate; and subsequent events show that it is so.[26]

Subsequent events had also shown that by the turn of the century the Scots (or some of them) had a pretty good grasp of the rhetoric of freedom, which, for example, pervades the Spanish brief alluded to above, and now dubbed the 'Bamburgh narrative' by Dr. Goldstein since it was apparently manufactured for unsuccessful peace regulations at Bamburgh in 1321. It clearly utilised materials dating from the 1290s but it is the rhetoric, employing as it does the *cursus*, which is of greatest interest. The 'ancient liberty and nobility of the kings and kingdom' had lasted for two thousand years 'with the unanimous consent of the entire people'. Following Edward's intervention the Scottish nobles appointed Bruce as king and he it was who 'restored the afflicted kingdom and desolate people to their former liberty'.[27]

Scottish concerns were, of course, part of a much wider European debate. Dante described freedom as God's greatest gift to human nature.[28] John of Salisbury believed that '*Libertas* means judging everything freely in accordance with private judgement'. He argued that liberty could not be separated from virtue and he continued in a most suggestive passage, in the present context, 'since all agree that virtue is the highest good in life and that it alone can strike off the heavy and hateful yoke of slavery, it has been the opinion of philosophers that men should die, if need arose, for the sake of virtue, which is the only reason for living'. The passage from *Policraticus* expands on this point:

> Virtue can never be fully attained without liberty, and the absence
> of liberty proves that virtue in its full perfection is wanting . . .
> none ever trod liberty underfoot save the open foes of virtue. The
> jurists know what good laws were introduced for the sake of
> liberty, and the testimony of historians has made famous the great
> deeds done for the love of it.[29]

Certain it is that the Scots invoked historical arguments in defence of freedom, particularly the freedom of the kingship and in so doing they stressed a unique Scottish identity.

Baldred Bisset incorporated many of the ideas from the 'Instructions' in his famous pleading addressed to Pope Boniface in 1301; it can be seen as part of a powerful sequence beginning with the responses to Edward's claims in 1291 and running through to the Declaration itself in 1320. The first point which Baldred stressed was common law - 'it is almost against natural law and astonishing for someone who enjoys legal independence to be subjected to the authority of someone else'. The Scots had been converted to christianity five hundred years before the English since which time they had always recognised the lordship of the Roman church and not that of England. At the negotiations over the Treaty of Birgham Edward had been forced to recognise that Scotland was a kingdom, quite separate, and entirely free from any kind of English subjection or lordship. Moreover, the Scots had 'a claim on freedom for a very long and immemorial period of time . . . as part of the nature of things'. King Alexander III had protested his freedom from Edward who took no action when, on the king's death, guardians were 'freely elected' to rule the kingdom, the point being that had Scotland been an English fief it would have reverted to Edward at that time. Instead, at the demise of the infant Margaret, daughter of Alexander III, Edward 'thrust himself forward in the guise of sheep's clothing' and asserted his lordship 'through oppression, force and fear'.

In order to refute Edward's historical arguments Baldred examines three time periods - most remote, past and present - the first pre-dating the birth of Christ, the second up to Edward's usurpation of the kingdom of Scotland, the present occupying the years since that disastrous event. He flatly rejects English assertions that Brutus in bequeathing his kingdom to his three sons made Albanactus (Scotland) subject to Locrinus (England). Instead he cites Scota the daughter of Pharaoh who sailed to Scotland bringing with her 'the royal seat', which Edward had recently removed forcibly to England, 'along with other insignia of the kingdom'. The children of Scota have ever since been free; English claims to overlordship based on events from Arthur to King John are forthrightly dismissed.[30]

The first real evidence that Robert Bruce's propaganda department was up and running is to be discerned in the Declaration by the Clergy of Scotland at the St Andrews parliament in 1309. There it is stated the 'the faithful people of Scotland always believed without hesitation, as they had understood from their ancestors and elders, and held to be the truth', that Robert the Competitor, grandfather of the king, was the true heir of Alexander III and his granddaughter. The denial of his claim had brought disasters upon the kingdom as 'experience of events, our mistress in politics, now often repeated, has manifestly shown'. To relieve the suffering caused by invasion and war, the people, 'by divine prompting', distinguishing their need for a captain and leader, and recognising that Bruce had inherited the rights of his grandfather, received Robert as king. 'By their authority he was set over the realm and formally established as king of Scots, and with him the faithful people of the realm (*fidelis populus regni*) wish to live and die, as with one who, by right of birth and by endowment with other cardinal virtues, is fit to rule, and worthy of the name of king and of the honour of the realm'. This fascinating text contains a reference to 'the consent of the whole people' - *consensum populi et plebis* - which seems somewhat more all embrasive than the *communitas regni*.[31] Furthermore the election of Bruce may echo the *Policraticus* V, chapter vi, in which the prince,

> is placed by divine governance at the apex of the commonwealth, and preferred above all others, sometimes through the secret ministry of God's providence, sometimes by the decision of His priests, and again it is the votes of the whole people (*totius populi*) which concur to place the ruler in authority.[32]

The jurists had long since decided that heredity alone did not confer the privilege of kingship and the example of King John must have reinforced such a view.[33] Freedom was undoubtedly catching. Around this same time three Scottish knights met up at Cambuskenneth abbey and swore in the presence of the abbot that they would 'defend the freedom of the kingdom and of Robert lately crowned king, against all mortals, French, English and Scots, to their last breath', a most interesting anticipation, as Professor Duncan points out, of the Arbroath declaration.[34]

The clergy's declaration conspicuously shares the rhetoric of both the Irish letter of 1317 and of the Declaration of Arbroath, a highly charged vocabulary and style already encountered in some of the earlier pleadings. Thus in 1309 the whole people, *populus et plebs*, of the realm of Scotland suffered many tribulations as the kingdom was reduced to:

> servitude, laid waste with great slaughter, and imbued with the bitterness of heavy sorrow, made desolate by the lack of good governance, exposed to every danger, given up to the despoiler, the inhabitants deprived of their property, tortured with strife, made captive, bound and imprisoned, oppressed with untold killings of blameless people, and with continual burnings, subject and in bonds, and nigh to perpetual ruin.[35]

The letter of the Irish to the pope is much more extreme in tone, recounting how Ireland's downfall is to be dated to 1170 when Pope Adrian, 'by a certain form of words', conferred the lordship of Ireland upon Henry II. 'And thus . . . he handed us over to be mangled by the cruel teeth of all the beasts. And those of us that escaped woefully flayed and half-dead from the teeth of crafty foxes and ravenous wolves sank violently into an abyss of sorrowful slavery'. The Irish, too, could boast a lengthy pedigree, of, in their case, one hundred and thirty six kings, 'without admixture of foreign blood', extending over a period of three thousand five hundred years all the way from Milesius. They too have a sense of the remote, the past and the present, rehearsing English treachery, betrayal and atrocity during the previous century and a half. In order to 'shake off the harsh and insupportable yoke of servitude' and to recover their 'native freedom', *libertas innata*, they have joined war with the oppressor. To aid their cause they have recruited Edward Bruce, brother of Robert, 'sprung from our noblest ancestors'. Since 'each person is free to give up his right and transfer it to another', they have established Edward as their king.[36]

Finally in the Declaration of Arbroath the Scots had lived in freedom and peace until Edward I,

> when our kingdom had no head and our people harboured no malice or treachery and were then unused to wars or attacks, came in the guise of friend and ally to invade them as an enemy. His wrongs, killings, violence, pillage, arson, imprisonment of prelates, burning down of monasteries, despoiling and killing of religious, and yet other innumerable outrages, sparing neither sex nor age, religion nor order, no-one could fully describe or fully understand unless experience had taught him.[37]

What is to be recognised in all three declarations is the rhetoric of tyranny. The universally acknowledged authority on tyrants and tyranny, on 'tyrannology' as a recent commentator has described it,[38] was John of Salisbury's *Policraticus*. 'The tyrant', he says, 'oppresses the people by rulership based upon force and regards nothing as accomplished unless the laws are brought to naught and the people are reduced to slavery'.[39] John, however, was forced to admit that tyranny must be a part of God's providential ordering of the universe. He asserted that 'tyrants are properly deserved by a stiff necked and stubborn people', so the Scots, and presumably the Irish, may be thought by some to have received their just deserts. John, as almost all writers on the subject, rather dithered as to what should be done about the tyrant, suggesting only prayer and forbearance until the offender was removed by God. But since the deity moves in mysterious ways he may employ an individual as his instrument. Both John and the authors of the declarations borrow heavily from the *Old Testament*. The Children of Israel,

> when the allotted time of their punishment was fulfilled . . . were allowed to cast off the yoke from their necks by the slaughter of tyrants; nor is blame attached to any of those by whose valour a penitent and humbled people were thus set free, but their memory

is preserved in affection and honour by posterity as servants of God.[40]

Elsewhere John seems to anticipate the Bartolean distinction of 'tyrants by abuse of power' when he remarks that whoever takes up the sword deserves to perish by it:

> And he is understood to take up the sword who usurps it by his own temerity and who does not receive the power of using it from God. Therefore the law rightly takes arms against him who disarms the laws and the public power rages in fury against him who strives to bring to nought the public force.[41]

John further reminds his readers that in the *Book of Isiah* the one 'who tried to build his throne in the north and make himself like unto the most high' was none other than Lucifer, the very antithesis of the true prince who should present 'a kind of likeness of divinity'.[42] Since the Scots were threatened with interdict in 1320 tact may have dictated that they refrain from baldly identifying Edward I and Edward II as tyrants, but they undoubtedly made the point implicitly through the language they employed. The Declaration made an appeal to natural justice in depicting Robert Bruce as the Lord's instrument chosen to free his people from tyranny.

The works of John of Salisbury were so well known that there is no particular difficulty in assuming that the author, or authors, of the Declaration would have access to them. Just who did mastermind the letter of 1320 is not known. An earlier generation was confident that it was composed by Bernard de Linton, chancellor of Scotland who became abbot of Arbroath about 1310. Professor Duncan has now demonstrated that Bernard de Linton and Abbot Bernard of Arbroath, the chancellor, were different people.[43] The latter first appears as chancellor in 1308 so he could have had a sight of the declaration of 1309, conceivably the Irish letter of 1317 and certainly the 1320 Declaration. Both of the Scottish pieces make extensive use of the *cursus*, but the attribution of various other documents to the hand of Abbot Bernard has been rejected.[44] The case against Bernard, however, is not absolutely conclusive, at least in respect of the three documents under review. No doubt his duties as chancellor kept him pretty fully occupied but he still found time to compose a significant body of Latin verse, including a poetic version of Bruce's speech at Bannockburn, which contained the line, 'My lords, my people, who lay great weight on freedom'. During the past eight years they had suffered great hardships, 'for our right to the kingdom, for honour and liberty', *pro regni jure, pro libertatis honore*.[45] At the very least Bernard could well have ensured compatibility of style and content. The candidate suggested for authorship by Professor Barrow is Mr Alexander Kinninmonth, a canon lawyer with considerable curial experience and future bishop of Aberdeen; he was one the ambassadors who accompanied the 1320 missive to the papal court at Avignon.[46] Authorship will probably never be conclusively proven but what is significant is the vein of rhetoric, metaphor and style shared, to a greater or lesser extent, by the documents under discussion. A degree of familiarity and expertise had clearly built up in Bernard's chancery which was often situated at Arbroath. There is a potentially interesting connection here for Arbroath was founded by William I in 1178 and dedicated to his good friend, Thomas Becket, on whose life John of Salisbury was the main authority.[47] The Irish letter, coincidentally perhaps, contains a reference to 'the false and wicked representation of King Henry of England, under whom and perhaps by whom St Thomas of Canterbury . . . suffered death for justice and defence of the church'.[48] At the very least there must be a strong possibility that John's works were available in the monastic library at Arbroath.

Robert Bruce who had lived by the sword was pragmatic enough to pay lip service to the idea that if he backtracked he might also perish by it at the hands of his own subjects. Most commentators have agreed that this section of the Arbroath letter is simply a concession to expedient rhetoric, but this is to seriously underestimate its significance. The momentous clause which stated that if Robert ever threatened to submit to English rule he would be driven out 'as our enemy and a subverter of his own right and ours' and that some other, able in defence, would be appointed as king, is the first national or governmental articulation, in all of Europe, of the principle of the contractual theory of monarchy which lies at the root of modern constitutionalism. Extraordinary though that claim might appear it is sustainable in the present state of our knowledge and it arises from the unique concatenation of circumstances that are cumulatively known as the Scottish Wars of Independence. Furthermore there can be little doubt that the statement should be taken seriously for lurking in the background was the shade of John Balliol, or, to give him his proper title, King John.[49]

There is a substantial body of secondary literature in existence which is devoted to the growth of early constitutionalism through the application to secular affairs of theories developed by canon lawyers.[50] The church had long confronted the problem of how to remove a lawfully appointed dignitary, especially one who had been ordained, when that individual was no longer fit for office. As canonical ideas impacted upon the secular sphere Pope

Celestine V, Adolf of Nassau and Edward II followed one another, in rapid succession, into the abyss of deposition, between 1294 and 1327.[51] Such 'depositions' took different forms; Celestine, for example, technically abdicated, but it will be here argued that Scottish King John should be added to the list and that the implications behind his departure were surely in the mind of whoever drafted the Declaration of Arbroath.

King John's success in the Great Cause was a victory for the principle of primogeniture, although, as is well known, Edward treated him as a feudal vassal and rapidly engineered his humiliation by encouraging appeals from Scotland to England and - in the final ignominy - demanding Scottish troops to fight in France. On 5 July 1295 John's subjects relieved him of the government of Scotland in an 'act of sober constitutional revolution'.[52] The episode is, admittedly, not well documented but clearly uncertainty about his intentions, or options, must have been a major motive, and a council of twelve, consisting of four bishops, four earls and four barons, was appointed to manage the affairs of the country *-pares sive custodes constituti sunt ad tuitionem at defensionem libertatis regni et communitatis eiusdem.*[53] Bower may have had the same incident in mind when he laconically reported that John summoned a parliament at which he recounted 'the injustices, insults, slights and shame which he had endured'. The next sentence may imply that John's decision was made for him:

> it was determined there that the same King John should utterly
> revoke the homage and fealty offered to the king of England
> because it had been wrung from him by force and fear; and that
> he could in no way obey him and his commands any longer to the
> detriment of his country's liberty.[54]

Exactly one year after the Stirling parliament John was forced, in agonising abjection, to resign his kingship to Edward I.[55] But, as is well known, when Andrew Moray and William Wallace took up the cause of resistance they claimed to be acting 'in the name of the eminent prince Lord John, by grace of God the illustrious king of Scotland, with the agreement of the community of the realm', while as late as 1301 Baldred Bisset was still referring to 'John our king', *rex noster*, and it has been convincingly suggested that his solution to Scotland's dire plight, as Edward sought 'the perpetual annihilation of all the blood, nation and name of the Scots', was to recommend to the pope the restoration of King John; indeed it was fear of just such an eventuality which explains Bruce's turnaround and his resubmission to Edward I.[56] It may be suggested that a separation of the powers had taken place at Stirling in 1295 or, to borrow the terminology of the canon lawyers, the *dignitas* was parted from the *administratio* while King John was *incapax*. The wretched John was Scotland's very own example of the *rex inutilis* or the 'useless king'. A revolution had taken place not only in Scottish, but in European, terms as well.

The question arises of why John did not suffer outright deposition. In the first place his claim seems to have been widely recognised. Furthermore there was no obvious successor, the Bruces untrusted and Robert, the future king, untried. There was clearly no desire to re-open the Great Cause and the 'English Justinian' had revealed his true colours. Most importantly, the council of twelve, in which reposed the *administratio,* reserved its right to reject or deny the legality of any future actions that might be carried out by, or visited upon, King John, as turned out to be the case.

In the twelfth century, the legal theorist, Huguccio, had preoccupied himself with the problems of the prelate who, through personal accident, such as illness or madness, or through criminality, was unfit for office. He concluded that the solution lay in the appointment of a curator or coadjutor who would be given the *administratio* while the *dignitas* remained with the individual who was incapacitated or *incapax*. To quote Edward Peters:

> Huguccio opened up a new line of thought which, although not strictly in keeping with contemporary political practice, was consistent with other canonist ideas about the nature of public authority and governance. Between 1190 and 1243, however, this approach existed solely in the commentaries upon the *Decretum.* It remained for a political authority to test Huguccio's alternatives.[57]

The test came with the case of Sancho II of Portugal in 1245 but on this occasion the pope took the initiative in the deposition. His Holiness was in no way involved in the demise of King John.

It is quite evident that the necessary expertise in canon law was present in Scotland in the last decade of the thirteenth century when the *Ecclesia Scoticana* could boast a galaxy of talent most it of aligned with the Bruce party. Such well known figures as bishop Fraser of St Andrews, bishop William Lamberton and the already mentioned bishop Robert Wishart of Glasgow, himself a guardian between 1286 and 1292, are only a few of the many. Baldred Bisset's credentials are not in doubt while Master William Frere, archdeacon of Lothian from 1285 to 1305 was not unique by Scottish standards in having spent the earlier part of his life as a regent in law at Paris.[58] There were canonical precedents in Scotland. Richard first abbot of

Melrose was deposed in 1148, as was Adam abbot of Alnwick (just on the English side of the border) in 1208. About 1184 abbot Gerard at Dryburgh became incapacitated and unable to manage the business of the house. The monk who would become famous as Adam of Dryburgh was elected in his stead, although he apparently felt unhappy about receiving episcopal benediction out of affection towards Gerard. Nevertheless this case seems a clear example of the separation of the *dignitas* and the *administratio.*[59]

To return to the removal clause in the Declaration, an important point should not be overlooked. When Bruce made his pact with Lamberton in 1304 and his bid for the crown in 1305-6, he was not only taking up the sword against the tyrant; he was also usurping the *dignitas* of King John. The fact that he did so makes it difficult, I think, to read the passage in the Arbroath letter concerning the possible future deposition of Bruce himself as pure bluff. He and his advisors were forced to refine a theory justifying his action to the world, the pope, and the people of Scotland. Here we might say with Professor Tierney,

> Our argument is not that hard-headed medieval statesmen behaved in such and such a way because some theorist in a university had invented a theory saying they ought to do so. The argument is rather that all men behave in certain ways, in part at least, because they adhere to certain ways of thinking. No doubt the ideas that are most influential in shaping actions are ones that the agent is hardly conscious of at all - he takes them so much for granted.[60]

In view of the foregoing it is worth considering, briefly, whether there was conceivably any echo of archaic kingship in the Bruce concept of the institution since it is well known that the ancient kings of Scots had sometimes lost their office 'for good seasons', that is, to restore the prosperity of their kingdom.[61] The earliest examples of books of advice for good rulers (later to be known as 'mirrors') are Irish and are thought to have inspired such writers as John of Salisbury.[62] The father of them all, *The Testament of Morand*, believed by Francis Byrne to date from around 600, attributes much to the prince's power of truth, or justice - prosperity, fertility for people, beasts and crops, and the avoidance of plague, famine and natural calamity.[63] The seventh century tract, *De duodecim abusivis saeculi*, states that the justice of the king,

> consists in oppressing no-one wrongfully through his might . . .
> However, let the king know that just as on his throne he is

established first among men, so too shall he hold the primacy in torments should he fail to do justice.[64]

Sedulius Scottus the Irish poet and philosopher who probably composed his *De rectoribus christianis* (*On Christian Rulers*) for Charles the Bald in the mid-ninth century, describes the eight pillars which sustain the just king - truth, patience, generosity, powers of persuasion, punishment of evil, friendship, lightness of tribute and equality of justice between rich and poor. False rulers, on the other hand, are rewarded with,

> sudden misfortunes, calamities, captivities, bereavements of children, slaughter of friends, barrenness of the earth's fruits, unbearable plagues, short and unhappy days, long illnesses, most miserable deaths and, above all, eternal torments.[65]

The logical remedy, in all cases, was the removal of the bad king who was thus sacrificed for good seasons. King John had undoubtedly opened the gates to Plantagenet tyranny. The invocation of Celtic ideas would have permitted Robert Bruce simultaneously to remove the *rex inutilis* and to resist the tyranny of the two Edwards. This is not to suggest that Bruce's advisers had read the Irish tracts but rather to imply that the ideas espoused by such literature could well have continued to circulate in thirteenth century Scotland, as they certainly did in Gaelic Scotland three hundred years later when it was believed that incompetent or incapable clan chiefs could be removed for the greater good.[66]

In the Turnberry Band of 1286 Robert Bruce the Competitor, in company with the Stewarts and the Macdonalds, had sworn allegiance to the person 'who will obtain the kingdom of Scotland by reason of the blood of the late King Alexander according to the ancient customs hitherto approved and used in the kingdom of Scotland'.[67] Old Bruce's claim was based upon 'nearness of degree', an argument which found sympathy with some European experts whose opinion was sought.[68] Much importance was clearly still attached to the kin-base. Certain earls had comparatively recently relinquished the grace title as in *dei gratia comes de Fyf* or *dei indulgentia comes Stradhern* which emphasised their status as princes in their own right and so blurring the distinction between themselves and the one who was *Dei Gratia Rex Scotorum*.[69] There is some evidence of a Celtic antiquarian revival in thirteenth century Ireland as a reaction to the Anglo-Norman presence; renewed interest in the Scota legend may indicate a parallel development in

Scotland.[70] Robert Bruce's interest in the *Gaidhealtachd* is well attested and he could appeal to a common heritage in addressing the Irish:

> we and you and our people and your people, free since ancient times, share the same national ancestry and are urged to come together more eagerly and joyfully in friendship by a common language and common custom, we have sent over to you our beloved kinsmen, the bearers of this letter, to negotiate with you in our name about permanently strengthening and maintaining inviolate the special friendship between us and you, so that with God's will *our nation* may be able to recover her ancient liberty (my italics).[71]

The remarkable letter to the Irish should be read in the context of what is undoubtedly the most spectacular example of Celtic revivalism. In 1307 it was reported to Edward that false preachers were telling the Scots that they had found a prophecy of Merlin stating that after the death of *le Roi Coveytous* 'the Scottish people and the Britons shall league together, and have the sovereign hand . . . and live in accord till the end of the world'. Bower records a Welsh and an Irish prophecy about the Scottish triumph.[72] After Bannockburn Edward Bruce was despatched to Ireland. The author of the *Vita Edwardi Secundi* nervously noted a rumour to the effect that if Robert's objectives in Ireland were achieved he would at once cross to Wales 'and raise the Welsh likewise against our king. For these two races bear hardly the yoke of slavery and curse the lordship of the English'. In fact there was contact between Edward Bruce and the Welsh and in 1315 Llewelyn raised a rebellion on the Welsh march.[73] Bruce envisioned nothing less than a pan-Celtic alliance, as prophesied by Merlin, and as popularised by Geoffrey of Monmouth in his *History of the Kings of Britain*:

> Albany will be angry; calling her near neighbours to her she shall give herself up entirely to bloodshed . . . (The Celts) shall load with chains the necks of the roaring ones and live again the days of their forefathers . . . The foreigners shall be slaughtered and the rivers will run with blood . . . The mountains of Armorica shall erupt and Armorica itself shall be crowned with Brutus' diadem. Kambria shall be filled with joy and the Cornish oaks shall flourish . . . [74]

Robert Bruce, in projecting himself as *Arthur Redivivant*, and so reclaiming Arthur as a Celtic hero for the Celtic peoples of Britain, was about to embark upon a universal crusade against injustice and tyranny. Freedom was to become Scotland's most precious export. In the process he orchestrated one of the greatest and most inspirational moments in all of Scottish - or for that matter British - history. It may indeed be the case that in Scotland's Celtic past, and in Bruce's reconstruction thereof, are to be detected Professor Tierney's 'certain ways of thinking' and the ideas of which the agent is hardly conscious at all since, 'he takes them so much for granted'.

There may, however, be a more immediate, if paradoxically distant, source of the Declaration's bold assertion that Bruce might be deposed and another set up in his place. All commentators are agreed that the most fruitful period of canonist theory embraced the years from c.1290 to the mid fourteenth century.[75] The thirteenth century rediscovery of Aristotelianism engaged the greatest mind of the era, that of Thomas Aquinas, who is the acknowledged link between classical thought and civic humanism. He wisely observed *civitas est nonnisi congregatio hominium*, 'the state is nothing but the congregation of men' and he suggestively opined, though he probably knew little or nothing of Scotland, that 'lesser evil follows from the corruption of a monarchy than from the corruption of an aristocracy'.[76]

Aquinas, like his predecessors, addressed the problem of tyranny, for the avoidance of which he posited three means. Firstly election should pertain to one section of the community which would exclude candidates with tyrannical tendencies. Secondly he seems to imply that tyrants may be removed by public authority and, thirdly, the king's power must be limited. Aquinas in this, his great work, *De regimine principum, On the Government of Rulers*, seems to be grasping for a theory which will accommodate the different types of polity that he knows to be in existence. Thus in certain circumstances it might be true to say that 'if the multitude has the right to choose its king, it has the right to depose him, for the king has broken his pact with his subjects; that is, to govern for the common good',[77] but that may be to read more into Aquinas than is actually there. Virtually all theorists who followed Aquinas wrote in his shadow. What is of greatest interest in the context of this paper is that all historians of medieval political thought concur that the first thinker to articulate the theory of the legality of deposition was John of Paris, also known as John Quidort, author of *De potestate regia et papali, On Royal and Papal Power* (1302). In this work, John, greatly exercised by the recent resignation of Pope Celestine V, joined the battle then raging between Boniface VIII and Philip IV of France, championing the latter and insisting upon the supremacy of the monarch in secular affairs. John, who was one of the greatest teachers at Paris in the 1290s may have actually taught some of the canon lawyers who, it has been suggested above, contributed to the Scottish political ideas which were to receive their finest expression in the Arbroath declaration. He believed that kingship offered the best type of government. To quote Arthur Monahan who puts the issues most succinctly:

> he maintained equally that this form of government is 'from God and the people electing'; that 'a king exists by the will of the people'; and that 'kingly power is from . . . the people who give their consent and choice' . . . He also draws a correlative conclusion concerning withdrawal of the people's consent from a temporal ruler: such withdrawal constitutes deposition from office.

Furthermore John assigns 'the function of expressing the popular will in both establishing and deposing a king to the barons and peers of the realm'.[78] The use of this latter phrase *barones et pares* and their precise relationship to the *populus* at large has given rise to as much contention and controversy as Geoffrey Barrow's interpretation of the *communitas regni*.[79] The point is that just as the cardinals represent the whole people in deposing a pope, so too would the barons and peers in deposing a king.[80] Similarly the *communitas regni* is, and is of, the whole people of Scotland. Those same people, the Scots, seem to be the first to exploit John of Paris' ideas for their own purposes thus demonstrating once again that Scotland in the early fourteenth century was 'amongst the most conceptually advanced kingdoms of medieval Europe'.[81]

The image of Bruce as a second Arthur of the prophecies of Merlin, chosen by God, elected by his people and sanctioned by heredity is undoubtedly inspirational as is his assigned role as liberator, defender of his people and battle champion. The metaphorical challenge to this paragon, however, was the awkward historicity of one, William Wallace, whose shade would stalk future centuries as surely as it did the kingship of Robert Bruce.

Seven hundred years after the battle of Stirling Bridge Wallace continues to confound historians. Even Geoffrey Barrow does not seem entirely at ease with his *persona*, observing with an uncharacteristic disregard for the lack of evidence that Wallace 'had the defects of his qualities, and one of these was lack of imagination'.[82] A superabundance of the latter commodity has informed almost every one of Wallace's biographers from Blind Harry to the present.[83] Wallace enjoys the role of Scotland's unimpeachable national hero, perhaps the only individual in Scottish history who never compromised in any manner whatsoever with the enemy. Yet, ironically for a national icon, almost everything that is known about the man and his deeds, in strictly contemporary terms, is derived not only from foreign, but from enemy, sources.

The earliest native account is contained in John of Fordun's *Chronica Gentis Scotorum* which was written about 1370. The story therein is that the hero rose from his 'den' to slay the English sheriff of Lanark. Despite the fact that his father was a knight, the Scottish nobility regarded him as lowborn. He triumphed at Stirling Bridge, raided into the north of England and suffered a brutal defeat at Falkirk thanks to the treachery of the nobility, notably Bruce who contrived to attack the Scottish army from behind. Fordun lamented that Scottish defeat at English hands was usually due to aristocratic jealousy. William thereafter resigned as Guardian, opting 'rather to serve with the commons (*plebs*) than to be set over them to their ruin and the grievous wasting of the people (*populus*). He alone stood out when the whole kingdom submitted to Edward. Betrayed by Sir John Menteith he was savagely executed at Smithfield.[84] Andrew Wyntoun in his vernacular metrical chronicle c.1420 notes the support of the 'lele comownys' for Wallace about whom 'gret gestis' had been composed. According to the chronicler a 'gret buk' could have been made about William but Andrew himself had neither the wit nor the leisure for such a task.[85]

The full blown legend of William Wallace is first encountered in the pages of Walter Bower's *Scotichronicon* compiled in the 1440s. Herein is depicted a man favoured by God and 'successful in everything'. In a passage which would be repeated and embroidered from century to century Bower has Wallace and Bruce meet up for a verbal exchange across an 'impassibly deep valley' after the battle of Falkirk in which, as in Fordun, William has been betrayed by Robert. When the latter asks the former why he wished to oppose not only Edward but the Scottish nobility, Wallace replies that it is Bruce's own inactivity, cowardice, feebleness and effete behaviour which has spurred him to action.[86] Though this passage has been largely ignored by modern historians - and irrespective of its historicity- it received prominence from virtually everyone who wrote on the wars of independence right down to the nineteenth century. The significance of the exchange is, of course, that aristocratic (and potentially monarchic) perfidy is countered by folk valour; the credentials of the heir to the throne are no match for the leader of the commons.

Contemporary Scottish attitudes towards Wallace are probably pretty well summed up in a section of the *Scotichronicon* discussing his position after all of Scotland has submitted to the English yoke in 1304, Wallace alone refusing so to do:

For the noble William was afraid of the treachery of his
countrymen. Some of them envied him for his uprightness, others
were seduced by the promises of the English, and others with
tortuous machinations and infinite care prepared traps for him,
hoping thereby for the favour of the king of England. In addition
persuasive arguments were offered to him by his immediate close
friends that he like the others should obey the king of the English,
so that they might thus obtain peace. Besides, others were sent by
the king himself to persuade him to do this, promising him on the
same king's behalf earldoms and wide possessions in England or
in Scotland, to be chosen by himself and held by his successors
for ever. He despised all these approaches, and speaking for the
liberty of his people like a second Mattathias he is reported to
have answered: 'Scotland, desolate as you are, you believe too
much in false words and are too unwary of woes to come! If you
think like me, you would not readily place your neck under a
foreign yoke. When I was growing up', he said, 'I learned from a
priest who was my uncle to set this one proverb above all worldly
possessions, and I have carried it in my heart:

> I tell you the truth, freedom is the
> finest of things;
> never live under a servile yoke, my son.

And that is why I tell you briefly that even if all Scots obey the
king of England so that each one abandons his liberty, I and my
companions who wish to be associated with me in this matter
shall stand up for the liberty of the kingdom. And . . . we others
shall obey no one but the king of Scots or his lieutenant.[87]

The fact that Wallace was not, strictly, a commoner, is irrelevant. He
was the younger son of a knight and was subsequently knighted himself; he
participated in embassies to the curia and to France where no less a personage
that Philip IV provided a letter of recommendation for 'our beloved William le
Walois of Scotland, knight'.[88] It is quite true, as Professor Barrow has
forcefully reminded us, that Wallace cannot be described as a 'man from
nowhere', nor did he act alone in 1297, but rather that he owed 'such standing
as he possessed in the community of the realm of Scotland to his place among
the feudal vassals of James Stewart'.[89] This is all true historically but as
medieval accounts make clear, such was not the perception of contemporaries;
in the eyes of English chroniclers, in particular, he was a hideous and
unnatural monster.

In the midst of so much that was revolutionary in the tumultious years between 1290 and 1320 the role of Wallace as military leader of a national revolt is surely the most remarkable of all. In a world that believed in the Great Chain of Being where everything had its natural place Wallace's actions threatened the very fabric of the cosmos. In another era he would have been accused of turning the world upside down and that perception, above all, explains the antipathy of the Scottish nobility as well as the near paranoid determination of Edward I to bring him to the scaffold; they would hardly have agreed that Wallace 'lacked imagination'. William was certainly a conservative who acted for his absent king, John, but History placed him in a revolutionary situation. The fact of his existence was potentially disastrous to a king like Robert I who belatedly adopted the mantle of Maccabeus while manipulating such volatile political ideas as election and deposition in the context of *communitas*, *populus*, and *plebs*. Professor Barrow may be correct in his intriguing suggestion that Bruce was described as *dux* or *capitaneus* in order to stress a continuity between himself and Wallace who, according to an English observer 'had been for long a captain of the Scottish people against King Edward'.[90] It is to be hoped that Barrow is correct though one might wish for more evidence since Bruce's rhetoric otherwise makes no mention of Wallace, presumably because to mention him would detract from the king's own heroic achievement as well as offending his aristocratic sensibilities. The point is that Wallace's memory was *not* subsumed or erased. His ghost lingered to haunt monarchy and nobility alike, an ever-present reminder that if they failed in their responsibilities these would be taken over in future centuries by Jock o' the Commonweil or Jock Uppaland or the commonalty of Scotland, all of whom represented the legacy of William Wallace whose career embodied the practical, secular, political counterpart to the Roman law maxim much favoured by the canonists - 'What touches all must be approved by all'.[91] Such a noble notion would, however laudable the sentiment, provide cold comfort to Scottish kings in future years.

It is often asserted that the Declaration remained unknown until the seventeenth century and hence its influence is questioned. Nonetheless it is important to note that Walter Bower not only transcribed the Declaration and the Irish letter of 1317 but that he also had access to a range of materials dating from the 1290s, some of which are discussed above. Indeed the Declaration was the first item in Bower's dossier of documents relating to independence. The dossier was copied in four manuscripts of Fordun's *Chronica* dating from the mid to the late fifteenth centuries and was probably an original component of the text left by Fordun or his continuator c. 1370.[92] Thus it is clear that the chronicle tradition via Fordun and Bower, not to mention the literary productions of Barbour and Blind Harry, transmitted the sentiments of 1320 to the fifteenth century. Further corroboration is to be gleaned from a number of scattered references.

The defenders of Stirling Castle claimed that they held the fortress on behalf of the Lion in 1304, a symbol which surfaced again in 1336.[93] In 1364 the Estates strenuously rejected David II's proposals that he be succeeded by the king of England.[94] A separation of the powers might be detected in the arrangement of 1384 whereby responsibility for the administration of justice throughout the realm was delegated by an enfeebled Robert II to his son and heir, the Earl of Carrick. Four years later power was removed altogether from the hands of Robert and Carrick due to 'the great and many defects in the governance of the realm'.[95] In 1398 it was judged that Robert III 'for seknes of his persoune may nocht travail to gouerne the Realme'.[96] There is some evidence that efforts were made to restrain James I before his tyranny engendered his murder in 1437.[97] Fifteenth century chroniclers such as the oft-cited Bower and the anonymous compiler of the *Liber Pluscardensis*, devoted much space to constitutional matters as did John Mair who noted that since King John 'permitted the subjection of Scotland to the English king, and, being otherwise of coward temper, the Scots drove him from his place'. All concerned had an obligation to maintain that 'mystical body', *corpus mysticum*, of which they were a part and he went on to argue:

> Whose it is to appoint a king, his it likewise is to decide any incident of a doubtful character that may arise concerning that king; but it is from the people, and most of all from the chief men and nobility who act for the common people, that kings have their institution; it belongs therefore to princes, prelates, and nobles to decide as to any ambiguity that may emerge in regard to a king; and their decision shall remain inviolable.[98]

When George Buchanan discussed bad kings and wayward clan chiefs in his *De jure regni apud Scotos* he specifically cited the case of John Balliol, 'deposed by our leading men on account of his having subjected himself and his kingdom to Edward the Englishman'.[99] Similar ideas were propounded and developed by the Melvillians, the Covenanters, Samuel Rutherford, Sir James Stewart and Alexander Shields, among others. It is perhaps fanciful, but metaphorically permissible, to imagine that at the time of Mary Queen of Scots' deposition (the single most important event of her reign) someone scrawled on an Edinburgh wall, *Communitas Regni Vivat*.

All of this is to suggest that the legacy of Arbroath survived in a distinguishable, and distinguished, Scottish political tradition. By the late fourteenth century a certain Scottish way of 'doing things' in respect of unworthy monarchs had been well and truly established. Yet more than a political identity is to be detected in such developments. There is also an identity - or empathy - of attitude, mindset and behaviour which can be traced to the heady years of 1290-1320, which received its finest articulation in the Declaration of Arbroath and which also owed much to the inspirational legend of William Wallace.

NOTES

[1] *Chron. Bower*, (Watt), 6, 147.

[2] E.L.G. Stones and Grant G. Simpson, *Edward I and the Throne of Scotland 1290-1296. An edition of the record sources for the Great Cause* 2 vols (Oxford 1978) i, 139. See too R. James Goldstein, *The Matter of Scotland: Historical Narrative in Medieval Scotland* (Lincoln, and London, 1993) chapter 2.

[3] The Scots were no novices in this respect. They had long cultivated the legend of St. Andrew and there were echoes of the identification between the Jews and the Scots in the twelfth century; the use of the name David was not accidental. See Edward J. Cowan, 'Myth and Identity in Early Medieval Scotland', *SHR*, lxiii (1984), 116-122.

[4] Translated in John Barbour, *The Bruce*, (Edinburgh, 1997) edited with translation and notes by A.A.M. Duncan, 779-782. This excellent, accessible and affordable edition will undoubtedly become the standard text well into the 21st century.

[5] Grant Simpson, 'The Declaration of Arbroath revitalised', *SHR*, lvi (1977), 11.

[6] Sir James Fergusson, *The Declaration of Arbroath*, (Edinburgh, 1970).

[7] Lord Cooper, 'The Declaration of Arbroath Revisited', *Supra Crepidam*, (London, 1951), 58-9.

[8] J.R. Philip, 'Sallust and the Declaration of Arbroath', *SHR*, xxvi (1947), 75-8.

[9] G.W.S. Barrow, *Robert Bruce and the Community of the Realm of Scotland* (London, 1965) xx-xxii. All other references are to the 1988 edition (Edinburgh).

[10] Ranald Nicholson, 'Magna Carta and the Declaration of Arbroath', *University of Edinburgh Journal*, xxii (1965), 140-44.

[11] A.A.M. Duncan , *The Nation of Scots and the Declaration of Arbroath (1320)* (London, 1970), 24.

[12] Simpson, 'Declaration revitalised' 22-24.

[13] Ranald Nicholson, *Scotland The Later Middle Ages*, (Edinburgh, 1974), 101.

[14] G.W.S. Barrow, 'The Idea of Freedom in Late Medieval Scotland' *Innes Review*, xxx (1979), 28-9.

[15] *Chron. Bower*, 6 135.

[16] A.A.M. Duncan, 'The Making of the Declaration of Arbroath' in *The Study of Medieval Records. Essays in honour of Kathleen Major*, (ed.) D.A. Bullough and R.L. Storey, (Oxford, 1971), 174-188; Fergusson, *Declaration*, 38-9.

[17] G.W.S. Barrow, *Robert the Bruce and the Scottish Identity,* Saltire Society (Edinburgh, 1984), 20.

[18] R. James Goldstein, *The Matter of Scotland,* 7, 87-98.

[19] *Tacitus On Britain and Germany,* trans. H.M. Mattingly, (Harmondsworth, 1948), 79-81.

[20] *The Poems and Songs of Robert Burns,* (ed.) James Kinsley, 3 vols, (Oxford, 1968), 707-8, 1438-1440.

[21] Barrow, 'Freedom', 18.

[22] Barrow, 'Freedom', 19; *Chronica de Mailros,* (ed.) Joseph Stevenson, Bannatyne Club, (Edinburgh, 1835), 98.

[23] Barrow, 'Freedom', 22; *Documents Illustrative of the History of Scotland 1286-1306,* 2 vols, (Edinburgh, 1870), i, no. 108.

[24] *Anglo-Scottish Relations 1174-1328, Some Selected Documents,* (ed) E.L.G. Stones, (Oxford, 1965), 81; *Chron. Bower,* 6, 29.

[25] Stones and Simpson, *Great Cause,* ii, 31; Barrow, *Bruce,* 32; Barrow, 'Freedom', 21-2; P.A. Linehan, 'A fourteenth century history of Anglo-Scottish relations in a Spanish manuscript', *Bulletin of the Institute of Historical Research,* xlviii (1975), 106-22.

[26] *Chron. Bower,* 6, 135-151; R. James Goldstein, 'The Scottish Mission to Boniface VIII in 1301: A Reconsideration of the Context of the *Instructionses* and *Processus*', *SHR,* lxx (1991), 1-15. These texts 'provide the earliest surviving historical narrative of the conflict with England to be produced on the Scottish side in the initial years of the Wars of Independence'. See also Goldstein, *Matter of Scotland,* 57-78.

[27] Goldstein, *The Matter of Scotland,* 85; Linehan, 'Spanish Manuscript', 121.

[28] Walter Ullman, *Principles of Government and Politics in the Middle Ages,* (London, 1961), 261.

[29] *The Statesman's Book of John of Salisbury Policraticus,* trans. John Dickinson, (New York, 1963), 323-4. A more modern translation is to be found in John of Salisbury, *Policraticus Of the Frivolities of Courtiers and the Footprints of Philosophers,* (ed.) Cary J. Nederman, (Cambridge, 1990), 'Liberty judges in accordance with the free will of the individual, and it is not afraid to censure that which seems to oppose sound moral character. Indeed, nothing except virtue is more glorious than liberty, if however liberty is ever properly separated from virtue . . . For this reason, because virtue is agreed to be the greatest good in life and that which alone banishes the heavy and hateful yoke of servility, philosophers strongly advise that, if assailed by necessity, one is to die for virtue, which is the sole reason for living. Yet this does not arise in its perfection without liberty, and the loss of liberty demonstrates irrefutably that virtue is not present . . . none has ever trampled on liberty except for the manifest enemies of virtue. The legal experts know that laws were introduced in support of liberty and the testimony of historians is continually mentioning what great deeds were done for love of it', 175-76.

[30] *Chron. Bower,* 6, 169-89.

[31] Stones, *Relations,* 281-5.

[32] Dickinson, *Policraticus,* 83.

[33] *Ibid.,* xlvi-xlvii.

[34] A.A.M. Duncan, 'The community of the realm and Robert Bruce. A review', *SHR,* xlv, 195.

[35] Stones, *Relations,* 283.

[36] *Chron. Bower,* 6, 385-403.

[37] Barbour, *The Bruce,* 780.

[38] Jan van Laarhoven, 'Thou shalt NOT slay a tyrant!' in *The World of John of Salisbury,* (ed.) Michael Wilks, (Oxford, 1984), 331.

[39] Dickinson, *Policraticus,* 335.

[40] *Ibid.,* 368-9.

[41] *Ibid.,* lxxiv.

[42] *Ibid.,* 335-6.

[43] RRS, v, 198-203.

[44] *Ibid* 165-6.

[45] *Chron. Bower,* 364-5.

[46] Barrow, *Bruce,* 305-6.

[47] Anne Duggan, 'John of Salisbury and Thomas Becket' in *World of John of Salisbury,* 427-38.

[48] *Chron. Bower,* 6, 387.

[49] It is deplorable in a book about Scotland and and a Scottish case to be told that to refer to this man as King John 'causes confusion with John of England'! Stones and Simpson, *Great Cause,* I 5n. One of the main problems about studying the entire period of the Wars of Independence is that so much of it has to be reconstructed using English sources, so that , for once, History is viewed through the eyes of the loser rather than the victor. King John suffered enough ignominy in his own lifetime without being further slighted by posterity.

[50] A selection, none of which discusses the Scottish situation, might include, Fritz Kern, *Kingship and Law in the Middle Ages,* (New York, 1956), Ernst Kantorowicz, *The King's Two Bodies. A Study in Medieval Political Theology,* (Princeton, 1957), Walter Ullman, *Principles of Government and Politics in the Middle Ages,* (London, 1961), Edward Peters, *The Shadow King. Rex Inutilis in Medieval Law and Literature, 751-1327,* (New Haven, and London, 1970), Henry A. Myers, *Medieval Kingship,* (Chicago, 1982), Brian Tierney, *Religion, law, and the growth of constitutional thought 1150-1650,* (Cambridge, 1982), Francis Oakley, *Omnipotence, Covenant and Order. An Excursion in the History of Ideas from Abelard to Leibniz,* (Ithaca, and London, 1984), Bernard Guenée, *States and Rulers in Later Medieval Europe,* (Oxford, 1985), Arthur P. Monahan, *Consent, Coercion, and Limit. The Medieval Origins of Parliamentary Democracy,* (Kingston, and Montreal, 1987), J.H. Burns (ed.) *The Cambridge History of Medieval Political Thought c. 350 - c. 1450,* (Cambridge, 1988), James M. Blythe, *Ideal Government and the Mixed Constitution in the Middle Ages,* (Princeton, 1992), Kenneth Pennington, *The Prince and the Law. Sovereignty and Rights in*

the Western Legal Tradition, (Berkeley, 1993), Joseph Canning, *A History of Medieval Political Thought 300-1450,* (London, 1996).

[51] Peters, *Shadow King,* 217.

[52] Barrow, *Bruce,* 63; Michael Prestwich, *Edward I,* (London, 1988), 372.

[53] Johannis de Fordun, *Chronica Gentis Scotorum,* (ed.) William F. Skene. 2 vols, (Edinburgh, 1871), i, 327-8.

[54] *Chron. Bower,* 43.

[55] Barrow, *Bruce,* 74.

[56] Stones, *Relations,* 155; *Chron. Bower,* 6, 189; Goldstein, 'Scottish Mission', 10-12; Duncan "Community of the realm', 195ff; Barrow, *Bruce,* 122-4; for much supplementary information on all of this see the excellent article by Norman Reid 'The kingless kingdom: the Scottish guardianships of 1286-1306', *SHR,* lxl (1982), 105-29.

[57] Peters, *Shadow King,* 134.

[58] G.W.S. Barrow, 'The Clergy in the War of Independence' in *The Kingdom of the Scots. Government, Church and Society from the eleventh to the fourteenth century,* (London, 1973), 233-54. See also D.E.R. Watt, *A Biographical Dictionary of Scottish Graduates to A.D. 1410 ,* (Oxford, 1977).

[59] James Bulloch, *Adam of Dryburgh,* (London, 1958), 19; *Chronica de Mailros,* 74, 108.

[60] Brian Tierney, 'Medieval Canon Law and Western Constitutionalism', *The Catholic Historical Review,* lii (1966), 14.

[61] Edward J. Cowan, 'The Historical MacBeth' in *Moray: Province and People,* (ed.) W.D.H. Sellar, Scottish Society for Northern Studies, (Edinburgh, 1993) 117-41. Not all kings suffered outright deposition; some seem to have been given the status of something like *rex emeritus,* for example Constantine mac Aed (900-943) who 'in decrepit old age' retired to the monastic life in St. Andrews. A.O. Anderson, *Early Sources of Scottish History A.D. 500 to 1286,* 2 vols. (Edinburgh, 1922), 1, 446-7.

[62] Hans Liebeschutz, *Medieval Humanism in the Life and Writings of John of Salisbury,* (London, 1950), 37-40; Dickinson, *Policraticus,* xix, lii.

[63] Francis J. Byrne, *Irish Kings and High Kings,* (London, 1973), 24.

[64] Dickinson, *Policraticus,* lxx.

[65] Sedulius Scottus, *On Christian Rulers and The Poems,* (trans.) Edward G. Doyle, (Binghampton, 1983), 68, 93.

[66] Edward J. Cowan, 'The political ideas of a covenanting leader: Archibald Campbell marquis of Argyll 1607-1661', in *Scots and Britons: Scottish Political Thought and the Union of 1603,* (ed.) Roger A. Mason, (Cambridge, 1994), 257-8.

[67] A.A.M. Duncan, 'The community of the realm ', 186.

[68] G.J. Hand, 'The Opinions of the Paris Lawyers upon the Scottish Succession c.1292', *The Irish Jurist,* v (1970), 141-55.

[69] *Carte Monialium De Northberwic,* (ed.) Cosmo Innes, *Bannatyne Club,* (Edinburgh, 1848), 4, *Charters of the Abbey of Inchaffra,* (ed.) W.A. Lindsay, J. Dowden and J. Maitland Thomson, *SHS,* (Edinburgh, 1907), No. 9; on this

subject see Jack Autrey Dabbs, *Dei Gratia In Royal Titles,* (The Hague, 1971), 105, at which, in what purports to be a serious study, we are offered the gratuitous information that Malcolm IV and Robert I were freemasons!

[70] Duncan, *Nation of Scots,* 31; Kathleen Simms, *From Kings to Warlords: The Changing Political Structure of Gaelic Ireland in the Later Middle Ages,* (Woodbridge, 1987), 15, 26-7.

[71] Barrow, *Bruce,* 314; Duncan, *Nation of Scots,* 32.

[72] *Chron. Bower,* 6 377.

[73] *Vita Edwardi Secundi monachi cuisdam Malmesberiensis; the Life of Edward the Second by the so-called Monk of Malmesbury,* (ed. and trans.) N. Denholm-Young, (Edinburgh, 1957), 61, 67, 69.

[74] Geoffrey of Monmouth, *The History of the Kings of Britain,* (ed.) Lewis Thorpe, (Harmondsworth, 1966), 174-5.

[75] e.g. Blythe, *Ideal Government,* 161; Canning, *History of Medieval Political Thought,* 135.

[76] Ullman, *Principles of Government,* 250; St. Thomas Aquinas, *On Kingship To the King of Cyprus,* (trans.) Gerald P. Phelan, (rev.) I.Th. Eschmann, (Toronto, 1949), 21.

[77] Blythe, *Ideal Government,* 48.

[78] Monahan, *Consent, Coercion and Limit,* 196.

[79] Thomas J. Renna, 'The Populus in John of Paris' Theory of Monarchy', *Tjidschrift voor Rechtsgeschiedenis,* 42 (1974), 243-68; Blythe, *Ideal Government,* 141-57.

[80] Blythe, *Ideal Government,* 157.

[81] Reid, 'Kingless Kingdom', 129.

[82] Barrow, *Bruce,* 92.

[83] The best modern study is Andrew Fisher, *William Wallace,* (1986). See too James Fergusson, *William Wallace, Guardian of Scotland,* (1938). A recent crop of books adds little to our knowledge - D. J. Gray, *William Wallace: The King's Enemy,* (1991), James Mackay, *William Wallace: Braveheart,* (1995), and Peter Reese, *William Wallace: A Biography,* (1996). For a somewhat fuller discussion of Wallace than is possible here see Edward J. Cowan, 'The Wallace Factor in Scottish History', in *Images of Scotland,* (eds.) Robin Jackson and Sydney Wood, *The Journal of Scottish Education,* Occasional Paper Number One. Northern College, (Dundee, 1997), 5-18.

[84] Fordun, *Chronica,* i, 331.

[85] Andrew of Wyntoun, *Orygynale Cronykil of Scotland,* (ed.) David Laing, 3 vols, (Edinburgh, 1872), ii, 339-49.

[86] Chron. Bower, 6, 95.

[87] Ibid., 299.

[88] Barrow, *Bruce,* 116.

[89] Barrow, *Bruce,* 81 cf. Duncan, *Nation of Scots* 'There was in Wallace's rising an undoubted element of protest by the 'poor commons' against their sufferings at the hands of a harsh and repressive society . . . Wallace was not just another

Guardian of the Realm chosen by the community thereof, but the leader of a popular movement with a measure of social discontent in its makeup'. 16.

[90] Barrow, 'Identity', 18; see too *Bruce,*   184, 223.

[91] Ullman, *Principles of Government,*   272.

[92] I am indebted to Dauvit Broun for this important information on the Bower dossier.

[93] Nicholson, *Later Middle Ages,* 67, 133.

[94] *Ibid* 170-1; *A question about the succession, 1364,*   (ed.) A.A.M. Duncan, *Miscellany of the Scottish History Society,*   vol. 12, (Edinburgh, 1994), 25-57.

[95] Nicholson, *Later Middle Ages,* 184, 200. On these matters see also S. Boardman,   *The Early Stewart Kings: Robert II and Robert III 1371-1406,* (Phantassie, 1996).

[96] *APS,*   1, 572.

[97] Michael Brown, *James I* , (Edinburgh, 1994), 175-7.

[98] John Major,   *A History of Greater Britain 1521,*   (ed.) Archibald Constable, *SHS,* (Edinburgh, 1892), 207, 214-5.

[99] George Buchanan, *De jure regni apud Scotos,*   (Edinburgh, 1843), cap. lvi.

Note - This paper has had an unconscionably long gestation. It was first presented to the Conference of Scottish Medievalists in July 1975 and was noticed by Grant Simpson in 'Arbroath Revitalised' 32 n. Some of the material was used, with permission, by Sandy Grant in his *Independence and Nationhood* (1984). Versions of the paper have also been presented at the universities of Edinburgh, Glasgow, Guelph, Toronto and Kalamazoo.

CHAPTER FOUR

Paragons and Patriots: National Identity and the Chivalric Ideal in Late-Medieval Scotland

Carol Edington

As evidenced by countless questionnaires printed in innumerable magazines, there is a popularly held belief that along with a favourite colour, food, or work of fiction, the identity of one's personal heroes offers a clear insight into character. Historians have frequently detected a similar process at work on a collective as well as an individual level, arguing that reverence for a unique pantheon of saints, heroes, and ruling dynasties, promotes a shared sense of national identity and lends 'significance and form' to social relationships.[1] Bearing this in mind, what follows aims to examine the creation of Scottish heroes in the later middle ages and to explore how these powerful images articulated deeply held beliefs about Scotland and the Scottish people alike.

Although the term 'hero' does not appear to have been commonly used before the sixteenth century, its use here is amply justified by the fulsome praise of various historical and quasi-historical figures which runs like a thread through the Scottish chronicle and literary traditions.[2] Even the most cursory examination reveals that these paragons are, for the most part, essentially military heroes lauded for their physical prowess and knightly accomplishments. There were of course several good reasons why this should be so. Such texts dealt largely (though not necessarily exclusively) with society's leaders—kings, magnates, lords, and knights—and, although this militarised élite rarely penned their own history, most clerical commentators, clearly recognising the chivalric code which informed secular attitudes, presented their material accordingly. Writing in the early 1530s, John Bellenden described his translation of Hector Boece's *Scotorum Historiae* as a 'marciall buke', written to show 'quhay hes bene of cheuelry the rois [rose]', and as this suggests, the work articulated a compelling and enormously influential story of a nation in arms.[3] Indeed, Scots frequently viewed their entire history as one of protracted warfare: as one commentator proudly declared, 'we have bene xviij hundreth yeire inconquest [unconquered]'.[4] Obviously, the values encapsulated in the chivalric creed, most notably those of physical bravery and loyal service, were particularly pertinent to a society at war and, as we shall see, Scotland's historical, and indeed national, identity was profoundly shaped by chivalric mores.[5]

Ultimately this was to produce an easily recognisable, hugely emotive, sense of what it was to be a Scot. Nevertheless, the fusion of chivalric and national—not to say nationalist—ideals was not as straightforward as has sometimes been assumed, and any examination of chivalric heroes raises important questions concerning the layered nature of perceived loyalties in medieval society.[6] Although some knight-heroes clearly possessed a broader appeal, chivalry was basically the ideology of the noble élite expressing a specific image of national identity which, albeit the most frequently articulated, was not necessarily the most widely held.[7] Moreover, this was a cosmopolitan aristocratic culture capable of forging bonds across national boundaries and reinforcing what Fiona Watson has identified as the often ambivalent attitude of Scottish nobles towards their English counterparts.[8] Within this international culture, there was plenty of opportunity to lavish praise on foreign—even English—heroes.

Additionally, the belief that 'the first and principal glory of the dignity of true chivalry is to fight for the faith' meant that the most heroic feats of arms were those fought on foreign soil.[9] The crusading ideal clearly exerted a powerful attraction for Scots of the middle ages and this gave rise to its own heroes.[10] Popular in the sixteenth century was *The Tail of Syr Valtir the Bald Leslye* which, as Rod Lyall has remarked, is surely an account of the fourteenth-century crusader, Sir Walter Leslie.[11] In addition there was at least one other sixteenth-century vernacular narrative set in the Holy Land. Concerned with the fantastic adventures of three kings' sons, this work was widely—albeit erroneously—taken to refer to the career of David, earl of Huntingdon, brother of William the Lion.[12] The circulation of such tales undoubtedly added lustre to the image of Scottish knighthood while at the same time cultivating a somewhat different breed of national icon, one which had little to do with events in Scotland itself.

The medieval habit of contemporising the past—that is, of conceptualising it in familiar images and language—increasingly helped reinforce the relationship between chivalry and Scotland's historical identity and the key figures of Scotland's early history were routinely, if anachronistically, viewed as knights. For example, writing in the fourteenth century, the English layman, Sir Thomas Gray, presented Scotland's mythical founder as the 'cheualerous' knight Gathelos who, like the knights-errant of Romance literature, quitted his father's kingdom in search of adventure and conquest.[13]

Such a vision of the past was butressed by the widespread belief in the classical origins of chivalry. For the anonymous fifteenth-century author of the *Liber Pluscardensis*, ancient Greece was renowned not only for its virtue and learning: it was also 'the flower of chivalry and arms'.[14] This view was also held by Andrew of Wyntoun who even went so far as to describe the jousts and tournaments held at the first Olympiad.[15] Of course Greece was also the home of Gathelos, husband of the eponymous Scota, and although the chroniclers do not make this connection explicit, it can not have failed to occur to their Scottish readers for whom their putative origins were a source of enormous pride: 'For sekerly we ar' cummyn of the mast famous & maist worshipfull nacioun that evire was in erd [earth] quhilk is of Grece'.[16] Underlying this conceit was the belief that the Greeks had conquered the world not just once but twice, and it is surely no coincidence that the most popular romance cycle in late-medieval Scotland concerned Alexander the Great.[17] Indeed, the Alexander legend would have had special resonance in a country beset by recurrent war, for its stirring depiction of martial valour articulated an important secular aspiration designed to fortify Scots in knightly virtue and prowess:

> Quha wald have honour, conquest, or victorie,
> Wirschip, hie vassaleg, or chaualrie,
> Thame nedis nane vther teching na doctour
> Bot this storie to be to thame mirrour.[18]

A further link between Scotland and ancient chivalry was provided by Wyntoun's account of the institution of 'knychthade' which, he explained, was the legacy of Noah's son, Japheth. As the chronicler went on to narrate, Japheth's direct descendant was the Scythian, 'Sir Newil', who settled in Greece where he fathered Gathelos.[19] Thus were Scots accustomed to accept what they saw as their special links with the glorious history of international chivalry.

This is not to claim that Scotland was in any way unusual in developing such an account of the past—the Trojan origin-legends of both England and France could be fashioned in similar terms. But the increasing application of this interpretative framework which can be detected in writers such as Wyntoun, Boece, and Bellenden, served to distort, if not entirely obscure, the Gaelic character of Scotland's early history. Although the bardic tradition also celebrated the Greek origins of the Gael, viewing Scotland's earliest heroes as chivalric paragons—or at least as recognisable knights—offered Scots an alternative cultural identity which had little to do with traditional Celtic society.[20] According to John Bellenden, the Scots were a people who from their earliest origins delighted in hunting and hawking:

practiced archers, generally clad in chain-mail, they were 'reddy at all tymes to defend thair lyvis, landis, & liberte'.[21]

As this passage illustrates, it was not just the physical appearance of a later age but also its preoccupations which determined how Scots thought about themselves and their history. Generations of intermittent conflict, particularly the wars against England, not only coloured accounts of the distant past, they also provided an important corpus of material which reinforced the links between traditional knightly ideals and Scotland's national history. As early as the fourteenth century, Thomas Gray had remarked that the adventures of Edward Bruce 'would be a great romance', while John Barbour did, in fact, characterise his great account of the Wars of Independence as a 'romanys'.[22] Certainly this would not be the first study to suggest that accounts of Scotland's recent past offered a Scottish equivalent of the great chivalric legends detailing 'the Matter of France', 'the Matter of Rome', or 'the Matter of Britain'.[23]

The evolution of this tradition can be traced to a number of different sources—notably the polemic produced during the course of the war, the great fourteenth-century account written by John Barbour, and the various versions of the story penned by later chroniclers. Military action against England in the early decades of the fourteenth century was accompanied by a vigorous propaganda war with both sides attempting to win papal support for their cause. Approaches to the papacy were, of course, written by clerics and framed with reference to the teachings of the church regarding the Just War. But the ideal of the Christian knight (itself born of the church's concern with secular conflict) offered another important conceptual weapon readily seized upon by both sides. In a letter sent by Edward I to Boniface VIII in May 1301, the Scots were portrayed as violating the central tenets of knighthood—the protection of the weak and defence of the church:

> Ruthlessly and with savage cruelty they even slaughtered babies in their cradles and women in labour; and what must horrify the listener, they cut off the breasts of many women. And after barring the doors of a school and lighting fires, they consumed with fire in their school some young clerics, about two hundred in number, who were learning their first letters and grammar.[24]

The Scots were not slow to respond in kind and the draft response to Edward's letter laid great emphasis on the English slaughter of women, children and priests, and the spoilation of religious houses.[25] Of course, this type of violent language was highly conventional: stressing atrocities committed against the civilian population was a common rhetorical device, one with impressive classical precedents, and a commentary not on actual events but on the perceived moral character of the perpetrator.[26] And although such bloodshed represented an obvious violation of canon law, it was just as much a crime against the chivalric creed. According to one commentator, attacking the defenceless showed no great courage: on the contrary, all knights and men-at-arms were duty bound to keep them from harm, 'and whoever does the contrary deserves the name of pillager'.[27] Significantly perhaps, when Walter Bower came to repeat the charges against the English king, he explicitly evoked the chivalric ethic, claiming that Edward began to stir up strife 'as soon as he became a knight'.[28]

In the end, the Scottish riposte was never formally presented to the Roman curia.[29] Another missive, however, certainly did reach papal ears. This was the famous Declaration of Arbroath written in 1320 with the aim of securing recognition of Bruce's kingship and, more specifically, of deflecting the papal hostility which had resulted in a series of bulls excommunicating the king and summoning four Scottish bishops to Rome.[30] This also emphasised the unholy and unchivalric character of Edward's conquests:

> His wrongs, killings, violence, pillage, arson, imprisonment of prelates, burning down of monasteries, outrages, sparing neither age nor sex, religion nor order, no one could fully describe or fully understand unless experience had taught him.[31]

Having condemned the English king in these terms, the Declaration went on to declare support for Robert Bruce who, 'like another Maccabeus or Joshua', had delivered his people from their enemies. The aptness of this comparison is unquestionable for, like these Old Testament heroes, Bruce had fought a desperate war against an imperialist aggressor. But the image did more than simply underscore the Scottish king's credentials as a military leader. The widespread admiration in which Joshua and Judas Maccabeus were held in the middle ages was a notable aspect of the cult of chivalry and, from an early stage, chivalric writers had ranked these two—and the latter in particular—foremost amongst the heroes of Christian chivalry.[32] This tradition had recently been reinforced by the *Voeux du Paon* written by Jean Longuyon around the year 1312. This new, extremely popular, addition to the Alexander legend first brought together the figures of *les Neuf Preux* or Nine Worthies, a revered company comprising three Jewish, three classical, and three Christian 'knights'. In this context, the comparison between Bruce, Joshua and Judas Maccabeus found in the Declaration of Arbroath seems designed to enhance Bruce's moral as well as his political position, claiming for him all the chivalric virtue necessarily attributable to this type of hero. For Geoffrey de Charny writing a few decades later, Judas Maccabeus represented the pinnacle of knightly achievement and anyone who could be likened to such a paragon was worthy of the highest honours of chivalry.[33]

It would, of course, be a great mistake to think that what might be termed the chivalric strand of the Declaration of Arbroath represents its most important message. Nor should the use of these few words and phrases obscure the much greater debts its authors owed to classical rhetoric on the one hand and similar contemporary petitions on the other.[34] Nevertheless, the Declaration does appear to have been drafted with at least half an eye on the chivalric mores which defined contemporary lay aspirations. The document was, after all, issued in the name of eight earls, thirty one nobles and 'the other barons and freeholders and the whole community of the realm of Scotland', and the evocation of chivalric ideals forcefully suggests that someone was concerned to draft a suitably secular appeal. Moreover if, as seems likely, the vision of national unity evinced by the Declaration rang decidedly hollow in 1320, then locating Bruce in a universally revered ethical framework would help smooth over the political differences which might still prove a powerful threat to his kingship.[35] In this respect, as in many others, the Declaration underlined how important the concept of kingship was to notions of Scottish identity and political autonomy.

Bruce's chivalric reputation was further enhanced by his association with the crusading ideal. This operated on two levels. On the one hand, it was possible to portray the Scottish struggle against England as a quasi-crusade.[36] On the other, Bruce himself was portrayed as a keen—if thwarted—crusader. Much enlarged upon by later writers, this image was also central to the Declaration of Arbroath. As has been pointed out, the 1320 petition was a product of the complex world of international diplomacy and, in particular, of a projected assault on the Holy Land.[37] In 1308 Philip IV had written to Bruce inviting him to go on Crusade, and it is clear that the Scots attempted to use this opportunity to make a political point: the Scots would take the cross when their freedom and peace were assured and Robert was recognised as king. Similar ideas undoubtedly lay behind the Declaration, and to debate whether or not it represented an honest representation of royal longing rather misses the point, that point being the creation of an appropriate image for the Scots hero-king. Moreover, in addition to recalling the Scottish attitudes of 1309, the argument used in 1320 seems to have been a calculated response to the contemporary image of Bruce's Plantagenet enemies: Edward I had actually been on crusade (and had also decorated his palace at Westminster with paintings depicting the career of Judas Maccabeus), while his son,

Edward II, had taken the cross in 1317.[38] But the crusading ideal appears to have been a more positive symbol of Bruce's kingship than a simple retort to English superiority in the crusading stakes, and the king's dying wish that his heart be carried in war against the Infidel swiftly became central to his almost mythic appeal.

The perception of Bruce as 'another Maccabeus' proved an attractive image. It would be reiterated by Fordun, and either source may have lain behind John Barbour's use of similar metaphors.[39] Bruce's absorption into the traditional canon of chivalric heroes is also illustrated by a three-line Latin doggerel found in a manuscript prepared for use at Sweetheart Abbey in the 1380s, and by the short poem known as *The Ballet of the Nine Nobles*.[40] Here, nine verses eulogising each of *Les Neuf Preux* are followed by a tenth detailing the accomplishments of Robert Bruce:

> *Robert the Brois throu hard feichtyng,*
> *Wytht few, vewcust the mychtthy kyng*
> *Off Ingland, Edward, twyse in fycht,*
> *As occupit his realme but rycht;*
> *At sumtyme wes set so hard,*
> *At hat nocht sax till him toward.*
> *Ye gude en that thir balletis redis*
> *Deme quha dochtyast was in dedis.*[41]

> 'Robert the Bruce through hard fighting,
> With few, vanquished the mighty king
> Of England, Edward, twice in battle,
> Who occupied his realm without right;
> That [Bruce] was sometimes pressed so hard,
> That not six [men] supported him.
> You good folk who read these ballads
> Deem who doughtiest was in deeds.'

The final line of this verse strongly recalls another tale designed to enhance Bruce's chivalric reputation. Writing in the 1440s, Walter Bower described how, on being asked by Edward II to name the greatest living knight, the royal herald, one King Robert (or Le Roy Robert), unhesitatingly awarded the prize to Bruce.[42] A condensed version of the tale was provided by the author of the *Liber Pluscardensis* in a passage which, encapsulating as it does so many of the central themes of the Bruce legend, is worth quoting at length:

> Note that a herald of the king of England, at a solemn festival,
> was publicly asked by King Edward who, according to his verdict,

was the most honourable, the most admirable in knightly
gallantry and in warlike deeds and in governing a kingdom and
also in perseverance in battling with his foes, both in his poverty
and in the excellence of his might, and in the end irresistibly
overcoming the enemy with a force small by the side of the
incomparably larger force of the enemy—who of all living that he
knew of in the chivalry of Christendom could truly and
reasonably be called the mightiest while he lived. So this herald,
repeating the remarks of some present who said the Emperor
Henry, while others said Sir Giles D' Argent, a Frenchman, was
the most gallant and mightiest and most approved, this herald
said openly before everybody that the most peerless and gallant,
the most daring and mightiest in warlike deeds, was that
invincible prince, King Robert Bruce; and this he openly
supported and made good by many arguments, and he offered to
defend his opinion with his body. Hence he incurred the great
displeasure of the English; but he earned the respect and good
word of the strangers who loved the truth.[43]

Despite the existence of a real herald or minstrel associated with the
English court in the early fourteenth century and known as the King Robert,
the conventional setting and stylised presentation smack of a more traditional
tale.[44] After all the Emperor Henry wore his three crowns only for a brief
period between 1312 and his death a year later—at which stage it was hard to
praise Bruce for his military exploits let alone his governance of the country.
What we have here is surely a fictional narrative rather than the product of an
actual episode, and it is tempting to suggest that the story was, in fact, a
somewhat later Scottish tale designed to stress the glory of the Scottish king.
The use of a real herald is no more to be wondered at than the catalogue of
real chivalric heroes. Indeed, having been garrisoned in Berwick between
1311-12, the King Robert could well have been familiar to at least some Scots
who might also have known of his presence at the Feast of the Swan in 1306
when, amidst great ceremony and feasting, an assembled company of English
knights swore an oath upon a swan—exactly the type of 'solemn festival'
which might have suggested such a tale.[45] Indeed, the story may even have
been a deliberate response to it—or at least to the feelings behind it—for in
1306 the English chivalric community, far from praising Bruce, had actually
vowed his destruction.

Although the provenance of this tale must remain a matter for
speculation, it appears to have been well known. A more elaborate version
may well have been the 'history made by the said king Robert' referred to by

the chronicler Jean le Bel who wrote in the mid-fourteenth century but who probably learnt of it when visiting Scotland in 1327.[46] Drawing on various unnamed sources, Thomas Gray's *Scalachronica* discussed the chivalric reputation of both the Emperor Henry and Giles D'Argentine (whom he linked together), while Barbour's description of the latter as the third best knight living in his day also appears to be an allusion to the judgement of the English herald.[47] In short, the acclamation of Bruce as a chivalric hero swiftly became a well-established—and long-lived—convention.

Although viewing the hero of the wars against England as a paragon of chivalric virtue clearly encouraged the conflation of nationalist and chivalric ideologies, it is important to recognise that longstanding and traditional chivalric assumptions frequently existed alongside, or even over-rode, patriotic considerations. Nowhere is this more clearly seen than in *The Bruce*, the great vernacular work written by John Barbour in the 1370s which, in attempting to marry chivalry and nationalism, often revealed the ideological tensions between the two. The characterisation of Bruce's faithful lieutenant, Sir James Douglas—generally reckoned a portrait of Barbour's 'ideal knight and subject'—is a case in point.[48] For, as vividly illustrated by the episode at Bannockburn when Douglas defied his king to ride to the aid of a comrade-in-arms, Douglas was more knight than subject. Like many a chivalric hero, he marched to the beat of more than a single drum. Throughout *The Bruce*, the defence of the Church—what Douglas described as his 'entent...To lyve or de in [God's] seruice'—and the quest for personal honour are used to explain Scottish motivation on the battlefield.[49] Whether this was indeed the case does not matter: Scots liked to think that it was so and they were accustomed to interpreting heroic action and national history in this way. Before the battle of Loudoun Hill, fought in response to Aymer de Valence's contemptuous challenge, Barbour portrayed Bruce rallying his men with the claim that they fought 'For to manytene her our honour', while at Bannockburn the cry was essentially the same: 'To wyn all or dey with honur'.[50]

The chivalric ideals with which Barbour sought to inspire his audience were most effectively linked to the patriotic cause in the person of Robert Bruce who, as the Scottish king, provided a powerful symbol of legitimacy and political independence as well as the peg upon which to hang the most exalted call to arms. Realising that he must face the English in open battle, Bruce called upon all those that loved him 'and the fredome off this countre'.[51] Similarly, before Methven, he roused his men declaring, 'he that deis for his cuntre / Sal herbryit in-till hewyn be' (he that dies for his country / Shall be received in heaven).[52] This quasi-deification of Scotland's military heroes needs to be located within a wider European intellectual tradition rooted in both classical and early medieval thinking.[53] Nonetheless, by transferring the chivalric ideals of personal lordship, service, and the type of thinking more usually found in a crusading context, Barbour was able to fashion an emotive model of heroic patriotism which, as we have seen, proved enormously influential in the fifteenth and early sixteenth centuries.

It would be a great mistake to think either that Scottish national identity was simply a product of the Wars of Independence or that it represented nothing more than a visceral reaction against the hostile 'other'—in this case England.[54] Nevertheless, recording this aspect of Scotland's past gave rise to what was arguably a new type of patriot hero and, in the creation of this new image, the ideals of Christian knighthood played a crucial role. Admittedly, the literary emergence of more specifically national heroes was by no means unique to Scotland.[55] Here, however, the chivalric ethic familiar to the country's military élite was deployed to discuss recent history whilst simultaneously promoting a self-consciously heroic image designed to inspire future generations. Examining the ways in which chivalric ideals were both understood and used in this respect illustrates not only how history coloured perceptions of national identity but also how these powerful images of Scotland's patriot champions shaped how the nation's history was written.

NOTES

1. *National Consciousness, History, and Political Culture in Early Modern Europe*, (ed) Orest Ranum (Baltimore, 1975), 3.
2. Morton Bloomfield, 'The Problem of the Hero in the Later Medieval Period', in *Concepts of the Hero in the Middle Ages and the Renaissance*, (ed) Norman T. Burns and Christopher J. Reagan (Albany, New York, 1975), 27-48, 28.
3. *Ballat apone the Translatione*, printed in *The Chronicles of Scotland compiled by Hector Boece Translated into Scots by John Bellenden, 1531*, (ed) R. W. Chambers and Edith C. Batho (hereafter *Bellenden, Chronicles*), 2 vols (STS, 1938-41), ii, 403-09, 403. Here Bellenden is using the word 'chivalry' to make a moral judgement; elsewhere, however, care must be taken not to read the word anachronistically. As has often been pointed out 'chivalry' had various meanings in the middle ages: sometimes it simply denoted a company of knights, often it was used to refer to the art of war. What Bellenden translated as 'chevelry', was generally something like re bellica; e.g. *Bellenden, Chronicles*, i, 183; Boece, *Scotorum Historiae* (Paris, 1527), folio edition, fo. lxxiiii[v].
4. *The Scottis Originale*, printed in *The Asloan Manuscript*, (ed) W. A. Craigie, 2 vols (STS, 1923-25), i, 185-96, 193.
5. Roger Mason, 'Chivalry and Citizenship: Aspects of National Identity in Renaissance Scotland', *in People and Power in Scotland: Essays in Honour of T.*

C. *Smout*, (ed) Roger Mason and Norman Macdougall (Edinburgh, 1992), 50-73, 57-58.

6. Susan Reynolds, *Kingdoms and Communities in Western Europe 900-1300* (Oxford, 1984), 330-31.

7. For discussion of a more popular national consciousness, see Alexander Grant, 'Aspects of National Consciousness in the Middle Ages', in *Nations, Nationalism and Patriotism in the European Past*, (ed) Charles Bjorn, Alexander Grant, Keith J. Stringer, (Copenhagen, 1994), 69-95, esp. 81-94.

8. Fiona Watson, see above.

9. The author of this statement was the crusading zealot, Philippe de Mézières. Quoted from *his Chevalerie de la Passion de Jesus Christ* by Maurice Keen, 'War, Peace and Chivalry', in *War and Peace in the Middle Ages*, (ed) B. P. McGuire, (Copenhagen, 1987), 94-117.

10. Alan Macquarrie, *Scotland and the Crusades 1095-1560* (Edinburgh, 1985).

11. R. J. Lyall, 'The Lost Literature of Medieval Scotland', in *Brycht Lanternis*: *Essays on the Language and Literature of Medieval and Renaissance Scotland*, (ed) J. Derrick McClure and Michael R. G. Spiller (Aberdeen, 1989), 33-47, 41.

12. This was almost certainly modelled on the fifteenth-century Burgundian romance, *Livre des trois filz de Roys*, a work subsequently translated into English around 1500 and printed in Paris four years later. The English version is printed as *The Three Kings' Sons*, (ed) F. J. Furnival (EETS, 1895). John Mair (in 1521) described this as a 'book well known among the French', and referred to 'a similar book we have in our own vernacular tongue'; *A History of Greater Britain as well England as Scotland*, (ed) Archibald Constable (SHS, 1892), 165.

13. *Scalachronica*, printed in W. F. Skene (ed.), *Chronicles of the Picts: Chronicles of the Scots* (Edinburgh, 1897), 194. The generic relationship between this literary approach and that of Romance literature (particularly Chrétien de Troyes's *Yvain*) is noted and discussed by R. James Goldstein, *The Matter of Scotland: Historical Narrative in Medieval Scotland* (Lincoln, Nebraska, 1993), 110.

14. *Liber Pluscardensis*, ed. and trans. F. H. J. Skene, 2 vols (Edinburgh, 1877-80), ii, 56. W. F. Skene argued (see *ibid.*, i, xix-xxiii) that the author was Maurice Buchanan, but this issue remains to be resolved conclusively.

15. *The Original Chronicle of Andrew of Wyntoun*, (ed) F. J. Amours, 6 vols (STS, 1903-14), ii, 339.

16. *The Scottis Originale*, 185.

17. Wyntoun did not detail Alexander's exploits as they were 'Contenyt in othir bukys' (*Chron. Wyntoun*, iii, 97). Two fifteenth-century versions were compiled, one probably in 1438; *The Buik of Alexander or the Buik of the Most Noble Valiant Conquerour Alexander the Grit*, (ed) R. L. G. Ritchie, 4 vols (STS, 1925-29); the other by Gilbert Hay, around the year 1460, *The Buik of King Alexander the Conquerour* by Gilbert Hay, ed. John Cartwright, 3 vols (STS, 1985-). Hay himself refers to the popularity of the legend and '...bukis of the auld translatioun, / Quhilk

hes bene in this cuntrie sa commoun' (ii, lines 6029-30). His though appears to have been the first Scots version (Epilogue, iii, lines 1933-34).

18. *The Buik of King Alexander the Conquerour*, (ed) Cartwright, ii, 268-71.

19. *Chron. Wyntoun*, ii, 191.

20. William J. Watson (ed.), *Scottish Verse from the Book of the Dean of Lismore*, (Edinburgh, 1937), nos. XX and XXVII. I am grateful to Dr S. Boardman for pointing this out.

21. *Bellenden, Chronicles*, i, 32-33.

22. *Scalachronica by Sir Thomas Gray of Heton, knight: A Chronicle of England and Scotland from AD MLXVI to ADMCCCLXII* (Maitland Club, 1836), 143; *Barbour's Bruce*, (ed) Matthew P. MacDiarmid and James A. C. Stevenson, 3 vols (STS, 1980-85), I, 446 (references cite the number of the book followed by the line number).

23. Ranald Nicholson, *Scotland: The Later Middle Ages* (Edinburgh, 1989), 276; Mason, 'Chivalry and Citizenship', 57; Goldstein, *The Matter of Scotland*, 143.

24. *Scotichronicon by Walter Bower*, gen. ed. D. E. R. Watt, 9 vols (Aberdeen, 1987-), vi, 125.

25. *Ibid.*, vi, 135, 165.

26. Notably Lucan's *Pharsalia*; Ruth Morse, *Truth and Convention in the Middle Ages: Rhetoric, Representation and Reality* (Cambridge, 1991), 117-18.

27. *The Tree of Battles of Honoré Bonet*, trans., G. W. Coopland (Liverpool, 1949), 185.

28. *Chron. Bower* (Watt), vi, 333.

29. *Ibid.*, vi, 261.

30. Nicholson, *Scotland, The Later Middle Ages*, 99.

31. Printed and translated by A. A. M. Duncan, *The Nation of the Scots and the Declaration of Arbroath*, Historical Association Pamphlet (1970), 35.

32. Maurice Keen, *Chivalry* (New Haven and London, 1984), 119-21.

33. *Le Livre de Chevalerie par Geoffroi de Charny*, printed in *Oeuvres de Froissart*, ed. le Baron Kervyn de Lettenhove, 26 vols (Brussels, 1867-77), i, part II, 463-533, 508-10.

34. Grant G. Simpson, 'The Declaration of Arbroath Revitalised', *SHR*, lvi (1977), 11-33, esp. 22-24.

35. A. A. M. Duncan, 'The War of the Scots', *TRHS* 6th series, ii (1992), 128-30.

36. Alan Macquarrie, 'The Ideal of the Holy War in Scotland', *Innes Review*, xxxii (1981), 83-92, 84.

37. Duncan, 'The War of the Scots', 131.

38. Michael Prestwich, *Edward I* (London, 1988), 119.

39. Johannis de Fordun, *Chronica Gentis Scotorum*, (ed) W. F. Skene & trans. Felix Skene, 2 vols (Edinburgh, 1871-2), i, 337. Bower also referred to Bruce in these terms but here he was simply lifting Fordun's words (*Chron. Bower* (Watt), vi, 301). Barbour likened the whole Scottish people to the Maccabees and compared Judas with Bruce's brother, Edward; *Barbour's Bruce*, I, 465; XIV, 312-16.

40. R. S. Loomis, 'Verses on the Nine Worthies', *Modern Philology*, xv no. 3 (1917), 18-27, 18.

41. Printed by W. A. Craigie, 'The Ballet of the Nine Nobles', *Anglia*, xxi (1899), 359-65; also by Ritchie in *The Buik of Alexander*, i, pp. cxxxiv-cl.

42. *Chron. Bower* (Watt), vii, 55, 57.

43. *Chron. Pluscarden*, ii, 194-95.

44. N. Denholm-Young, *History of Heraldry 1254 to 1310: A Study of the Historical Value of the Rolls of Arms* (Oxford, 1965), 55.

45. *CDS*, iii, 399, 417.

46. *Chronique de Jean le Bel*, (ed) Jules Viard and Eugene Dèprez, Société de l'Histoire de France, 2 vols (Paris, 1904), i, 111.

47. *Scalachronica*, 132; *Barbour's Bruce*, XIV, 322-23.

48. Lois A. Ebin, 'John Barbour's *Bruce*: Poetry, History and Propaganda', *Studies in Scottish Literature*, ix (1972), 218-242, 224. Anne M. McKim gives a verbatim endorsement of this opinion, 'James Douglas and Barbour's Ideal of Knighthood', *Forum for Modern Language Studies*, xvii (1981), 167-80, 167. For a contrasting view, see Sonja Väthjunker (now Cameron), 'A Study of the Career of Sir James Douglas—The Historical Record versus Barbour's Bruce', unpublished Ph.D. thesis (Aberdeen University, 1992), 178.

49. *Barbour's Bruce*, XX, 461-62.

50. *Ibid.*, VIII, 252; XI, 407.

51. *Ibid.*, XI, 63.

52. *Ibid.*, II, 343-44.

53. Ernst H. Kantrowicz, '*Pro Patria Mori* in Medieval Political Thought', *American Historical Review*, lvi (1951), 473-92.

54. See earlier chapters in this volume. Also E. J. Cowan, 'Myth and Identity in Early Medieval Scotland', *SHR*, lxiii (1984), 111-35; Dauvit Broun, 'The Origins of Scottish Identity', in *Nations, Nationalism and Patriotism*, (ed) Bjorn, Grant and Stringer, 34-55.

55. Peter Coss, *The Knight in Medieval England 1000-1400* (Stroud, Glos., 1993), 143; Susan Crane, *Insular Romances: Politics, Faith and Culture in Anglo-Norman and Middle English Literature* (Berkeley, 1986), 67.

CHAPTER FIVE

A Nation Born Again?
Scottish Identity in the Sixteenth and Seventeenth Centuries

Michael Lynch

The sixteenth and seventeenth centuries hold an ambiguous place in the framing of Scottish identity. For many, the Reformation of 1560 is the central fact of Scottish history, when the Scots were born again - as a Protestant nation. In 1960, at its quatercentenary, familiar claims were restated that the kirk was a 'national symbol' and that 'one may doubt whether there could be a Scotland without it'.[1] Yet there was also a degree of discomfort within a presbyterian establishment already in defensive mode, under attack from two directions. The effect of Gordon Donaldson's carefully crafted, episcopalian claim to the new Protestant church of 1560 - a kirk without presbyters as well as priests - was considerable; his discovery of the 'moderation' of the first generation of Protestant reformers, in contrast to the neo-Calvinist dogmatism of the next generation of Andrew Melville, threatened to undermine part of the authentic presbyterian inheritance as well as the automatic linkage between post-Reformation kirk and nation.[2] As for Knox, some of the moral certainties often attached to the founding father of the kirk had been called into question by the recent discovery of Catholic historians that Knox had been ordained a Catholic priest before rediscovering himself as a Protestant preacher.[3] Both reinterpretations provoked outrage but little by way of scholarly rebuttal.[4] The next set-piece anniversaries received scant attention; the celebrations in 1972, the 400th anniversary of the death of John Knox, were muted;[5] and the tercentenary of the landmark of 1689, when the kirk was 'by the law established', passed almost unnoticed.[6]   The more the late twentieth century has progressed, the more, it seems, that Scots have begun to think what in 1960 seemed unthinkable - the faltering of a Protestant national identity, displaced by the rediscovery of a rival invented past, which leapfrogs the Reformation period. It promises an age when there seems to have been a more clear-cut sense of *patria*, born of war - against England. It is Bruce and Wallace who have been born again in the 1990s. This is a curious reversal of the cultural experience of the later nineteenth century, when - apart from a cult of William Wallace as a restyled hero of national liberation movements in Italy and elsewhere - the Middle Ages were increasingly passed over in favour of the pursuit of the post-Reformation period which lent a more sharply etched sense of Protestant identity. The 1840s and 1850s were the period when the Bannatyne and Maitland Clubs, which had done so much to recover a medieval past, foundered and the Wodrow Society, the voice of a branch of Protestant dissent in search of its roots, emerged.[7] In the second half of the nineteenth century, cults of Knox and Andrew Melville vied - in the Scottish diaspora as well as in the Scottish homeland itself - with cults of Wallace and Robert Burns.

It did not take long for the minority Protestant movement, once it had captured power in the Reformation-rebellion of 1559-60, to claim that it had erected a new national church. Yet the new Scots were also, at least potentially, new Britons, protected by a new-found 'amity' with their English brethren, and perhaps new internationalists as well, welded together by an increasingly common fear of a Catholic international.[8] These were extra dimensions which would give depth to a new-found, but still flimsily constructed sense of identity, but there were also serious flaws. The dilemmas of post-Reformation Scotland, a nation in search of an identity which needed to be refashioned after centuries of seeming certainty, may more easily be appreciated today, by a society which is seeing a crisis in Britain's national identity; the key institutions which are the guardians of the nation's identity - a British monarchy, British parliament, English law and an established church - have all in the recent past had their own crises of confidence, which have in turn exaggerated a more general crisis - of British unionism. The situation described here has certain similarities: until the Reformation the icons of national identity were the crown and the church. Certain other factors conditioned Scottish identity, including Scots language and law, but they were as yet only of secondary importance.[9] The cause of the Lords of the Congregation came to be portrayed as a crusade against French domination, and to a certain extent the propaganda stuck.[10] Yet for some time after 1560 the Reformation had little positive to substitute for a pro-French monarchy or a national church which it had managed to discredit but not as yet fully replace. There was, as a result, a partial but crucial vacuum in Scots' sense of themselves, which lasted for two or three generations after 1560; it was a gap which was exploited by James VI from the mid-1590s onwards with a barrage of propaganda about the attractions of a greater Britain and a 'perfect union', as he termed it. Few were convinced by the spectacle of a new Arthur, king of a greater Britain, but the state's near-monopoly of the communication lines of political culture, in the absence after 1596 of regular meetings of the General Assembly, gave it an unwonted prominence. A comparison with England is instructive. In its case, national identity had been inflated by the unlikely successes of England in the Hundred Years' War against France; as early as

1377 the English chancellor was comparing the English nation to the 'people of Israel'. At the Reformation, it was but one short step for the Englishman to claim as John Aylmer did in 1559, that 'God is English' and that the English were God's own privileged people. The true Englishman had become the true born Englishman, born again and saved from Rome. The day of Queen Elizabeth's succession (17 November) became a Protestant saint's day, a direct replacement of one of the two greatest Catholic feast days of the year, the Assumption of the Blessed Virgin Mary.[11] For Scotland, national identity was also first born out of what might well have been called Scotland's Hundred Years War, otherwise termed the Wars of Independence. As has recently emphatically been stated, these were *people's* wars and Scottish national identity was inextricably bound up with that fact.[12] After the 'Rough wooing' of the 1540s, however, there were no people's wars in the sixteenth century to underpin identity.   Was there instead a people's Reformation? Did Scotland experience a popular Reformation which had a galvanising effect on Scots' sense of themselves, giving them a new identity as a chosen people, free of both Rome and France, and overwhelming a sense of place conditioned by long-established local or regional horizons? The notion of a people's Reformation was a reputation which was, at best, a convenient myth used first, not by the hagiographers of Protestantism, but by authority to avert a recurrence of the danger of the many-headed monster - the people. There were in Scotland in 1560 only muted rallying cries of a covenant with Israel; the most effective propaganda of the Lords of the Congregation finessed on a term which had been in use since the 1530s - the notion of the commonweal, the product of Sir David Lindsay of the Mount.[13] This, far from being a revolutionary slogan, underpinned a deeply conservative caste of mind. The works of Lindsay, playwright, court poet and royal herald, reached a new and much wider reading public after 1570, when they were published in successive editions by Edinburgh booksellers; in the process, the *Ane Satyre of the Three Estatis*, an anticlerical *tour de force* of which reflected shifting opinion which was as yet still short of outright heresy in the critical second quarter of the sixteenth century, acquired an explicitly Protestant message after 1560.[14] Yet populism as a literary device should not be confused with popular feeling; the primary audience for whom Lindsay wrote was the privileged circle of the royal court. And even in the rediscovery of Lindsay's works in printed form after 1570, the new audience was almost certainly professional or middle class and not drawn from the lower orders.[15]

More is known of the progress of the Reformation in Scotland, but much is still in dispute. The new Protestant church claimed as early as the autumn of 1560 that it was the 'church of Scotland', meaning the whole of

Scotland.[16] By the end of 1561, by the most optimistic estimates, it had ministers or readers - though usually readers - placed in only one in four of Scotland's 1,000 parishes, with a heavy preponderance in Fife and Angus.[17] By 1574, there were incumbents in most parishes outside the dark corners of the land, in the Highlands and borderlands. Yet the counting of ministers is as accurate an exercise as the counting of sheep in assessing the spread of Protestantism. What needs to be borne in mind are two qualifications, commonly used to measure the success and failure of other reformations in Europe - the quality and motivation of the parish ministry and the authenticity of the religious experience.[18] Here, mere conformity needs to be distinguished from genuine conversion. Using the first of these criteria, it can readily be shown that it would take until the end of the sixteenth century for there to be fully qualified ministers in place in the bulk of Lowland parishes; in the borderlands such as the south-west it would take a further generation after 1600; but in much of the Highlands provision was patchy throughout most of the seventeenth century.[19] The second criterion is more difficult to assess with certainty, although orthodox presbyterian historiography has usually had few such qualms. In England, by contrast, it is commonly acknowledged that the second and third decades of the seventeenth century saw a real, if partly paranoid crisis of the Protestant intellect and a withdrawal into the moral certainties of the religious autobiography, diary or spiritual exercise.[20]

In this vein, what is the historian to make of claims such as that made by John Knox in or about 1566, in the preface to Book IV of his *History of the Reformation*, that 'as regards doctrine and the administration of the sacraments' there was no church upon the face of the earth that had them in a purer form. This was a myth which would be repeated at regular intervals after 1560. In 1616, for example, the General Assembly claimed that its was the 'purest church under Heaven'. But this was largely whistling in the wind, to keep up the flagging morale of a ministry which was by then undergoing a serious crisis of confidence in its ability to reach out to the populace as a whole, as were its counterparts in England. In 1566 Knox made this claim while the General Assembly was complaining about the spread of the pollution of the Catholic mass throughout all parts of the country; in 1616 the Kirk was trying to emphasise its own purity against a background of increasing worry about the 'irreverent behaviour of the vulgar sort' during services as well as by the calculated onslaught of James VI and his bishops.[21]

If a stricter definition of conversion is used than mere conformity, it becomes likely that it took two or three generations for the new Protestant church to evangelise Lowland society. Real progress, in the sense of bring the Reformation to the people as a whole, was probably not achieved much before the 1620s or 1630s at the earliest. That argument is closely intertwined with the current issue, of when the new kirk successfully fashioned an image of itself as a national church. Before 1560, the idea of national identity was a highly developed, aggressive and mythical construct, fostered largely by a mandarin class of clerics and based on the supporting pillars of medieval kings and the Church. It was not easy to replace quickly. When James VI came of age, in 1579, the messages were still mixed: the precociousness of the godly boy prince was celebrated in the formal entry into his capital in 1579 but the central message was of an old-style rather than a new monarchy; the central image, seen in a specially commissioned set of portraits hung at the Salt Tron in the High Street, was of the previous five kings before him called James.[22] No new national histories were commissioned, at least before James VI left for London; and after 1603 the new king of Great Britain would become the patron of British rather than Scottish histories. It was only in the 1620s and 1630s that a new-style history of Scotland and its new national church began to be written. By then, rival ecclesiastical histories, episcopalian and radical presbyterian, competed for the centre ground of Scottish political culture. And in the process, old myths were repolished, by both of the contending parties, including the hoary argument that Christianity had come to Scotland centuries before it reached the English.

The Reformation in Scotland was most successful, in the short term, where it chose to draw on the rich cultural heritage of late medieval Scotland; it was far less successful, in the short to medium term, where it offered change, disruption or uncertainty. Because of the significant amount of iconoclasm and destruction in and after 1560, which was designed to produce a cleansing of the mind as much as a stripping of the altars, the new Protestant preachers had less evangelical tools with which to combat ungodly congregations than the priests of the old Church. There was, in Scotland, virtually nothing like the quasi-canonization of Martin Luther which has been described in Germany to help replace the old Catholic cult.[23] Knox surfaced again, as presbyter reborn, only in the 1620s and 1630s, in the work of David Calderwood and other radicals seeking to claim for their own party their spiritual forebears.

There was no equivalent in Scotland to match the Protestant civic pageantry associated with England's Eliza, even after the young godly prince, James VI, came of age in 1579. Equally, Scotland had was no national saint's day. One of the first mentions of St Andrew after 1560 came in 1603, when it was intended that the first of the triumphal arches in London greeting James I of England should represent St Andrew and St George; the idea was dropped for lack of interest. In the 1660s, so a jaundiced English observer in London noted, the exiled Scots treated St Andrew's Day only as another chance to get drunk. It had nothing of the symbolic significance heaped upon St George's Day since early in the reign of Elizabeth.[24] In the *Complaynt of Scotland*, the patriotic, pro-Catholic tract written by Robert Wedderburn, vicar of Dundee, against the background of the foreign invasion of Scotland in the 1540s and the bombardment of his town of Dundee by the English, Dame Scotia had symbolised the distresses of the commonweal.[25] In the royal entry of 1579, she had reappeared in the guise of Dame Religion, who greeted the young king on the steps of St Giles'. This was a rare appearance of an iconic figure which seems to have fallen into disuse after 1560; it was also a pallid imitation, for Dame Religion had greeted the young king in Hebrew.[26] This was not an image for the populace to understand or rally behind.

Where was the new popular literature of a Protestant nation? It is hard to find, at least before 1600. The two most significant 'popular' religious works were the *Good and Godly Ballads*, first published in a uncensored version in 1565, and known by the 1580s as the Dundee Psalms and an otherwise half-forgotten diatribe against Regent Morton, a poem called *A Winter's Night*. What was probably more influential in the shorter term was a patriotic publishing campaign, which began in the early 1570s. It largely consisted of the re-publication of the masterpieces of late medieval Scotland - or at least those masterpieces which contained wholesome messages. The works of Robert Henryson, and especially the 'Testament of Cresseid' and the works of David Lindsay were published and republished in successive cheap editions in the late sixteenth and seventeenth centuries.[27] It may be significant that the late medieval heroic verse epics - Barbour's *The Brus* and Blind Harry's *Wallace* - were published by the king's party printer during the civil war, anxious to claim, as had the Lords of Congregation a decade before, the high ground of Protestant patriotism. There is a hint here of a clash of rival remembered pasts: in one vein, the king's party relied on the heroic, chivalric traditions which had emerged in the course of the later fourteenth and early fifteenth centuries; in another, in tracts such as *The Chameleon* and *Ane Admonitioun to the Trew Lordis*, it was concocting the first drafts of the 'revolutionary tradition' which would appear, in more mature form, in George Buchanan's later work.[28]

Where were the basic tools of Protestant evangelisation? England, of course, had had Tyndale's New Testament since 1529 and its own prayer book since 1558, written by exiled English ministers in Geneva. The first Bible produced in Scotland was published in 1579; at £40, it cost the equivalent of a craftsman's annual wage. The act which enforced its sale was limited to greater lairds and, at best, to one urban household in twenty. But

this, the Arbuthnot Bible, named after its printer, was in English. There was
no readily available Bible in Scots. Cheap editions of bibles began to appear
in Edinburgh booksellers' inventories only in the 1630s.[29] The Bibles of
ministers, godly magistrates, lawyers and humanists - the key makers of
opinion - might be well-thumbed before then, but it is only in the 1630s, by
which time perhaps one quarter of adult males in urban society were literate,
that it begins to be possible to argue the case for a widespread impact of the
Bible on society at large.[30] The debate is usually cast in the wrong terms - of
a contest between Scots and English. In reality, the battle was between Latin
and the vernacular. In England, it has been argued, the force of the plain
'ploughboy's English' of Tyndale's New Testament had allowed it to overtake
Latin by the middle of the sixteenth century.[31] In Scotland, its impact must
have been lesser, both amongst a wider reading public which still spoke Scots
and amongst a literati where the neo-Latin tradition was much stronger.
Equally, there was no popular catechism in Scots, although there were a
series of publishing failures from the 1580s onwards. Scottish schoolchildren
had to rely on Calvin's catechism in a quasi-foreign language - in English. The
most important tool in the hands of preachers and schoolmasters was the
psalter - either the Psalms of David or the Dundee Psalms.

How else can the 'imagining of Scotland' be measured? Although
much can be - and has been - made of the emergence of a covenanted nation
in the 1630s, with its roots three or four decades earlier,[32] the case has still
convincingly to be made on a wider and more inclusive basis than the political
theology of what emerged as a radical party in the kirk or the slogans of one
side in the Wars of the Covenants. Where in Scottish dialectic was the new
civic and national consciousness which John Pocock has detected in English
political culture of the century after 1558? Much of the late medieval
reshaping of Scotland had been due to the efforts of clerical historians ranging
from John Barbour writing in the 1370s to Walter Bower, who had compiled
the massive *Scotichronicon* by the 1450s. Yet often, in other early modern
states, it is not only clerics or chroniclers who can create or refashion the
perception of a national community. Lawyers, heralds and map-makers can
do so as well.[33] It was in the 1590s that Scotland was first extensively and
systematically mapped, by Timothy Pont, the son of a minister. But (unlike
England which saw extensive publication of the county maps of John Speed in
the late sixteenth century) these maps were not easily available before the
1650s, when they were published in Amsterdam.[34] County maps of Scotland,
drawn by John Adair, and an accurate map of the coastline belong to the last
quarter of the seventeenth century. It was in that period that a rediscovery of
Scotland in different and wider ranging dimensions can be detected - variously

seen in the work of Robert Sibbald in geography, geology and archaeology, the rediscovery (first made by George Mackenzie of Rosehaugh) of the customs of Gaeldom which would climax rather than begin with McPherson's *Ossian* three quarters of a century later,[35] the reinstitution of the Order of the Thistle (defunct since 1542), as well as the mapping of Scotland. It seems clear - although relatively little has been made of the phenomenon - that a widespread, multi-layered exploration of Scotland's identity had emerged by the last quarter of the seventeenth century.

Another measure of a more widely visualized national community might be the point at which learned histories reach a wider reading public. Here, the dating of the phenomenon is rather earlier. A useful comparison can be gleaned from Denmark. By 1600, an authoritative, compendious history of Denmark, written by a nobleman, courtier and member of the king's council, Arild Huitfeld, was influential within the privileged confines of government and royal court; it ran to nine volumes. It was reprinted in a severely abridged version of 138 pages in 1645; this went through a second edition in the same year and was reprinted again in 1649. An 'official' history had reached the people. The same phenomenon can be traced somewhat earlier in Scotland, with the first appearance of abridged editions of longer chronicles about 1600. There are two earlier editions, compiled by John Monipenny, which appeared in 1597 and possibly as early as 1594. Most examples of the more popular form of almanacs, however, belonged to the period after 1610.[36]

This was an abridged version, not of the presbyterian canon - taught by Andrew Melville and his academic disciples in the universities - of George Buchanan's *History* of 1582, but a translation and greatly shortened version of Hector Boece's *Chronicle* which, in its original form, had first been published in Latin in 1527 and first translated into the vernacular, by royal commission, in 1536. The first manifestations of a wider, popular identity were drawn, it might be said, not from new George but old Hector.[37] The basis was a chronicle of the kings of Scots compiled, like a series of late medieval chronicles before it, to enhance the image of kingship rather than the foremost example in the century after the Reformation of the genre of 'Calvinist humanism'[38] designed to allow lesser magistrates or ministers' godly consciences to censure kings. It was royalist rather than presbyterian history which first reached a wider audience.

Two distinctions need to be drawn at this point. The first is the need to separate from each other ideology - the political culture of the makers of opinion - and *mentalité*, or opinion itself.[39] A concentration on the concept of history as the prime ingredient of national consciousness, which has become fashionable amongst recent Scottish historians of the early modern period, perhaps because it can readily fashion the Scottish past into a coherent thread of sorts, can obscure this difference. It threatens to become a new, more sophisticated kind of establishment history. The second is the need to trace the linkage between the two, or at what point - for there is often a considerable drag factor in time involved - an ideology gained a wider currency. Few would wish to deny the force of the case that Buchanan's *History* played a key role in fashioning a distinctively Protestant Scottish identity, succinctly described as an 'ongoing process of Scottish self-definition - and redefinition - which began with the Reformation of 1560 and was to culminate ... in a second Reformation in the late 1630s and 1640s'.[40] but the direct effect of a work which remained in its original Latin version throughout the seventeenth century must largely have been limited to the opinion makers. In Ireland, the emerging phenomenon in the middle of the sixteenth century of an apparently strident Gaelic nationalism in reality was confined to a cloistered order of literati until the early decades of the seventeenth century.[41] How continuous or unbroken amongst the makers of opinion in Scotland was this process of self-definition, which from the 1610s onwards began to take the form of competing versions of a post-Reformation ideology, with historians of the rival presbyterian and episcopalian parties each claiming as its own not only the Reformation of 1560 but also its mythical pre-history? David Calderwood and Archbishop Spottiswoode, for example, squabbled in print over squatters' rights to the tradition of Columba and the culdees.[42] At what point in the passage of time of eight or nine decades between 1560 and the 1630s or 1640s - a period which makes the Reformation as remote to the experience of the contemporaries of the Covenanters as the First World War would be to today - did that process of redefinition achieve a wider influence? In England, the sense of a new covenant with the Lord was already explicit and popular by 1559. In Scotland, it seems difficult to claim the same much before the 1630s.

Why should there have been so divergent experiences between England and Scotland? One obvious answer lies communications. With England, the 'dark corners of the land', in England as distinct from its far-flung possessions in Wales and Ireland, were sharply receding in the course of the sixteenth century. It was not until late in the sixteenth century that a 'road to the Isles' across mainland Scotland was laid out in the minds of Lowland Scots. And the decisive period marking an improvement in inland networks and trade seems to have been the last four decades of the seventeenth century, when almost 250 new market centres were licensed. The result was that by 1700 less than a fifth of mainland Scotland was situated more than a dozen miles distant from a market centre. By then, too, Scotland had begun to be mapped and its towns surveyed on a much more extensive scale.[43]

A further obvious answer lies in war. The reign of Elizabeth saw England's involvement in war in Scotland in 1560, in France in 1562, in the Netherlands in the 1570s and again in the mid-1580s, the threat of the Armada in 1588 and a surrogate role in the Thirty Years' War after 1618. Wars of religion in the period 1560 to 1650, Professor Collinson has affirmed, were vital to the development of the English Protestant notion of a 'beleaguered isle'. In much the same way, Linda Colley has argued that a second Hundred Years War - between 1690 and 1815 - was what fashioned Protestant Britons.[44] For the first sixty years of its existence - until the Thirty Years' War - Protestant Scotland had no such galvanising experience. Foreign invasion was feared - but also lobbied for - during the inconclusive struggle between the king's and queen's men in 1568-73, but this was a civil war in which the religious issue stubbornly refused to take primacy of place, despite the best efforts of king's party propagandists such as Buchanan.[45] In the more godly atmosphere of James VI's personal reign, Scots congregations, it is true, from time to time made collections for the relief of their distressed European brethren in some of these European wars of religion; and the kirk arranged its own private chain of communications in 1588 to give early warning of a Spanish landing.[46] Yet there was no serious perceived threat to Scottish identity before the 1630s, no national army before the Wars of the Covenant, and little sense of a nation under threat until the Montrose campaign of 1644.

Does this suggest that the decisive moment in Scotland's rediscovery of itself was the Wars of the Covenant? These were, in a real though limited sense, wars of religion just as the English Civil War has recently been acknowledged as a war of religion. But there is an important difference, which deserves fuller recognition in the conceptual framework of Scotland's history: the century after 1638 brought saw a different kind of Hundred Years' War. The Scottish variant of 'people's wars' was civil wars, which dominated much of the history of Scotland from the breakdown of the forced consensus that lay behind the National Covenant until Culloden. The intervening period saw intermittent warfare between Scot and Scot and between the Lowlands and the so-called 'conservative north' (meaning non-Highland society north of the Tay),[47] as well as between Lowlander and Highlander.

The Covenanters fought under the national flag of the saltire and banners which variously proclaimed their cause as 'For Religion, Country, Crown and Covenant' and 'For Covenant, Religion, King and Kingdom'.[48] These were striking images, but they were exclusivist rather than inclusive, and they reflected the internal frontiers which had descended on Scottish society in the course of the century before 1640. It has been said that a civil war has the effect of tearing back the veil which usually conceals the secrets of society.[49] The wars of the 1640s, in their various guises - the Wars of the Covenant, the Scottish Revolution and the War of the Three Kingdoms - revealed a society in which the natural horizon of the locality, and the network of kin, lineage and personal loyalties which underpinned it, reasserted itself. The wars began in 1639 with the expedition of the Campbell network against the power structure of the Gordons which challenged it at the margins of its authority in the north-west; the 'conservative north' reasserted itself in the 1640s as well as in 1715 against a Campbell coalition which had been the first to use the term 'north Britons' to describe itself.[50] The second half of the 1640s saw the emergence of a 'radical south-west', which had generally been late in the process of conversion to Protestantism and which lacked a powerful magnate of the dimensions of the king's traditional lieutenants in the west and the north - the earls of Argyll and Huntly. The rise to influence within Covenanting ranks of elements from the south-west revealed not only illicit developments in worship which had been generally ignored by mainstream presbyterianism but also sharper social tensions, both of which carried hints of a revolutionary recasting of society.[51] The wider War of the Three Kingdoms was fought by expeditionary Covenanting armies in Ireland to defend recently established Scots colonists who saw themselves as the first 'Britons', a transmutation of identity which anticipated the redefinition of the new English settlers as 'west Britons' by at least a decade,[52] but they also were defending the extended Campbell local network on both sides of the North Channel, in Ulster as well as in Argyll. Campbell localism, in effect, was now been promoted on a British as well as a Scottish stage. North-east localism, orchestrated by the powerful Gordon network, by contrast, retreated into its *laager*.[53] If space permitted, the contrasting examples could be multiplied.

The Covenanting regime proved in the course of the 1640s to be more centralist, demanding and authoritarian - as well as more British in its aspirations[54] - than the regime of Charles I against which it had rebelled. The problems which it encountered within Scotland reflected a serious crisis of identity of a kingdom with an absentee king. Throughout most of the medieval period, it is commonly argued, both Scottish kingship and society had been hybrid;[55] that ceased to be the case sometime in the early modern period. Although the notion of a Highland 'problem' had begun to arise in the very late fourteenth century, kingship itself remained hybrid for at least another century. Kings still saw themselves as descended from Celtic kings; at his entry into Edinburgh in 1633 Charles was greeted by a tableau which hailed him as a descendant of kings who had conquered both the Romans and the Picts who were equally 'broken in war and repelled by destiny'.[56] The sixteenth century, however, was the last to embrace both Lowland and Highland culture as equal constituent parts of Scottish identity. When a mock fort representing the divinity of the royal house of Stewart was erected outside Stirling Castle at the time of the baptismal celebrations for the son of Mary Queen of Scots in 1566, it was assaulted by the enemies of the realm, who included Highlanders as well as the conventional villains of European Christendom - the Moors. At the entry of James VI's bride, Anna of Denmark into Edinburgh in 1590, the only representation of Gaelic culture was a sword dance, put on, it seems likely, by local performers.[57] By the 1590s, the Highlands had reached that ambiguous double status they were to enjoy for the next two centuries - both barbarous and kitsch. The calculated stigmatisation of Gaelic culture had begun in the royal court in the 1580s, when the poet Alexander Montgomerie had made fun of Celtic origins legends. A new divide between civilised society and the barbarous Highlands had opened up. It was precisely the same stigmatisation of Gaelic society that can be detected amongst English humanists and propagandists, like Edmund Spenser, in his *View of the Present State of Ireland*, published in 1596.[58] Amongst Scotland's literati, this consensus seems to have lasted about a century, until antiquarians such as Mackenzie of Rosehaugh began in the 1670s to break ranks by taking seriously the customs and manners of the Gaeldom. Amongst the wider populace, the image of Highland barbarity persisted widely until well after Culloden.

For centuries, the monarchy had provided most of the institutional unity in the realm as well as the most compelling image of national identity. The monarchy by the 1590s was urging, with distinguished eccentricity, a new pan-British identity. The kirk, as yet, was immersed in its own problems of underfunding, increasingly aware of its deficiencies in converting the ungodly masses and little concerned as yet with the dark corners of the land where the new Gospel had scarcely reached - in the south-west, in the Highlands and the Isles. James Melville in his long spiritual autobiography which runs to 804 pages in print, mentioned the Highlands only a handful of times. Inverness and even Aberdeenshire were Scotland's *gulags* where offending radical ministers, including Robert Bruce and Samuel Rutherford, were sent by the king as a punishment, into internal exile.[59]

What of lawyers, also guardians of part of the nation's identity? It is true that considerable effort was being made, in the 1580s or before, to codify Scots law, but the most prominent legal brains in the country were, in the 1590s, for the most part happy enough to stress James the lawgiver rather than the distinctive nature of Scots law.[60] Where were the preservatives of Scottish identity? It was their virtual absence that allowed James VI to get as far as he did with the seductive images of a British union. It produced a generation of intellectuals whose ideology flirted with a new identity: Robert Pont, grand old man of the Reformation of 1560, fulminated to order in the first decade of the seventeenth century, against Borderers, Highlanders and papists as the enemies of the new greater Britain; David Hume of Godscroft, historian, neo-Latin poet and the most important lay figure in Scottish Calvinism in the age of Andrew Melville, consistently thought of himself as Scoto-Brittanus.[61] A great deal was seemingly on offer: not just new flags and a coinage but a new history, an apocalyptic vision of king and kingdom and an attempt to forge a common Calvinist religion out of three previously separate state churches. It produced the first generation of convinced British unionists - and perhaps the last for over a century and a half. They were, however, confined either to a rarefied strain of Calvinist humanism or to special interest groups, such as the septs of Clan Campbell.

In part, the rise of such new exotic species of identity came about because of the weakness of an alternative. There was a patriotic literature which seems in the course of the last three decades of the sixteenth century to have has found a new reading public; Blind Harry's *Wallace*, Barbour's *The Brus*, Lindsay's *Three Estatis* with the figure of John the Commonweill at its centre were amongst the best sellers of the 1590s.[62] However more sharply etched this new sense of *mentalité* was, amongst the various branches of the middling sort which constituted this new audience for a patriotic printing campaign, this widening sense of *patria* had as yet found no clear alternative to the monarchy to protect or foster it: the icons of Dame Scotia, metaphor of a Catholic priest for the beleagured homeland, and of Lady Veritie, creation of a court poet and royal herald, but without the royal court to offer it a home after 1603, had yet to find a new protector.

It was the nobility rather than the church which first showed signs of filling the void, though hardly as new-style Calvinist ephors to the design of George Buchanan. The last quarter of the sixteenth century was marked by a vogue for commissioning the histories of noble families and concocting their genealogies - by fair means or fake. In an age when there was a sharp increase in the number of noble creations, an inflation of honours, and increased formal ritual and ceremony (both before and after 1603),[63] it tended to be those families on the make who were most conscious of the need to find an impressive noble pedigree. Two well-known examples illustrate the fashion: the Seton armorial, which traced both its own family and kings of Scots back into distant Scotch mists, and the striking collection commissioned by the Campbells of Glenorchy of twenty-four portraits of kings and queens of Scots and thirty-four lords and ladies from their own ancestors. The renewed stress on noble lineage naturally complemented the habitual but growing emphasis in the last quarter of the sixteenth century on the antiquity of the Stewart royal line. Without a personal king after 1603 to complement it, however, noble chivalry and lineage could have the effect of reasserting the locality at the expense of the centre.

This was certainly the case in Ireland, which offers a number of parallels and an ironical commentary on the rebirth of a Scottish identity in the early seventeenth century. There, the bards at and after the flight of the earls in 1607 fed much the same fashion for noble lineage but rarely escaped from the nostalgic or the local. The Glenorchy portraits and the Seton Armorial resemble much of Irish Gaelic culture of the same period - patriotic but only in a vague sense; the focus is with lordship, lineage and the locality. In the same way, Gaelic poetry in both Scotland and Ireland was more concerned with the threat to its own patrons rather than an attack on Celtic society as a whole; for the most part, it did not rise above defence of the local or individual lord, whether MacDonald or Macdonnell. Even when it did, it was concerned with a class of Gaelic lords rather than Gaelic society as a whole.[64] It would be a mistake to suggest that an alternative notion of *patria* was available in the Gaidhealtachd. Quite the opposite.

Ireland again offers further instructive parallels in trying to assess the fall-out after the 'perfect union' of James VI failed to materialise, in most of its promised parts after 1607. In the 1630s and 1640s a new kind of Irish identity and self-consciousness was forged. Increasingly the Irish were compared with the Israelites, for their hour of deliverance from their oppressor was at hand. The job description of a noble now went beyond merely being a godly magistrate to acting as an exemplar of the true Christian way of life. This new Irish identity was backed by a reawakened interest in Gaelic sources and history, which was reinterpreted for the period since 1560 in stark confessional terms.[65] Every one of these points has an obvious parallel in Scotland. By the 1630s, in the thought of radical presbyterians, Scotland and Israel were the 'only two sworn nations of the Lord'; Samuel Rutherford urged on delinquent Scottish noble their duty to be 'little nursing fathers' of the kirk. In Ireland, Irish history became a battleground, between the Protestant Church of Ireland and a new Catholic mission, led by the Jesuits, each claiming to represent the authentic Irish church with its roots deep in the past. In Scotland, the battle lay between episcopalian historians like Archbishop Spottiswoode and a growing weight of presbyterian historiography, with David Calderwood's massive *History of the Kirk* prominent among it.[66]

There is a further ironic analogy to be made. When the Jesuits had first visited Ireland in 1539, they had cast off the native Irish as barbarous and incapable of conversion to the true faith. By the 1630s, the Irish were being praised for their primitive simplicity; post-Tridentine practice was supposed to fit in with the existing customs of Gaelic society. Patrick was rediscovered as a Jesuit, born eleven centuries before his time, and also recast by Archbishop Ussher as a useful native forerunner of the colonialist Protestant Church of Ireland. In Scotland, much the same propaganda battle went on although the contenders were different; Spottiswoode and Calderwood vied over the grave of Columba, a defender of the true primitive Scots religion against Rome - as a bishop or a presbyter ten centuries before *his* time.[67] In both Ireland and Scotland in the 1620s and 1630s, new personae and new icons of national identity emerged; they were remarkably similar. In Ireland, in Gaelic literature from the 1640s onwards, there appears with increasing embroidery, the figure of 'mother Ireland', a woman in captivity or mourning. In Scotland, Dame Scotia had by the later 1630s become the kirk itself, the suffering bride of Christ.[68]

There is one further irony. Many of the presbyterian concoctors of this new Scottish identity had been exiles; such as Calderwood in the Netherlands or other clergy in France or Ireland until expelled by Richelieu or Strafford in the course of the 1630s. Radical presbyterians such as these returned to the homeland fuelled by a sense of injustice. Here, it is perhaps worth recall the words of Michael Walzer about some of the very radical tracts of the Marian exiles of the 1550s, Knox among them; that only an exile, a rootless figure divorced from the homeland, could have written them.[69] There is an element of truth in the analogy, but it is only a half truth. Who were these ministerial refugees from Ireland? Andrew Knox, bishop of the Isles, is well known for his activities as the architect of James VI's Highland policy after 1603, which included kidnapping and the forced education of sons of Gaelic chiefs. His career as bishop of the Irish diocese of Raphoe after 1610 is less well known, at least in Scotland. He was one of the first of a minor exodus of Scots presbyterian ministers who joined the Church of Ireland. This was by then a thoroughly colonialist church; these Scottish clergy were generally not Gaelic speakers; they were English-speaking colonialists, bent on a mission to civilize a people 'as barbarous as the Moors'. They belonged to a British church.[70] Many of the stoutest defenders of the independence of the Scottish church from the mid-1630s onwards were ex-unionists or disillusioned Britons. The Protestant mission exploring the darkest corners of the Protestant Isles had turned sour; amongst the clerical missionaries it had the effect of turning old Britons into new Scots or old colonialists into born-again patriots.

To sum up, in both Ireland and Scotland, a new national identity crystallised in the 1630s and 1640s. In each case, it was a defence mechanism which reflected the failure of an absentee king, based in London, to mould a society to his will. It came about as a result of the failure of the notion of a British *patria*. That notion of Britain - or a Greater Britain - as a new-style nation state had had a certain cachet amongst sections of the Scottish intelligentsia for perhaps a generation from the 1590s onwards and amongst special interest groups, such as settlers and colonists in Ulster. The threat of a British patria and its subsequent collapse produced a nation born again, in both Scotland and Ireland. This was no longer based on kingship or local lordship or on ethnic consciousness. It was a notion, in each case, of the nation as a new Israel.

What is suggested here is that nations are not forged overnight - even with events such as 1560 which later take on a reputation of inevitability or unstoppable dynamic. That may surprise some and enrage others. Yet it should not surprise those familiar with the tangled web of recreating a national identity in both Protestant and Catholic societies after the impact of Reformation or Counter-Reformation. Wha's like us? Damn' few? In fact, damn' many. The Scots were far from being the only tribe of Israelites in early modern Europe. The queue claiming to be God's authentic people included English Protestants, Irish Catholics, French, Poles and Spaniards.

For historians of earlier periods of Scottish history this argument should also seem familiar. Scottish identity has never been a fixed, immutable idea, whether held in the head or in the gut. The story of much of Scotland's past up to the sixteenth century is largely one of how identities change, develop and recast themselves. This is true as well of the untouchable century - the century or so after the Reformation of 1560 - in which there is so much emotional investment amongst those who see Scotland as fulfilling its destiny, as a Protestant nation. Before reasserting that 'We are the people ...', it would be better try to answer the question, 'what people?' in order to address a more difficult question: whose past, and whose present? Some of the most enduring myths of Scotland's Protestant identity were, like Ireland's Catholic identity, creations of the nineteenth century: they included Jenny Geddes as a Protestant Dame Scotia throwing a stool into the works of an Anglican-style church and the Magdalen Chapel in Edinburgh, the home of a staunchly Catholic craft guild throughout much of the 1560s, becoming the 'workshop of the Reformation' in John Knox's time.[71] Invented traditions were a feature of Lowland Scotland as well as Highland in the Victorian age. They were often the work of dissenting off-shoots of the established church, each anxious to claim for itself the authentic tradition of a Protestant national culture.

The mature form of that culture, like its equivalent in Catholic Ireland, was a creation of later centuries rather than the century of its first emergence - the seventeenth. Also, other distinctions need to be made. If historians are to try to rediscover the people's past, and not simply the past as forged and recast by an intelligentsia, a wider *mentalité* has to be distinguished from ideology. Within the former, there is usually an add-on factor that lies somewhere within Scots' sense of themselves. In early modern Scotland, as in England, ministers preaching from the pulpits of a radical Protestant church scarcely acknowledged the local community or the ambiguities inherent within a localised patriotism; the new Jerusalem offered one nation Protestantism and a transcendent Protestant international.[72] It largely passed over what many of their parishioners as well as those who were scarcely touched by the new kirk still saw as their 'country'. Within most Scots there was usually a locality - whether barony, shire, burgh, region or kinship network - waiting to get out.

For much of the medieval period, so far as can be discerned (and the nature of the evidence means that this is much more limited in scope than for later periods), that sense of localism could usually be overridden by a greater sense of *patria*, fuelled by one of the central features of Scottish history of the period - war with England. The sixteenth century brought about a decisive change but not, as is often thought, in the direction of a nation reborn and reunited. An alternative route can be staked out. The century between 1560 and 1660 produced the first, decisive episodes in a very different history. It brought a new questioning of a single national identity as well as novel definitions of it. Clashes between Catholics and Protestants, presbyterians and episcopalians, presbyterians and dissenters,[73] Highlanders and Lowlanders, north Britons and Scots all made their first appearance in this period. Each would think of themselves as Scots - but each had a different version of the past, and some also had different paths to the future. The early modern period, if taken to mean the two centuries before Culloden, saw at work centrifugal forces - locality, creed, religious faction and kinship - as well as the centripetal pressures, including a new national church, a body of distinctive codified law and the evolution of a 'mainstream' historiographical tradition, which until very recently have usually formed the core of most treatments of the period by historians. The result was twofold: early modern Scotland was a nation divided as never before as well a 'historical nation' reborn and reunited. Much of the latter agenda was the creation of successive generations of presbyterian historians, happier to find comforting answers than to pose uncomfortable questions. Scotland's past deserves more dispassionate analysis; the myths about the traumatic century and a half after 1560 need to be challenged by a generation more sceptical of easy answers to questions of national consciousness and identity.

NOTES

[1] J.M. Reid, *Kirk and Nation* (London, 1960), 173.

[2] G. Donaldson, *The Scottish Reformation* (Cambridge, 1960); it was heavily criticised for its 'unabashed partisanship' by Rev. Professor A. Cheyne of the Divinity Faculty of Edinburgh, who was used to a different brand of committed scholarship.

[3] P.J. Shearman, 'Father Alexander McQuhirrie, SJ', *Innes Review*, vi (1955) 22-45; W.J. Anderson, J.H. Burns, I. Mclaren [J. Durkan], 'The ordination of John Knox', *Innes Review*, vi (1955), 103-04, 102-03, 104-06. Cf *SHR*, xxxv (1956), 80, 180.

[4] The restatement of the orthodox presbyterian view of the Reformation, and the discovery of fresh material to make it more plausible, had to await the appearance of J. Kirk, *Patterns of Reform: Continuity and Change in the Reformation Kirk* (Edinburgh, 1989).

[5] The main product of 1972 was the slim proceedings of a conference on Knox: D. Shaw (ed.), *John Knox Quatercentenary Papers* (Edinburgh, 1975). The suggestion made by Stewart Lamont, author of the most recent biography of Knox, *The Swordbearer* (London, 1991) that a national day should be established in Knox's memory received little favour, even from the establishment of the Church of Scotland.

[6] See also D. Stevenson, 'Twilight before night or darkness before dawn? Interpreting seventeenth-century Scotland', in R. Mitchison (ed.), *Why Scottish History Matters* (2nd edn., Edinburgh, 1997), 53-64.

[7] M. Ash, *The Strange Death of Scottish History* (Edinburgh, 1980), 82-5.

[8] P. Collinson, 'The Protestant nation', in *Birthpangs of Protestant England: Religious and Cultural Change in the Sixteenth and Seventeenth Centuries* (London, 1988), 16-17.

[9] James V had acknowledged the importance of Scots as a language by his commissioning of a translation by John Bellenden of Hector Boece's *Chronicle*, which took on the status of a quasi-official national history: R. Mason, 'Scotching the Brut: politics, history and national myth in sixteenth century Britain', in R.A. Mason (ed.), *Scotland and England* (Edinburgh, 1987), 60-84. Royal patronage, in the form of the first printed edition in 1566 of the acts of parliament, also had a galvanising effect on law: it was followed by a dictionary of Scots law produced by David Chalmers, one of the editorial team of 1566, and by series of manuals of

precedents, culminating in the Practicks of Sir James Balfour of Pittendreich, compiled 1574-83; see *An Introductory Survey to the Sources and Literature of Scots Law* (Stair Society, 1936), 25-6.

[10] R. Mason, 'Covenant and commonweal: the language of politics in Reformation Scotland', in N. Macdougall (ed.), *Church, Politics and Society, 1408-1929* (Edinburgh, 1983), 97-126.

[11] Collinson, *Birthpangs*, 4-7; R. Hutton, *The Rise and Fall of Merry England: the Ritual Year, 1400-1700* (Oxford, 1994), 147-51; D. Cressy, *Bonfires and Bells: National Memory and the Protestant Calendar in Elizabethan and Stuart England* (London, 1989), 50-57.

[12] A. Grant, 'The Middle Ages: the defence of independence', in Mitchison (ed.), *Why Scottish History Matters*, 34-6.

[13] Mason, 'Covenant and commonweal', 108-12.

[14] Eight editions of Lindsay's Works were printed 1568-97 and a further eighteen in the seventeenth century: H.G. Aldis (ed.), *A List of Books printed in Scotland before 1700* (Edinburgh, 1970), 140, 167. See also 'Collection of the wills of printers and booksellers in Edinburgh between the years 1577 and 1687' in *Bannatyne Miscellany*, ii (Bannatyne Club, 1836), 191-296; see C. Edington, *Court and Culture in Renaissance Scotland: Sir David Lindsay of the Mount* (Amherst, 1994), 180-98, 210-11, for Lindsay's religious views, which never quite crossed the boundary into Protestant heresy.

[15] T. van Heijnsbergen, 'The interaction between literature and history in Queen Mary's Edinburgh: the Bannatyne Manuscript and its prosopographical context', in A.A. MacDonald, M. Lynch and I. B. Cowan (eds.), *The Renaissance in Scotland* (Brill, 1994), 183-225.

[16] Knox, *History*, i, 255.

[17] J. Kirk, *Patterns of Reform*, 130-31; cf F.D. Bardgett, *Scotland Reformed: the Reformation in Angus and the Mearns* (Edinburgh, 1989), 88-9, which shows that the incumbents in Angus and the Mearns accounted for a quarter of the national total in 1561.

[18] E. Cameron, *The European Reformation* (Oxford, 1991), 390-91, 396-400.

[19] M. Lynch, 'Preaching to the converted? Perspectives on the Scottish Reformation', in MacDonald *et al*, *The Renaissance in Scotland*, 306-14, 319-27; cf J. Kirk, *Patterns of Reform*, 305-33, 449-87. See also J. Dawson, 'The Gaidhealtachd and the emergence of the Scottish Highlands', in B. Bradshaw and P. Roberts (eds.), *British Identity and Consciousness* (forthcoming, Cambridge, 1997). I am grateful to Dr Dawson for an early sight of this piece.

[20] J. Bossy, *Christianity in the West, 1400-1700* (Oxford, 1985), 133; Collinson, *The Religion of Protestants: the Church in English Society, 1559-1625* (Oxford, 1982), 221-6, 232-3; M. Steele, 'The "politick Christian": the theological

background to the National Covenant', in J. Morrill (ed.), *The Scottish National Covenant in its British Context, 1638-51* (Edinburgh, 1990), 31-67.

[21] Knox, *History*, ii, 3; *Acts and Proceedings of the General Assemblies of the Kirk of Scotland* (Bannatyne Club, 1839-45), i, 77-81 (1566); iii, 1116-39 (1616). See Lynch, 'Preaching to the converted', 302-05. Cf Collinson, *Religion of Protestants*, 190-91, 199-205, 221-6.

[22] M. Lynch, 'A royal progress: court ceremony and ritual during the personal reign of James VI', in J. Goodare and M. Lynch (eds.), *James VI: Court and Kingship* (forthcoming, Tuckwell Press, East Linton).

[23] See R.W. Scribner, *Popular Culture and Popular Movements in Reformation Germany* (London, 1987), 301-22.

[24] Hutton, *Merry England*, 146-51, 186-7; K. Brown, 'The vanishing emperor: British kingship and its decline, 1603-1707', in R.A. Mason (ed.), *Scots and Britons: Scottish Political Thought and the Union of 1603* (Cambridge, 1994), 71.

[25] The figure of Lady Veritie, which appeared in Lindsay's *Satire of the Three Estatis*, had both a larger and narrower role: she was a conventional figure in medieval allegories but here also represented the Word of God. See Edington, *Court and Culture*, 138. The later Protestant icon of Dame Scotia, it is likely, was intended to combine the moral force of both Wedderburn's and Lindsay's emblematic figures.

[26] Lynch, 'A royal visit'.

[27] Aldis, *List*, p 137; 'Wills of printers and booksellers', 191ff.

[28] Aldis, *List*, nos. 82, 98; *Vernacular Writings of George Buchanan* (STS, 1892), 18-53.

[29] Lynch, 'Preaching to the converted', 329-30; 'Wills of printers and booksellers', 259.

[30] For England, where even in godly areas such as Essex ownership of Bibles was not widespread much before 1600, see R. Whiting, *The Blind Devotion of the People* (Cambridge, 1989), 183, 190.

[31] *Tyndale's New Testament*, ed. D. Daniell (Yale, 1993).

[32] S.A. Burrell, 'The covenant idea as a revolutionary symbol: Scotland. 1597-1637', *Church History*, xxvii (1958), 339-43, 48; idem, 'The apocalyptic vision of the early Covenanters', *Scottish Historical Review*, xliii (1964), 1-24.

[33] J. Pocock, 'England', in O. Ranum (ed.), *National Consciousness, History and Popular Culture in Early Modern Europe* (Baltimore, 1975), 98-105.

[34] J.C. Stone, *The Pont Manuscript of Scotland: Sixteenth Century Origins of a Blaeu Atlas* (Tring, 1989), 5-9.

[35] I am grateful to Dr William Ferguson for this point.

[36] S. Oakley, *The Story of Denmark* (London, 1972), 108; Aldis, *List*, nos. 247, 303.5. See also Mason, 'Scotching the Brut', 75-6.

[37] I am grateful to Dr Roger Mason for this point.

[38] D. Allan, *Virtue, Learning and the Scottish Enlightenment: Ideas of Scholarship in Early Modern History* (Edinburgh, 1993).

[39] Ranum, *National Consciousness*, 3-4, 18.

[40] Mason (ed.), *Scots and Britons*, 4.

[41] Cf B. Bradshaw, *The Irish Constitutional Revolution of the Sixteenth Century* (Cambridge, 1979) and N. Canny, 'The formation of the Irish mind: religion, politics and Gaelic Irish literature, 1580-1750' *Past and Present*, xcv (1982), 92-3.

[42] M. Lynch, 'National identity in Ireland and Scotland, 1500-1640', in C. Bjorn, A. Grant and K. Stringer (eds.), *Nations, Nationalism and Patriotism in the European Past* (Copenhagen, 1990), 123-4: Calderwood, *History*, i, 39-42; Spottiswoode, *History*, i, 6, 17-19.

[43] J. Dawson, 'The origins of the "Road to the Isles": trade, communications and Campbell power in early modern Scotland', in R.A. Mason and N. Macdougall (eds.), *People and Power in Scotland: Essays in Honour of T.C. Smout* (Edinburgh, 1992); 'I.D. Whyte, 'The growth of periodic market centres in Scotland, 1600-1700', *Scottish Geographical Magazine*, xcv (1979), 13-26; see K. Cavers, *A Vision of Scotland: The Nation Observed by John Slezer, 1671 to 1717* (Edinburgh, 1993).

[44] Collinson, *Birthpangs*, 6-7, 133-6; L. Colley, *Britons: Forging the Nation, 1707-1837* (New Haven, 1992).

[45] G. Donaldson, *All the Queen's Men: Power and Politics in Mary Stewart's Scotland* (London, 1983), 83-116.

[46] 'The Scottish contributions to the distressed church of France, 1622', *Scottish History Society Miscellany*, iii (SHS, 1919), 179-202; Melville, *Diary*, 260-61; Calderwood, *History*, v, 681.

[47] G. Donaldson, 'Scotland's conservative north in the sixteenth and seventeenth centuries', *Transactions of the Royal Historical Society*, 5th series, xvi (1966), 65-79.

[48] E. Furgol, *A Regimental History of the Covenanting Armies, 1639-1651* (Edinburgh, 1990), 11-12, 32.

[49] A. Everitt, *The Community of Kent and the Great Rebellion* (Leicester, 1966), 1.

[50] A.I. Macinnes, *Clanship, Commerce and the House of Stuart, 1603-1788* (East Linton, 1996), 60.

[51] W.H. Makey, *The Church of the Covenant, 1637-1651: Revolution and Social Change in Scotland* (1979), 131-9, 165-79.

[52] Macinnes, *Clanship*, 60; T. Barnard, 'Crises of identity among Irish Protestants, 1641-1685', *Past and Present*, cxxix (1990), 42, 48. See also D. Stevenson, *Scottish Covenanters and Irish Confederates: Scottish-Irish Relations in the Mid-Seventeenth Century* (Belfast, 1981), esp. 56-7, 60-61, 295, 297-9.

[53] See D. Stevenson, *King or Covenant? Voices from Civil War* (East Linton, 1996), 95-103, for John Spalding.

[54] By 1650, the Life Guard of Horse's banner proclaiming 'Pro Religione, Rege et Patria', displayed an imperial crown of Britain: Furgol, *Covenanting Armies*, 320.

[55] A. Grant, 'Scotland's "Celtic fringe" in the late Middle Ages: the MacDonald Lords of the Isles and the kingdom of Scotland', in R.R. Davies (ed.), *The British Isles, 1100-1500* (Edinburgh, 1988), 118-41.

[56] See E. McGrath, 'Local heroes: the Scottish humanist Parnassus for Charles I', in E. Chaney and P. Mack (eds.), *England and the Continental Renaissance: Essays in Honour of J.B. Trapp* (London, 1990), 257-70.

[57] M. Lynch, 'Queen Mary's triumph', *Scottish Historical Review*, lxix (1990), 1-21; idem, 'A royal progress'.

[58] V.E. Durcacz, *The Decline of the Celtic Languages* (Edinburgh, 1983), 4-5; Edmund Spenser, *A View of the State of Ireland*, ed. W.L. Renwick (Oxford, 1970).

[59] *Diary and Autobiography of Mr James Melville* (Wodrow Society, 1842); 318, 420, 434, 640.

[60] M. Lee, *Great Britain's Solomon: James VI and I in his Three Kingdoms* (Urbana and Chicago, 1990), 67-8, 78, 82-3.

[61] Robert Pont, 'Of the Union of Britayne' (1604), in B. Galloway (ed.), The Jacobean Union (SHS, 1985). David Hume, *De unione Insulae Britanniae* (1605); F. Gilfillan, 'David Hume of Godscroft: His Life and Work' (unpublished Edinburgh University Ph.D., 1994). See also D. Reid (cd.), *David Hume of Godscroft's The History of the House of Douglas*, 2 vols. (STS, 1996).

[62] 'Wills of printers and booksellers', 191ff.

[63] Lynch, 'Royal progress'.

[64] T.J. Dunne, 'The Gaelic response to conquest and colonisation: the evidence of the poetry', *Studia Hibernica*, xx (1980), 12-16; R. Foster, *Modern Ireland, 1600-1972* (London, 1988), 28, 42-3

[65] T.W. Moody, F.X. Martin and F.J. Byrne (eds.), *Early Modern Ireland, 1534-1691* (New History of Ireland, iii, Dublin, 1976), pp. xliii, 67, 530-41, 568-9; N. Canny, 'Formation of the Irish mind', 94-9.

[66] Lynch, 'National identity', 127-34.

[67] A. Ford, *The Protestant Reformation in Ireland, 1590-1641* (Frankfurt-am-Main, 1987), 221-2; Calderwood, History, i, 39-42; Spottiswoode, History, i, 6, 17-19.

[68] Dunne, 'Gaelic response', 16-20; B. Bradshaw, 'Native reaction to the Westward Enterprise: a case study in Gaelic ideology', in K.R. Andrews, N.P. Canny and P.E. H. Hair (eds.), *The Westward Enterprise: English Activities in Ireland, the Atlantic and America, 1480-1650* (Liverpool, 1978), 72-3. A. Bonar (ed.), *Letters of Samuel Rutherford*, (Edinburgh, 1891), 457, 519.

[69] M. Walzer, *The Revolution of the Saints: A Study in the Origins of Radical Politics* (London, 1966).

[70] Ford, *Reformation in Ireland*, 33, 123, 142, 159-68.

[71] This is the claim, based on an obscure nineteenth-century history, made by the Twentieth Century Reformation Society, current owners of the Magdalen Chapel.

[72] Collinson, *Birthpangs*, 6-9.

[73] The 1640s saw serious local disputes in a number of parishes which anticipated the later divisions between Resolutioners and Protesters. In both St Michael's Church in Linlithgow and the Holy Rude in Stirling, for example, walls were built within the church to separate rival ministers and congregations.

CHAPTER SIX

The Scottish Parliament and National Identity from the Union of the Crowns to the Union of the Parliaments, 1603-1707

John R. Young

The concept of national identity is a difficult one to define and currently attracts the attention of a wide range of historians on an European basis.[1] Culture, language, ethnicity, religion and group identity all play central roles. Less fashionable, perhaps, but equally important is that of an institutional national identity. It has long been recognised that one of the major successes of the Treaty of Union has been the maintenance of a distinct Scottish institutional identity through the Scottish legal system, the Scottish education system and the Church of Scotland (as the national church).[2]

As a national institution, however, the Scottish Parliament has remained a relatively neglected and undervalued area of the Scottish historical experience. This can be explained by a variety of reasons. Previous generations of scholars in the early twentieth century focused on a Whig interpretation of history, with history being fundamentally equated with progress, and viewed the Treaty of Union of 1707 as an act of liberation which civilised Scotland and freed her from the shackles of a barbaric past. Equated with this interpretation was the unparalleled success of the British Empire and the key role played by the Scots in it. It also reflected a view that Scottish institutions pre-1707 were fundamentally flawed and inferior to the dominant English constitution and Mother of Parliaments. Such anglocentricism ultimately resulted in a distorted picture of Scottish parliamentary developments. The related problem of political Darwinism also affected the interpretation of Scotland's institutions, whereby `weaker' institutions were subsumed by the more dominant and `politically fit' institutions of larger and more powerful neighbouring states.[3]

However, it is now the case, and rightly so, to `see Scottish institutions and constitutional procedures as worthy of examination in their own right and of assessment in their own terms'[4] and `Scottish institutions evolved their own peculiar identities and ways of working'.[5] Such a conceptual approach is not uniquely Scottish, however, and should be applied across the board to representative assemlies in general. Richard Bonney writing in 1991 in *The European Dynastic States 1494-1660* wisely noted that each European parliamentary institution should be `viewed in terms of its own successes or failure'.[6]

Dr William Ferguson, one of the elder statesmen of the Scottish historical profession, has recently noted that `A new spirit of enquiry...has arisen among students of Scottish constitutional history'.[7] It is in this regard that the new project for re-editing the *Acts of the Parliaments of Scotland* and incorporating new manuscript material, based at the University of St Andrews, is to be welcomed. Hence the neglect of Scotland's constitutional heritage is being currently redressed.[8]

The Union of the Crowns and Scottish national identity
The history of the British Isles in the seventeenth century has been defined as `The Century of the Three Kingdoms'.[9] The Union of the Crowns was to have a profound impact not only on the political and constitutional relationship between the kingdoms of Scotland and England, but also on the relationship between the Scottish Crown and the Scottish political nation. In terms of power politics from 1603 onwards the political focus of a `British' monarch (in the sense that each individual monarch held the crowns of both Scotland and England) was directed towards of the English Crown and the English political nation. The creation of a `dual monarchy'[10] was essentially dynastic and personal (under James VI and I). The Scottish and English Crowns remained independent in constitutional terms, albeit the imperial vision of James was exemplified in his proclamation as King of Great Britain in 1604.[11] Yet the dynastic union of 1603 did not imply a merging of the Scottish and English legal systems, a merging of Scottish and English political institutions, nor a merging of the Scottish and English churches.[12] Despite the establishment of respective commissions in the Scottish and English Parliaments to treat for union[13], the attempts of James VI and I to secure a `perfect' union between the kingdoms including a union of the laws and common citizenship[14] failed for a variety of reasons. There was a perceived threat to English national identity, such as in the status and prestige of English Common Law, and also a fear of a `swarming of the Scots, who, if the union were effected, would reign and rule all'[15]. English domestic difficulties did not enhance the prospects of the success of the union `project', especially the constitutional clash between James as King of England and the opposition within the House of Commons. This was most apparent in the dispute over the Buckinghamshire Election Case of 1604 and the Apology of 1604, which emphasised the Common's control over its own membership.[16] By 1607-8 the attempt to establish a `perfect' union was dead in the water.[17]

In the longer term and from the perspective of Scottish political and economic interests, however, the end result of the Union of the Crowns was `provincial relegation'.[18] By the close of the seventeenth century and the early years of the eighteenth century it had become apparent that the Anglo-Scottish dynastic union had exhausted itself and the relationship between the two kingdoms required some form of *redefinition.*

A theoretical *structural* analysis can pinpoint several key features which developed in the long term which affected Scottish national identity. Firstly, the removal of the Scottish Crown to London weakened the ties between the Scottish Crown and the Scottish political nation in terms of sheer geographical distance. Secondly, the 'Scottish Court' was removed to London and had to compete with English courtiers for the attention of the monarch.[19] Thirdly, the Union of the Crowns facilitated the process of anglicization (which was already underway), although recent research has emphasised that in the post-1603 period the leading Scottish families were not greatly anglicized and a traditional Scottish aristocratic identity was maintained in terms of elite integration within the wider British context.[20]

Such a *structural* analysis is based on the premise that the relationship between the Scottish Crown and the Scottish political nation was fundamental to the concept of Scottish national identity and that the political, social, and economic relationship was weakened in the long term, albeit there was to be no strong creation of a British identity in the immediate post-1603 period. On the one hand, the accession of Scot to the English throne, one of the most powerful and prestigious in Europe, may be interpreted as the enhancing of 'Scottishness' on a wider European basis. According to this analysis, the Scottish royal line, the House of Stewart, was imposed on the English royal line and the Scottish monarchy became incorporated into the first rank of European monarchy. Therefore, the accession of James VI to the English throne can be viewed as a major diplomatic, political and dynastic achievement for the Scottish Crown over its traditional and ancient rival. Indeed the influx of Scots to London in the post-1603 period to be near their native king led to an adverse reaction by the English political nation against the incoming Scots precisely because they perceived that their own English national identity was under threat. The lack of development of a British national identity can be attributed to a strong sense of Englishness and the wish to safeguard the *name* and *institutions* of *England* as opposed to full incorporation within *Britain*. Such logical partisan national sentiment explains the rejection by the English Parliament of the plans of James VI and I for closer union in 1604 and 1607. Such English fears had been highlighted in the appointment of four Scots to the English Privy Council in 1603.[21]

The fact that cracks began to appear in the dynastic union following the death of James VI and I in 1625 can be explained quite simply by the fact that all holders of the Scottish Crown, 1625-1689, were Scots in all but name only and from 1689 to 1707 were foreigners with little concern for, or interest in, Scottish affairs. In turn, it can therefore be argued that the Union of the Crowns functioned with greatest success under James VI and I, a Scot himself. His political pedigree was essentially Scottish: He had a detailed knowledge and appreciation of the Scottish political community. This political ability to deal with his own native land stood James in good stead when his political power base was transferred to London. In the 36 years from 1567 to 1603 16 Parliaments and 68 Conventions of Estates were held under James VI, whereas in the 22 years from 1603 to the accession of Charles I in 1625 only seven Parliaments and eight Conventions of Estates were held.[22] Recent research has noted the frequency of parliamentary sessions during the civil war era of 1570-73 and has also indicated that only six Parliaments were held in the period 1586-1603.[23] Nevertheless, the basic political fact remains that in the post-1603 period James VI and I was essentially an English monarch (in political terms) and the possibilities for personal contact between the king and the Scottish political community had been reduced.

The breakdown of the Union of the Crowns under Charles I and the rise of Scottish nationalism
Under Charles I 'the debilitating effects of regal union slowly began to become apparent'.[24] The anglocentric policies pursued by this absentee monarch gave rise to the Scottish Covenanting Movement which initiated the British Civil Wars. Traditionally historians have attributed the outbreak of the Covenanting Revolution in Scotland in 1637-38 to religious origins and have assumed that religious motives constituted the driving force behind the Scottish Covenanting Movement. Recent historiography and research has convincingly argued that relgious tension was only one of a variety of factors in the explosion of protest against the rule of Charles I in Scotland.[25] The Covenanting Movement can be defined as a nationalist movement which sought to reassert and defend Scottish political and religious identity in the face of what it saw as an unprecedented assault on Scottish institutions by an anglicised and absentee monarch.[26]

Scottish political institutions were to be reformed according to the nationalist agenda articulated by the Covenanters. Much of the demand for political and constitutional reform came from the Scottish localities in the form of petitions from the shires and burghs. The National Covenant had demanded 'free' Parliaments and General Assemblies: 'free' in the sense that the voice of the political nation could be heard and not be stifled via royal influence and management. The 1621 Parliament[27] (convened under the authority of James VI) and the Coronation Parliament of 1633 (convened under the authority of Charles I) had witnessed the use of the Lords of the Articles as a parliamentary instrument of royal control. Parliament was to be controlled according to Crown interests and the Articles acted as a clearing house for parliamentary legislation. Thus legislation was to be enacted which was amenable to Crown interests. In the words of the contemporary Royalist commentator Sir James Balfour, the 1633 Parliament:

> was led one by the Episcopall and courte faction, wich therafter proued to be that stone that afterwardes crusht them in pieces, and the fewell of that flame wich sett all Brittane a fyre not longe therafter.[28]

The employment of clerics within Scottish political institutions was to cease. The clerical estate within Parliament (Archbishops and Bishops) was to be abolished and therefore clerics would be removed from the Lords of the

Articles. The employment of clerics on the Privy Council was also to cease and the use of proxy voting (used extensively in the 1633 Parliament) and English peers in Parliament was to be banned. The nomination of Scottish Officers of State (such as Treasurer and Clerk Register) was to be transferred from the Crown to the Scottish Parliament.

The Covenanting agenda formulated in 1639 received formal constitutional sanction in the Scottish Constitutional Settlement of 1640-41. The royal prerogative in Scotland was curtailed and effective political power in the kingdom of Scotland was transferred to the Scottish Parliament, which now controlled the executive and judiciary. A Triennial Act ensured that Scottish Parliaments were to be convened on a regular basis every three years. Furthermore, the Scottish Constitutional Settlement also had important British ramifications as it provided a constitutional model which the English Long Parliament could draw on for its challenge to Charles I's royal authority in England.

The 1640s witnessed the unprecedented development of the Scottish Parliament as a political institution in its own right. A complicated but efficient committee structure evolved in the form of session and interval committees and was accompanied by detailed procedural innovation. The supremacy of the Estates was emphasised, whilst the royal prerogative in Scotland was limited.[29]

The Scottish Parliament, Scottish national identity and the British Civil Wars

Following the 1641 Parliament a de facto revolution had taken place in the operation of Scottish political institutions. Parliament had become the ultimate political force and authority at the expense of both the monarchy and the Privy Council. Indeed the Scottish Privy Council, the traditional instrument of royal administration was effectively marginalised in the period 1641-44. As an institution, the Scottish Privy Council disappeared into virtual oblivion until it was revived by the Royalists in the Restoration Settlement of 1660-1661.[30] In the immediate aftermath of the 1641 Parliament effective political power was exercised by three parliamentary interval committees which had been appointed by the 1641 Parliament and had been given parliamentary authority to sit until the next Parliament in 1644 (which was to be convened according to the Triennial Act of 1640). These three committees were the Committee for Common Burdens, the Committee for the Brotherly Assistance and the Committee for the Conservators of the Peace. The first two committees possesed financial remits and actually sat as a single committee, although they were constitutionally distinct. The Committee for the Conservators of the Peace was a diplomatic committee which was designed to liaise with the English Parliament concerning the Treaty of London of 1641. It was these three parliamentary committees, staffed and controlled by the radical wing of the Covenanting Movement, which brought

Scottish military, financial, diplomatic, political and religious involvement into the English Civil War on the side of the English Parliament in the conflict against Charles I.

Such a political alignment on the side of the English Parliament, symbolised in the Solemn League and Covenant and the Treaty of Military Assistance of 26 August 1643, has led several historians to argue that the Scottish Covenanters sought a redefinition in the relationship between Scotland and England in favour of federalism.[31] Nevertheless, the Solemn League and Covenant did *not* provide for, nor intend, a closer *parliamentary union* between the two kingdoms. Article Three of the Solemn League and Covenant pledged to `preserve the rights and priviledges of the parliamentes and the liberties of the kingdomes'.[32] Certainly a closer formal contact with the English Parliament was sought, and was attained, in the establishment of the Committee of Both Kingdoms for the direction and conduct of military policy in the English Civil War. Nevertheless, the Committee of Both Kingdoms was essentially a committee of the English Parliament and its Scottish members were outnumbered by English personnel.[33]

The Solemn League and Covenant stipulated that there was to be no reduction in the constitutional authority and legitimacy of the Scottish Parliament. Rather, the main intention of the Solemn League and Covenant was the imposition of Presbyterianism on a British basis in exchange for Covenanting military involvement in the English Civil War. Robert Baillie, minister of Kilwinning in the Covenanting heartlands and representative at the Westminster Assembly of Divines, noted that `the English pressed chiefly a Civil League and the Scots a Religious one'.[34] There was to be no fundamental development of a `British' religious identity, but Scottish presbyterianism was to be imposed on England and Ireland. The Scottish Covenanters were well aware of the fact that the success of the `Scottish Revolution' was dependent on the success of the English Parliament in its struggle against Charles I and his defeat on a British basis. Therefore, the Solemn League and Covenant was ultimately concerned with the transportation and imposition of the Scottish Revolution on a British basis as the appropriate means to defend that revolution in religious, military and constitutional terms.[35]

Covenanting military commitment in the English Civil War, driven by the dominant radical element in the Covenanting Movement, resulted in civil war within Scotland in 1644-45. The marginalisation of the Scottish Privy Council and the securing of the Solemn League and Covenant and Treaty of Military Assistance marked a personal defeat for James, third Marquis and first Duke of Hamilton who had operated as the main political mediator between Charles I and the Covenanters on a British basis. However, Hamilton had fallen out of favour during 1643 after he had failed to secure a Royalist revival in Scotland and had been humiliated politically by the calling of the

1643 Convention of Estates and the signing of the Solemn League and Covenant.

Hamilton's reward from Charles I for political failure in the 1643 Convention was imprisonment in Pendennis Castle in Cornwall until 1646. The mantle of a Royalist revival was taken up instead by that heroic failure and romantic historical icon, James Graham, fifth Earl and first Marquis of Montrose. Covenanting hegemony in Scotland was challenged militarily and Montrose scored an impressive six victories over Covenanting forces between September 1644 and August 1645 before being finally defeated at the Battle of Kilsyth on 15 August 1645. The defeat of Montrose at Kilsyth secured the power base of the radical wing of the Covenanting Movement, which then proceeded to pursue a policy of widespread punishment and purging of those who had collaborated with Montrose. For the Royalist section of the Scottish political nation Scottish national identity was inexorably linked to the fate and authority of the king.

In terms of the military conduct of the English Civil War, by November 1646 it had become clear that the military alliance between the Scottish and English Parliaments had become increasingly strained and the position of the king, Charles I, had become the focal point of diplomatic tension. Under the jurisdiction and protection of the Scottish army in England, Charles I had consistently refused to meet Scottish negotiating demands and he refused to subscribe the National Covenant and the Solemn League and Covenant. The weakening of the Scottish Covenanting position on a British basis and the dimunition of its ability to dictate and formulate a British agenda was reflected in the claims of the English Houses of Parliament that they had *sole* jurisdiction over what should be done with the king, *despite* the fact that he was also *King of Scotland* and despite the objections of the Scottish diplomatic commissioners (as representatives of the Scottish Parliament).[36] Whereas in 1643 the Scottish Covenanters had sought to dictate a British religious agenda (the imposition of Presbyterianism) and were tolerated to do so because their military strength was required by the English Parliament to defeat the Royalist military forces in England, by 1646 the English Houses of Parliament had relegated the Scottish Covenanters to a subordinate role in terms of their struggle with Charles I as *King of England*. In return for the payment of £400,000 sterling (£4.8 million Scots) due as arrears to the Scottish military forces, the Scots were to hand over their native king to the official jurisdiction of the English Parliament and were then to return to the Kingdom of Scotland.[37] Such an agreement received formal ratification in the Sixth Session of the First Triennial Parliament (3 November 1646-27 March 1647) on 16 January 1647, yet this was 'utterly contrary to his Majesty's expectations'.[38] Charles I would now be formally handed over to the English Parliament which would deal with him at its own discretion.

The exchange of Charles I in return for financial reward, amidst claims that the Scottish Covenanters had 'sold' their native king, raises two crucial issues concerning the Anglo-Scottish dynastic union. Firstly, the English Houses of Parliament perceived Charles I to be first and foremost an English king. In their claim for sole jurisdiction over Charles they simply disregarded the fact that he was also King of Scots. Therefore there was clearly no relationship of 'equal partners' in the status of the two crowns of Scotland and England. Secondly, despite the fact that that such an attitude on the part of the English Houses of Parliament aroused Scottish hostility, the 'disposal' or 'sale' of the king did receive legal and constitutional sanction from the Scottish Parliament. In technical terms, therefore, the Scottish Parliament handed over the King of Scotland to his political fate at the hands of the English Parliament. That such legislation secured a safe passage through the Scottish Parliament may be attributed to the skills of parliamentary management of the predominant radical faction. Nevertheless, it still indicates that there was a significant number of Scottish parliamentarians who were prepared to sacrifice the king.

The political fallout and backlash from the 'sale' of the king provided for an alteration of the political balance of power within the Covenanting Movement. 1646-47 witnessed the rise and eventual ascendancy of Covenanting conservatism in the Scottish Parliament, primarily under the auspices of James, third Marquis and first Duke of Hamilton, who had been released from imprisonment in 1646. The conservative element of the Covenanting Movement combined with 'pragmatic Royalists' (Royalists who were prepared to subscribe to Covenanting oaths and obligations, such as the National Covenant, in order to hold public office) to secure the Engagement Treaty with the king in December 1647. Alterations had also taken place in the balance of power concerning English political factionalism and had resulted in the ascendancy of the New Model Army and the Independents. Therefore, within the wider British dimension, the Engagement Treaty was essentially a compromise political settlement with the ultimate goal of safeguarding the king.The Engagement Treaty itself contains a strong federalist tone, yet it was a document based on political realism and was designed to attract as much support as possible in a volatile and everchanging situation. Presbyterianism was to be established in England for a trial period of three years and free trade was to be established between the two kingdoms. Scots were to be accorded an increased role and stature within the 'British' polity. In this instance, the concept of 'closer union' meant the employment in equal numbers of Scotsmen as Englishmen in foreign negotiations, the employment of Scotsmen on the English Privy Council (Englishmen were also to be admitted to the Scottish Privy Council), and the employment of Scotsmen in places of trust within the royal household. In addition, the king or the Prince of Wales was to reside in Scotland at regular intervals. Hence the Anglo-Scottish dynastic union was to be redefined. Scottish monarchy was to be revitalised but this could only be achieved via the *structure* of the Union of the Crowns and a wider `British' redefinition and settlement in light of what had taken place in both Scotland and England in the 1640s.

The executive demands of the Engagement Treaty are similar to Covenanting demands articulated in 1640 and Scottish Royalist proposals which were formulated for the redefintion of the Anglo-Scottish dynastic union with the restoration of the monarchy in 1660. The lesson, which was to become all too apparent in 1651, is clear: Scottish monarchy could not stand alone but could only be safeguarded within a British monarchical context.

The Scottish Engagement Parliament of 1648 represented the formal political and constitutional ascendancy of the conservative-pragmatic Royalist alliance, albeit a vocal radical rump was still represented in the House. A military invasion of England resulted in the summer of 1648 with the mission of securing Charles I. Paradoxically, a new British agenda was being formulated and articulated from Scotland once again which resulted in a military invasion of England, albeit there was a sustained resistance to the Engager invasion by the small radical rump in Parliament and also the ministers of the General Assembly.[39] In 1643 a Scottish military invasion of England had been led by the radical section of the Covenanting Movement to fight the cause of the English Parliamentarians against Charles I. Now, in 1648 the conservative and Royalist section of that movement invaded England to fight the cause of Charles I against the New Model Army and the Independents and secure his English Crown as well as his Scottish one. The political and military equilibrium of England was once again to be challenged from the troublesome Scots. Yet, a subtle distinction in the political motives in the respective invasions of 1643 and 1648 was noted by one contemporary Scot, `Alexander Hamilton of Kinkell':

the brave army that now entered England as Principals and not as Auxiliaries and Assistants in the war as the Scots army did in the 1643, being only Accessories to the Parliament of England not Principals in the war.[40]

Political and constitutional upheaval was continued and intensified in the aftermath of the defeat of the Engager forces by Oliver Cromwell at the Battle of Preston on 3 September 1648. Radical Covenanters quickly seized their opportunity and took their revenge in the infamous Whiggamore Raid in September 1648. Emanating primarily from south-west Scotland, the heartland of Covenanting radicalism, an anti-Engager regime of diehard Covenanters was established in Edinburgh, backed militarily by Oliver Cromwell, and the institutions of Scottish government were purged of the `ungodly'. The Scottish Parliament was used as the appropriate tool and institutional device to establish a Covenanted state which pursued a political, religious, social and moral revolution. Aristocratic power in Scotland was challenged and reduced and men from lower down the social scale secured a new political voice and parliamentary representation, albeit the radical caucus which had been active throughout the 1640s continued to dominate the Covenanting agenda.[41]

The execution of Charles I by the Cromwellian regime in London in January 1649 had profound ramifications which reveberated around the British polity. In conjunction with the Cromwellian abolition of the office of monarchy in England itself, the Anglo-Scottish dynastic union (the Union of the Crowns) which had been in existence since 1603 was destroyed. This left a newly-established Covenanted state in Scotland, supported by Cromwell himself, yet at the same time the King of Scotland had been executed without the support or even the consultation of the Scottish political nation. During the trial of the king in London, Scottish diplomatic commissioners in London (whose commission had been issued by the Scottish Parliament) were given formal instructions on how they were to react when a judgement against the king was reached by the English judicial court:

> If they proceede and pronounce sentenynce against the king, that yow enter your dissent and protest that this kingdome may be free of all deviations, miseries and Blood-shed that probablye will follow thereupon, without offering in your reasons that princes are exemplified from tyrall and injustice.[42]

Charles I had been required to be a Covenanted monarch of three Covenanted kingdoms and his royal prerogative within the Kingdom of Scotland had been reduced, but regicide was simply out of the question for the Scots. Rather, Charles was to see the error of his ways and be 'reformed' and educated in line with Covenanting ideology.[43] Within a wider British perspective, a more fundamental paradox can be detected. The British problem and the difficulties of ruling 'multiple kingdoms' under a single monarch had now moved on to a new plateau, but on this occasion the political, ideological, and intellectual initiative had been taken by a minority group in the southern kingdom, England.[44] Monarchical problems were to be resolved in an English context by the execution of Charles I as King of England and the abolition of the English monarchy.

The reaction of the radical Covenanted state to the execution of Charles I was immediate. On 5 February 1649 the Scottish Parliament proclaimed Charles, Prince of Wales as King of *Great Britain*, France and Ireland. Yet admission to the office of monarchy on a *British* basis was not unconditional and the conditions required to be met were stated in the Act anent the Securing of Religion and Peace of the Kingdom of 7 February 1649. In common with his father, Charles II would be required to subscribe the National Covenant and the Solemn League and Covenant and Presbyterianism was to be established in all three kingdoms (Scotland, England and Ireland). Therefore the radical Covenanted state resurrected and *reimposed* the Anglo-

Scottish dynastic union on a British basis. Radical Covenanters clearly did not envisage a Covenanted state outwith a wider British polity. Various options were available following the execution of Charles I and the abolition of monarchy in England. First, the Covenanters could have accepted the termination of the Union of the Crowns, however distasteful that may have been through regicide, and established an *independent Covenanted state outwith the Scottish monarchy*. This truly would have been the most `radical' policy option, but in reality the *office* of monarchy in Scotland had not been abolished although the *person* of the current King of Scots had been executed; the two were separate and distinct. In turn, this provided for a second and more realistic option: an independent Covenanted kingdom with a *Covenanted King of Scots*, but with no resurrection of the Union of the Crowns (ie England and Scotland would go their own ways and Scotland would be a Covenanted kingdom). Yet the option which was eventually adopted transcended a Scottish settlement and continued to embrace a wider Covenanting imperial vision of `Britain'. Hence, the future Charles II was not merely King of Scotland. He was primarily King of Great Britain. This imperial vision of a Covenanted king ruling three Covenanting kingdoms via the *reimposed structure* of the Union of the Crowns was a de facto act of outright hostility to Cromwell and the English Independents. Once again, a new British vision was envisaged and was to be imposed by the Scottish Covenanters. Scottish Covenanting radicalism and a new `Britain' clearly went hand in hand. A new Anglo-Scottish war between two `godly nations' ensued and the Cromwellian conquest of Scotland in 1650-51 can be fundamentally traced to the events of 5 and 7 February 1649 and the proclamation of Charles II as King of Great Britain, France and Ireland. Paradoxically, the Scottish diplomatic commissioners in London at the time of the king's trial had been ordered to undertake `nothing that may import any breache or give any ground or seed of a new warre'.[45] Alexander Hamilton of Kinkell was acutely aware of the implications of the proclamation of Charles II as King of Great Britain following the execution of his father:

> the Scots interposed and opposed these tragick Actions and what a dangerous war they drew upon themselves thereby, which end not, but with the subjugation of this Kingdom unto the English, under which it continued ten years time.[46]

The much sought after purity of a Covenanted state consisting of the godly had resulted in a process of political purging from public office and purging of the Scottish armed forces.[47] On the second anniversary of the rout of the Engagers at Preston, the military debacle of the Battle of Dunbar on 3 September 1650 marked the beginning of the end of the radical regime. Dunbar had opened up the way for a military conquest of Scotland and the defence of the kingdom was now the main priority. National unity was to take priority over political factionalism. Royalists and former Engagers could no longer be excluded from the political process and the army for the defence of the kingdom. Cromwellian hostility towards the radical regime had also intensified because of its relationship with Charles II. A rapprochement had been effected between the new king and the radical Covenanters, primarily because each of Charles's options to secure the restoration of his English Crown had been destroyed one by one and he was forced to fall back on the radical Covenanting regime in Scotland. The option of taking Scotland through a second military campaign led by Montrose was lost after the failure of the Montrose Rising in the north of Scotland in 1650, whilst Ireland had been conquered and subjugated by Cromwellian forces. The only road through which Charles II could secure the English throne was through Scotland. In turn, this intensified the need for the military defeat of the Scots for the strategic safety of the Independent regime in England.[48] The British problem had now turned full circle.

A Scottish patriotic accommodation was slowly secured throughout the winter of 1650 and the spring of 1651 which involved a national political rapprochement between Charles II and the various political factions in Scotland. Parliament was the focal point for this rapprochement. Thus, a continuum can be detected for the 1640s as a whole. From 1639-46/7 the radical wing of the Covenanting Movement had enjoyed parliamentary supremacy, whilst the Engagers had triumphed in 1647-48. By 1651 factionalism was increasingly subordinated to the needs of national unity. Parliament and its committees provided the forum for the resurgence of nationalism.

Following military defeat at Dunbar the Committee of Estates (which operated as a provisional government between parliamentary sessions) called for factional military rapprochement to `solicit unity for the good of the kingdome'.[49] The Northern Band and Oath of Engagement was issued by north-eastern Royalists involved in the Atholl Rebellion of October 1650. Although formulated and initiated by Royalists, the Band and Oath was essentially a `nationalist' document directed against an English military occupation which would `reduce the whole [Scotland] to a Province, except the Lord in his mercy prevent it, by joining his Ma^tys subjects in a band of unity, wch is the only meane (in our Judgement) to preserve Religion, King & Kingdome'.[50] The conciliatory nature and tone of the Band and Oath was stressed by the emphasis on joining ranks and avoiding division in church, state and the armed forces. Ultimately, it was designed to appeal to as broad a section of Scottish political groupings as possible. Presbyterianism, the National Covenant and the Solemn League and Covenant were to be defended, as well as the king's person, authority and the royal prerogative. The privileges of the Scottish Parliament were also to be defended. General Middleton, one of the main protagonists in the Northern Rebellion, commented 'we are Scotishmen, we desyre to fight for our countrie; religion, king and kingdome are in hazard'.[51]

The lamentable condition of the kingdom was described by John Nicholl, a contemporary commentator, in October 1650:

> The Kingdome being thus in a moist pitifull and deplorabill conditioun, and sad estait, nane to ryse aganes the enymie, nor to defend the kingdome, severall meetingis wer appoynted by the Estais to meet and to consult on the effaires of the land; sum tymes at Sterling, uther tymes at Peerth, quhair dyveris dyettis of Parliament, Committee, and the Commissioners for the Kirk met and wer holdin, and for the crowning of the King; bot all wes to small purpos, the divisiones both of Stait and Kirk incressing to the great advantage of the enymie, quha esteemed these inward divisiounes of this land to be worth to him and moir profitable than twenty thowsand men, as it evidentlie appered.[52]

National unity was hindered by the issue of the Western Remonstrance in October 1650. The Western Remonstrance constituted a hard-line ideological stance of extreme radicals from the Covenanting heartlands. Although the Remonstrants resolved to expel English armed forces from Scotland, they also stressed that the king's cause was an ungodly one and that the Scots should refrain from meddling in the affairs of the English Commonwealth. The Remonstrants were marginalised politically and carried no great support within the Scottish political nation at large. The Committee of Estates, followed by Parliament, condemned and legislated against the Western Remonstrance and the Commission of the Kirk (the standing committee of the General Assembly) noted that the Remonstrance was 'apt to breid divisions in this Kirk and Kingdome'.[53] Facilitated by the Resolutioner majority in the General Assembly, the rehabilitation of former Engagers and Royalists was initiated by the issue of the Public Resolutions on 14 December 1650. Political and factional rapprochement on a national basis continued throughout the parliamentary sessions of 1651. This rapprochement climaxed in the establishment of the Committee for Managing the Affairs of the Army (which allowed for the admission of former Engagers and Royalists into the Scottish armed forces) and the repeal of the Acts of Classes of 1646 and 1649 (which had banned former Engagers and Royalists from public office). This rapprochement increasingly focused on the monarchy. Charles II had regularly attended Parliament since November 1650 and he was crowned King of Great Britain at Scone in Perthshire on 1 January 1651. Nevertheless, the British Civil Wars were effectively ended by the military defeat at the Battle of Worcester on 3 September 1651 and the end result was not only a Cromwellian military occupation of Scotland, but also the loss of national independence and constitutional subjugation by the English Commonwealth until 1660. Under the Cromwellian occupation there was no Scottish

Parliament. Thus there was no formal political or institutional forum for the Scottish political nation to convene. Scotland was incorporated within the English Commonwealth and Protectorate and was accorded limited representation in the Cromwellian Parliaments of 1654, 1656 and 1659. That representation was based on English influence and only a small group of Scots, ideologically and politically aligned to Cromwell, secured election.[54]

The Restoration Settlement, the reassertion of the royal prerogative and the management of Scottish politics from London
The Restoration Settlement in Scotland witnessed a full reassertion of the royal prerogative in tandem with the abolition of Scottish incorporation in the Cromwellian union and the subsequent renewal of the Anglo-Scottish dynastic union.[55] Large numbers of the Scottish nobility and gentry had hurried to London to secure royal favour after the restoration of Charles II in his English kingdom. In response to a petition from the 'Nobility and gentry of Scotland then at London, July 1660'[56] and in light of the recent Cromwellian occupation, the last Committee of Estates established in 1651 was recalled and was to operate as a provisional government until the Scottish Parliament itself could formally meet.[57] The pre-Cromwellian Scottish political institutions were to be restored (including the Scottish Privy Council). In terms of the *mentalité* of the Scottish political nation in 1660, however, its national identity was focused firmly on the monarchy and the reassertion of the royal prerogative. 'Monarchical Government [was] restored to the great comfort, and joy of the Kingdom of Scotland'.[58] Parliament was to provide the appropriate constitutional forum for that reassertion and this was stated publicly in the aforementioned petition:

> according to the desirs of the Petitioners his M. will speidily call a Parliament in Scotland whereby his antient royal prerogative may be asserted and the just liberties of that kingdom settled which they have for so many ages enjoyed under his Royal Ancestors.[59]

The parliamentary session of 1 January to 12 July 1661 witnessed the rescinding of the legislation of the Covenanting era in tandem with the restoration of the royal prerogative. The Scottish Constitutional Settlement of 1640-41 was rescinded. The king was accorded sole power in the calling of the Conventions of Estates and Parliaments. Likewise, he was accorded sole authority in the naming of Privy Councillors, Officers of State and Lords of Session. The Lords of the Articles were reintroduced as an instrument of crown control within Parliament for the process of parliamentary business, albeit at this stage clerics were still excluded. Archibald Campbell, eighth Earl and first Marquis of Argyll, the epitome and personification of Covenanting radicalism, was executed as an example of what usurpers of royal authority could expect. The Oath of Allegiance demanded personal loyalty to the king and required acknowledgement that the king was the supreme governor of the kingdom. Sir Archibald Primrose, Clerk Register, in correspondence with John Maitland, second Earl and first Duke of Lauderdale, Secretary, on 19 January 1661 (eighteen days into the parliamentary session) commented that 'Never was ther a Parliament so frantic for the King'.[60] By the close of the 1661 parliamentary session it had become clear that real political power in Scotland had been transferred back to the Crown. It had also become apparent that in future the operation and direction of Scottish political affairs would be increasingly controlled from London. This feature was emphasised by the establishment of a standing council on Scottish affairs, with a permanent English majority, and headed by Edward Hyde, first Earl of Clarendon, at that stage the most influential English minister. Hence the Union of the Crowns was restored but the dynastic union was *redefined* once more and *redirected* more firmly towards Whitehall. During the 1661 session of Parliament, Franceso Giavarina, the Venetian Ambassador in England, reported back to his superiors that the Scottish Parliament had continued to 'act in accordance with the wishes of the Court'.[61]

Following the 1661 parliamentary session, two further sessions of the Restoration Parliament were held: 8 May-9 September 1662 and 18 June- 9 October 1663.[62] The two most notable achievements in terms of the advancement of Crown control were the reintroduction of Episcopacy as the appropriate form of government of the Church of Scotland and the remodelling of the Lords of the Articles along the lines followed in 1633 and the reintroduction of the clerics.[63] During the 1661 session the Act Recissory had abolished all ecclesiastical innovation in the Kirk since 1633, that is both the Laudian reforms and the Presbyterian reforms. Furthermore, the Act anent Religion of 1661 had stipulated that the settlement of the Church of Scotland should be determined by the Crown. The fact that Episcopacy had been restored in England acted as an added incentive for its reintroduction in Scotland, both in terms of 'British' relgious uniformity and also in terms of royal control of the Kirk. The ascendancy of Episcopacy was secured in 1662 and received formal parliamentary ratification. The clerical estate was reintroduced into Parliament in 1663 and the mode of election of the Lords of the Articles reverted to that of 1633 (which secured an in-built majority amenable to the Crown). By the close of the 1663 parliamentary session the Restoration Settlement in favour of the Crown was virtually complete.

Two Conventions of Estates were held in 1665 and 1667 with the primary objective of securing financial provision for Charles II's Dutch Wars.[64] The Parliament of 1669-74 consisted of four parliamentary sessions, whilst there was a Convention of Estates in 1678 (again for taxation purposes), a further Parliament in 1681 (consisting of one parliamentary session) and a Parliament held under the authority of James VII and II in 1685-86 (again consisting of one session). Increased factionalism was a noted feature of the operation of Restoration politics, notably under the administration of John Maitland, first Duke of Lauderdale, circa 1667-1679. Lauderdale gained the ascendancy in Scottish affairs after the fall from grace of Clarendon in England and John, first Earl of Middleton, and John Leslie, seventh Earl of Rothes, in 1667. Parliamentary opposition to Lauderdale emerged in 1669, 1670, 1672, 1673 and 1678, most notably around 'the party' of William, third Duke of Hamilton and his allies.[65]

As evidenced by the conduct of the Restoration Parliaments and the Convention of Estates of 1665 and 1667, Parliament was to be governed and controlled according to the royal interest. This process has been described as 'ministerial government'.[66] That Lauderdale exercised political power in Scotland for so long can be attributed to the fact that he was prepared to loyally serve the royal interest within Scotland and employ any means to secure that end.[67] It has been observed that Charles II attempted to operate as an absolutist monarch, in awe of Louis XIV of France, and that he wished to circumvent Parliament. In that sense, Lauderdale has been described as 'subservient, a yes-man pure and simple'.[68] The Restoration period witnessed an increased move towards Stuart absolutism in which the royal prerogative became 'absolute and uncontrollable'.[69]

Several key issues emerge in terms of Scottish national identity and the operation of the Scottish Parliament in the post-Restoration period. Firstly, in comparison to the parliamentary developments of the 1640s, factionalism was conducted within the confines of personal rivalry (Lauderdale, Rothes, Middleton, Hamilton and Tweeddale) for political favour with the king, precisely because the *monarch* had re-emerged as the focal point of political power and patronage. As the Earl of Kincardine observed to the Earl of Tweeddale prior to the meeting of the 1669 Parliament:

> Mens conjecturs of the occasione of the ensuing Parliament are according as their fears or hopes prompt them; generally people hope very well from it, but the rich men feare their purses, evrybody lands a new occasione of his oune.[70]

The second observable trend is that Parliaments were held with the clear objective of the enhancement and retrenchment of royal authority. Thirdly, the contentious issue of union reared itself again in the period 1667-70. Initiated by Charles II, the initial union proposals were concerned with an economic union, whic aroused Scottish support due to the protectionist nature of the English Navigation Act. When negotiations commenced between the commissioners from both kingdoms, Charles moved the agenda on to an incorporating union, as informed to the Scottish Privy Council in June 1669. Nevertheless, the political climate in both Scotland and England was not ripe for an incorporating agenda. From a Scottish perspective, the memory of the

Cromwellian occupation and union in the Commonwealth and Protectorate was relatively recent, whilst the English political nation did not want an increased financial burden imposed on them by the impoverished Scots. The proposed incorporating union of 1669-70 envisaged a united Parliament, free trade, but separate legal systems. In terms of Scottish representation within such a Parliament, Scotland was to be awarded 30 seats in the Commons and 10 peers and two bishops in the Lords. The fact that negotiations broke down can be attributed to Charles II himself, diplomatic intrigue and the signing of the Secret Treaty of Dover with Louis XIV of France in May 1670.[71]

The political fallout of the demise of Lauderdale in 1679[72] resulted in an increased role in Scotland for James, Duke of York, brother of Charles II and heir to the thrones of England and Scotland.[73] The fact that James was a devout Roman Catholic threatened the security of the Protestant Succession. James, Duke of York, acted as King's Commissioner to the Scottish Parliament of 1681. Indeed the 1681 Parliament marked a personal triumph for James, given the experience of the Exclusion Parliaments in England. Not only was legislation enacted which secured his hereditary rights in spite of his Catholic faith, but the Test Act stipulated that all members of Parliament, the electoral nation and all office-bearers in church and state were to acknowledge the royal supremacy and swear not to make any alterations to civil or ecclesiastical government.[74] Moreover, according to the Act of Supremacy James would still enjoy ultimate ecclesiastical authority, despite his Roman Catholicism.[75]

The experience of the 1681 Parliament in Scotland would suggest that Scottish national identity was not *necessarily* linked to Protestantism, in the form of the religious beliefs of the monarch *per se*.[76] Here was a future Roman Catholic monarch who had secured his succession, his royal authority, and his royal supremacy in church and state. An alternative explanation is that the 1681 Parliament was essentially 'tame'.[77] That the Protestant Succession was indeed linked to Scottish national identity was apparent in the Parliament of 1685-86, whereby James advocated a policy of free trade with England in return for religious toleration for Roman Catholics. Having come to the throne as James VII in 1685, this may well have been the case of James showing his true colours, in the form of the ascendancy of Roman Catholicism, having first secured the crown. Such fears were intensified in the conversion to Catholicism of the Earl of Perth, Lord Chancellor, and the two Secretaries of State, Lord Melfort (Perth's brother) and the Earl of Moray, as well as the appointment of the Catholic Duke of Gordon as Governor of Edinburgh Castle.[78] In the words of Sir John Reresby, a contemporary English diarist, 'This declared favour to persons of that religion gave great disgust in that kingdome'.[79] Sympathy for James was also ultimately weakened by Melfort's comments on the Scottish Presbyterians: 'when we get the power, we will make these men hewers of wood and drawers of water'.[80]

Opposition to the policy of religious toleration for Roman Catholics emerged in the Lords of the Articles and within the House generally. James VII had clearly misjudged the mood of the Scottish Parliament.[81] Parliament wrote to James personally 'not doubting that your majesty will be careful to secure the protestant religion established by law'.[82] The result of such parliamentary opposition was the adjournment and dissolution of the 1686 Parliament. The threatened Protestant identity of the Scottish political nation had led to conflict with a Catholic monarch, despite his political and constitutional triumph in the 1681 Parliament.[83]

The Revolution Settlement of 1689-90 and the reassertion of Scottish parliamentary power

In 'British' terms there were two separate and distinct revolutions in Scotland and England.[84] The end result, however, was similar and two constitutional settlements were enacted which checked and limited the power of the crown. In a Scottish context, this resulted in the reassertion of the political and constitutional power of the Scottish Parliament which was to ultimately lead to an incorporating union with England in 1707.[85]

The 1689 Convention of Estates (composed of a majority in favour of William) resolved on 4 April that the Scottish Crown had been *forfeited* by James VII. Hence theoretical distinctions were employed in Scotland and England for the justification of the deposition of James VII and II. James II as King of England had *abdicated* the English Crown. James VII as King of Scotland had *forfeited* the Scottish Crown. In this respect, therefore, the Scottish political justification was far more radical than its English counterpart.[86] Indeed, the notion of a contractual monarchy/limited monarchy in Scotland received further sanction in the Scottish Claim of Right enacted on 11 April 1689. Therefore, divine right monarchy was rejected in favour of a limited monarchy.[87] The Scottish Claim of Right stressed that there was to be free and regular Parliaments (including freedom of speech), parliamentary consent was to be required for the raising of supply, no Catholic could succeed to the throne or be employed in public office, whlist statute law gained supremacy over the royal prerogative.[88] The Articles of Grievances, enacted on 13 April 1689, focused on the condemnation of the Lords of the Articles and the declaration of Episcopacy as a grievance. Having proclaimed William and Mary as King and Queen of Scotland on 11 April, a parliamentary delegation was despatched to London with the *offer* of the Scottish Crown. This was accepted on 11 May according to the terms of the Claim of Right and the Articles of Grievances. The 1690 Parliament secured the formal constitutional abolition of the Lords of the Articles, which had been pressed for by the constitutional reform group known as 'the Club'. In addition, the 1669 Act of Supremacy was repealed and the Presbyterian form of the government of the Church of Scotland was restored.[89]

Against the background of the Restoration Settlement, with its emphasis on the royal prerogative, and increased parliamentary management from Whitehall in favour of the Crown, the Revolution Settlement of 1689-90 in Scotland can be viewed as a renewal of the Scottish Parliament as the most important political institution in Scotland at the expense of the Crown. Moreover, the Revolution Settlement of 1689-90 harked back to the Scottish Constitutional Settlement of 1640-41 and the Scottish Covenanters.[90] Scottish national identity in its institutional format was to be reasserted. One contemporary rumour, emanating from `a great lord of Scotland' and circulating in influential circles south of the border, stated that Scotland would `be noe longer a province to England, or dance attendance at the door of an English court'.[91]

The Crisis of the Union of the Crowns, Anglo-Scottish Relations, Scottish national identity and the Treaty of Union
Parliamentary developments and proceedings in the post-1690 period centred on increased Court interference and corruption in the management of Scottish parliamentary politics.[92] William of Orange, in conversation with Lord Halifax, English Lord Privy Seal, predicted that `Scotland by their divisions would give him more trouble than anything'.[93] Sir John Clerk of Penicuik, Member of Parliament for Whitburn 1703-07, writing in 1730 and commenting on the nature of pre-1707 Scotland, noted that:

> As to our Civil Government...it was an entire state of dependence on the Councils of England. We had frequent sessions of Parliament, a constant Privie Council, a Treasury and Exchequer, but all these subservient to such administrators as the chief ministers in England thought fit to recommend to the Soveraign. Our Commissioners for holding the aforesaid sessions of Parliament had always their instructions from the Cabinet Council of England and never gave the royal assent to any one act till the same was layd before their constituents at Court and in a word we were in the same or a worse condition than Ireland.[94]

Clerk's perspective is important here as he was one of the Scottish parliamentarians commissioned to negotiate the Treaty of Union. Albeit he was pro-incorporationist, Clerk had enjoyed a rich pedigree of parliamentary experience and deployment on specialised committees, such as the Commission to Investigate Public Accounts, in the period 1702-1707.[95] Writing in 1744 towards the end of his life, Clerk reiterated his stance on the pre-1707 period:

> Our seperat and, as we thought, independent parliaments were meer phantoms of power, and perfect Burlesques on free national Assemblies.

They met always under the influence & direction of the Ministry of England and therfor nothing of consequence was transacted in them but what flowed from sign'd Instructions given to the King's High Commissioners who presided in their several sessions...I own indeed that some matters were, now and then transacted in our parliaments which in Appearance did not seem to be calculated altogether for the benefit of England, but still every thing passed under English Ministerial Influence to bring about some favourite point which the Court had in view, for their own particular interest & often to thwart the projects of an opposite party.[96]

Increased Court interference in Scottish affairs was partly a reflection of the strength of the Revolution Settlement of 1689-90 itself, following the abolition of the Lords of the Articles, which meant that a new process of parliamentary management had to be found.[97] William's unpopularity in Scotland, exemplified by his role in the Massacre of Glencoe and the Darien fiasco, increased the political hostility between the Scottish Parliament and the English Court. That the Union of the Crowns was destabilising into a state of crisis was highlighted by the fact that William had sabotaged the Darien Scheme as King of England, via collusion with the English East India Company and the international financial markets at Amsterdam, although he had previously approved the new venture as King of Scotland.[98] Attempts to create an independent maritime empire and to facilitate the process of economic modernisation by the Scots were deliberately scuppered by vested commercial interests in the form of the English Board of Trade and the English East India Company. Spain was William's principal ally in the European conflict with Louis XIV and a Scottish commercial outpost would clearly antagonise and encroach on a perceived Spanish sphere of influence. The commercial interests of William's northern kingdom were to be subordinated to a rapprochement with the Spanish and the threat of Bourbon hegemony and the creation of a French universal monarchy.[99]

Prior to his death in March 1702, William was already advocating a closer union between the two kingdoms, as articulated to both the Commons and the Lords in 1700 and 1702 respectively, precisely because his Scottish kingdom had become increasingly ungovernable. Under his successor, Queen Anne, and in terms of the mentality of the English political nation, Anglo-Scottish relations had decidedly worsened and the Union of the Crowns had essentially collapsed. Dynastic crisis over the Hanoverian Succession, an independent Scottish foreign policy as articulated by the Scottish Parliament, and an increasingly confident and powerful Scottish Parliament, led the Marlborough-Godolphin ministry to the conclusion that an incorporating union was the only viable solution to the `Scottish problem' in an era of major European warfare.[100] `The Scottish Parliament...was maturing into an institution with an independent, nationalist bent. From an English imperial point of view this was intolerable'.[101]

Initial negotiations for an incorporating union, conducted in 1702-03,[102] failed. Following the English elections of July 1702, the English Tory ministry was less than lukewarm in its enthusiasm for an union of incorporation. In combination with Scottish negotiating demands for recognition of the rights of the Company of Scotland and English hostility to the establishment of free trade, this ensured that the union project was dead and buried by February 1703. Crucially, it was the 1703 session of the Scottish Parliament which marked the turning point in Anglo-Scottish relations. The Scottish Parliament pursued an independent dynastic policy distinct from that of England which had been articulated in the English Act of Settlement of 1701. The Scottish Act of Security stated that the successor to the Scottish throne was to be nominated by the Scottish Parliament and the successor should be a Protestant and of the Scottish royal line. However, if the sovereignty of the Scottish line was not secured then the successor to the Scottish crown need not necessarily be the same successor as that designated to the English throne. Therefore the Scottish Parliament was prepared to implement an independent dynastic policy. In addition, the Act anent Peace and War advocated an independent Scottish foreign policy (crucial from an English perspective for Scottish involvment in any future British war effort). When the 1703 parliamentary session ended on 16 September, with the King's Commissioner refusing to touch the Act of Security with the sceptre, Anglo-Scottish relations had reached a crisis point.[103]

Despite changes in the personnel of Court representatives (Queensberry being dropped and replaced by Tweeddale and the New Party), the 1704 parliamentary session brought further problems. By the end of the 1704 session the Hanoverian Succession had still not been secured. Ideas of a federal union with England were being forwarded as was further reform of the Scottish constitution.[104] Nevertheless, the English response to the protracted Scottish problem was precise. Under the terms of the English Alien Act of 1705, Scots would be treated as aliens in England and Scottish exported goods would be banned from English markets, unless the Scottish Act of Security was repealed and the Hanoverian Succession accepted by Christmas Day 1705. In addition, there were threats of an invading English military force into Scotland.[105] Considerations of dynastic instability, the possible restoration of Jacobite on the Scottish throne and the primacy of the strategic safety of England's northern borders during major military and financial commitments in the War of Spanish Succession ensured that a resolution to the instability of Scottish affairs had to be found.[106]

The parliamentary incorporating union of 1707 can be traced to a bizarre series of events in 1705-1706 involving the political ineptitude of the Duke of Hamilton. Hamilton was the key figure in the parliamentary opposition to the Court in the 1705 Parliament. Shortly after the opening of the 1705 session, the majority of the Scottish Estates refused to consider the recommendations of Queen Anne to secure the Hanoverian Succession and for an incorporating treaty with England. Although Secretary of State Mar had succeeded in passing the draft of an act with England on 20 July, the pivotal events centred on 24 August and 1 September 1705.[107] On 24 August the parliamentary opposition to the Court argued that the Scottish Estates should elect their own commissioners for the treaty negotiations. If this position had been maintained then it is doubtful whether an incorporating union could have been secured. Late in the evening of 1 September 1705 Hamilton stood up in the Scottish Parliament with most of the members absent and moved that the nomination of the Scottish commissioners to negotiate a treaty should be chosen by Queen Anne. This was quickly seized upon by the Court and an immediate vote was taken on Hamilton's motion, which secured a majority. Thirteen days later on 14 September the 1705 session of the Scottish Parliament was adjourned. The political result in favour of the Court and Queen Anne was secured when the Queen named the commissioners for union on 27 February 1706. Only one of the Scottish negotiating team, Sir George Lockhart of Carnwath, was anti-unionist (in terms of incorporation). Therefore the Scottish commissioners who negotiated the incorporating union with England were distinctly *unrepresentative* of the Scottish political nation at large.[108] Moreover, when the union negotiations commenced on 16 April 1706 the two sets of commissioners did not negotiate directly with each other. Instead the two bodies sat apart and only communicated in writing. The principle of an incorporating union had been accepted by the Scottish commissioners by 25 April 1706. The Treaty of Union, consisting of 25 articles, had been agreed on by 23 July 1706.[109]

The passage of the Treaty of Union through the Scottish Parliament deserves further consideration as does extra-parliamentary activity as a gauge of the reaction of the wider Scottish community to the incorporating union. When the 1706 session opened on 3 October, the Articles of Union were read to the House. Article One of the Treaty of Union was put to the House on 4 November and secured a majority of 115 votes to 83 votes.[110] Similarly, on 4 November the Church of Scotland was pacified by the act guaranteeing the Presbyterian establishment (the General Assembly had previously come out against the Treaty). This secured enactment on 12 November and the 'immediate result' was to 'neutralise the institutional leadership of the Kirk' and provide a leadership vacuum for 'coherent anti-unionism', albeit Presbyterian hostility to the union remained at the lower echelons of the Church of Scotland.[111] On 16 January 1707 the Treaty of Union secured ratification by 110 votes to 67. The Scottish Parliament was dissolved by proclamation on 28 April 1707 and the English Parliament had passed the treaty and Act of Union by 1 May 1707.[112]

No less than 15 of the 25 articles of union were concerned with economic issues and these certainly appealed to members of the various political factions in the House. This particularly applies to Article IV, concerning freedom of trade, which only secured 19 opposition votes.

However, the Court's policy of buying off the various interest groups was especially applied to the Squadrone Volante, which had 25 votes. Two main inducements were held out to the Squadrone. Firstly, the Squadrone was led to believe that it would secure a majority of the positions for the 16 elected peers in the House of Lords. Secondly, the Squadrone leadership had been prominent stockholders in the Company of Scotland. Therefore, as a financial inducement, the Squadrone leadership was also led to believe that it would be allowed to distribute the Equivalent (financial compensation contained within the treaty for the failure of the Company of Scotland/Darien Scheme). The fact that the incorporating treaty secured a safe passage through the Scottish Parliament can be attributed *more* to the *weakness* of the Scottish opposition than to the *strength* of the Court Party per se. The £20, 000 sent up to Scotland by the English Treasury for distribution by the Scottish Treasurer, the Earl of Glasgow, was carefully deployed to secure key votes or abstentions, in particular with the Squadrone Volante.[113] The passage of the treaty through the Scottish Parliament can therefore be attributed to the voting behaviour of the Squadrone Volante. If the Squadrone had voted otherwise then there would have been no incorporating union in 1706-07.[114]

The relationship between Scottish national identity (in its institutional format) and an independent Scottish Parliament can be gauged by reference to extra-parliamentary activity in Scotland. Anti-union riots took place in Glasgow, Edinburgh and Stirling, whilst copies of the articles of union were publicly set alight in Dumfries. Rioting in Glasgow was so intense and such a threat to public order that 200 dragoons were sent to the west. A small force of around 1500 men was located in the vicinity of Edinburgh.[115] Clerk of Penicuik noted that the incorporating union was `contrary to the inclinations of at least three-fourths of the Kingdom'.[116] Petitioning against the incorporating union can be interpreted as a representative voice of the nation. Petitions against the union were presented to Parliament from three main sources: shires, burghs, and parishes, as well as the Convention of Royal Burghs.[117] No less than 15 of the 33 shires (46%) and 21 of the 67 royal burghs (31%) in Scotland petitioned against an incorporating union. Crude numerical analysis in its own right, however, can be misleading. Whereas it has been argued that `three-quarters of the burghs and two-thirds of the shires did not petition at all',[118] this has to be balanced with the fact that there was *not one* petition received in *favour* of incorporation. What should be more pertinent is a systematic analysis of anti-union petitions from the three above sources to assess the reasoning behind anti-incorporation from the Scottish localities. J.R. Jones, one of the leading English historians of the Restoration and Revolution era has observed that anti-union petitions `were a more authentic and accurate indication of opinion'[119] in Scotland.

The freeholders of Dunbartonshire convened at Kilpatrick on the banks of the Clyde on 28 October 1706 (when the articles of union were going through Parliament) where they drew up a petition to be presented to the Scottish Parliament against incorporation. They had already examined a copy of the articles of union where they reached several conclusions. Firstly, 'ane incorporating union' as outlined in the twenty-five articles was:

> contrary to the honour fundamentall lawes and Constitution of this Kingdom, claim of right, and rights and priviledges of the barrons and ffreeholders, and Church as by law established, And that the same is destructive to the trew interest of the nation...[120]

Secondly, they petitioned Parliament not to allow of any incorporating union, but to:

> support preserve entire the soveraignty and Independancy of the crown and Kingdom and the rights and privileges of parliament, which has been so valliantly maintained by our heroike ancestours for the space of near two thousand years, that the samine may be transmitted to the succeeding generations as it hes been conveyed to us...[121]

The contemporary writings of Andrew Fletcher of Saltoun, the Scottish patriot and constitutional theorist, provide a further insight into the relationship between Scottish national identity and an independent Scottish Parliament.[122] Saltoun had certainly advocated a unification of the Parliaments and free trade in 1689, but the Darien fiasco and the experience of the 1690s had led Saltoun to abandon these beliefs. Saltoun's writings embrace a variety of complex issues,[123] and he has recently been described as 'perhaps the most creative political analyst in Britain'.[124] One of the key areas of his writings focused on Scottish parliamentary representation within a united British Parliament.[125] Fletcher's observations must also be viewed within the context of the 'pamphlet war' which erupted in response to the economic, political, constitutional and dynastic crisis of Anglo-Scottish relations.[126] Pamphleteering represented a crucial medium in the formation of political opinion[127] and a significant number of pamphlets also argued for the necessity of an incorporating union[128], most notably William Seton of Pitmedden's *Scotland's Great Advantages By An Union with England: Showen in a Letter From the Country To a Member of Parliament* (1706).[129] The plethora of pamphlets on the issue and the standard of its intellectual debate have moved the historical terrain to appreciate the Union of 1707 as an 'episode in intellectual as well as political history' which 'generated a significant body of political thought'.[130] Recent scholarship, based on the construction of inter-relational historical databases and detailed analysis of voting behaviour, has also persuasively argued for the reaccommodation of the issue of political principle for those Members of Parliament who voted in favour of an incorporating union.[131]

Under the terms of the Treaty of Union, Scotland secured 45 members out of 568 in the House of Commons and 16 seats out of 206 in the House of Lords. Scottish representation in the Commons therefore amounted to 7.9% of its total membership, whilst that of the Lords amounted to 7.8%.[132] Saltoun observed that:

> It is much easier to corrupt 45 Scots at *London*, than it is to corrupt 300 at *Edinburgh*: and besides, there will be no occasion of corrupting them, when the Case shall occur, of a difference betwixt the South-Britons and the North-Britons: for the Northern will be out-voted, without being corrupted. As the first can be practis'd with ease, so the Scots may be injured in a united Parliament with greater safety.[133]

Furthermore:

> In a word, a Separate English Parliament may perhaps invade the Scots Rights by their Laws: and perhaps a Scots Parliament may find means to move them to repeal those Laws: But in the case of a united Parliament, the Scots do make a formal Surrender of the very faculty itself, and are for ever left to the Mercy of the English, with respect to all their Interests, both united and separate. ....[134]
> This will be the Issue of that darling Plea, of being one and not two; it will be turned upon the Scots with a Vengeance; and their 45 Scots Members may dance round to all Eternity, in this Trap of their own making. ...And do we doubt whether an English ministry, or a Scots Parliament will be most for the interest of Scotland ?[135][136]

Such an analysis is valid within the context of a structural overview of the representation of Scottish political interests. The de facto absorption of the Scots into the Westminster system was confirmed by the Lord Chief Justice of Common Pleas as the Articles of Union were considered by the Committee of the Whole House in the House of Lords. Accordingly, `the Scots come into the Parliament of England. Nothing can be stronger to imply the Parliament of England does continue'.[137] Colin Kidd has noted that `by strict constitutional criteria, there was no less reason for Scotsmen than Englishmen to take pride in the British Parliament as a palladium of their historic liberties'.[138] Whilst this may be the case, it does not resolve the structural problem of Scottish representation within an effectively enlarged English institution. As John Robertson has commented on the willingness of the *English* Parliament to accept an incorporating union with Scotland, it did so on the grounds that `in every respect bar its style and a limited addition to its membership the new Parliament of Great Britain would be as its English predecessor'.[139] The central function of Scottish political managers operating within the British system after 1707 was to provide a solid and reliable phalanx of personnel amenable to the Westminster government of the day.[140]

Conclusion

The concept of Scottish national identity must embrace all of its component parts. This paper has addressed the issue of an institutional identity in the form of the Scottish Parliament. The Scottish Parliament was not inherently `weak' and two major reform programmes were enacted in 1640-41 and 1689-90. Constitutional and institutional innovation continued throughout the 1640s and in the period 1689-1707. Parliament played host to intense political factionalism and personal rivalry in the Restoration era, but this was a product of the ramifications of the partisanship and factional rivalries of the wider British political scene and not an institutional structural deficiency *per se*.[141] By the early eighteenth century, a resurgent Scottish Parliament, in tandem with divergence from the dominant strategic interests of the English fiscal-military state,[142] ensured that the only viable political solution to containing or eliminating the `Scottish problem' was via a parliamentary incorporating union. `Constitutional advancement within Scotland was sacrificed to the personal pursuit of office and profit under the British Crown'[143] and `as soon as the Scottish Parliament tried to assert an independent line on a matter of consequence, it was abolished'.[144] The final word lies with a contribution from the devolution debates of the 1970s:

> That the Scottish Parliament advanced as far as it did
> gave Scotland an institution far ahead of most comparable
> European states in what was still the age of absolutism.
> By comparison with England, the Scottish Parliament fell
> short, but by European standards the conclusion that
> Scotland was anywhere but among the front-runners in
> political advance is inept.[145]

NOTES

[1]. For example, Anthony Nicholls, `The Problem of German Identity in the Nineteenth and Twentieth Centuries', 52-71, and Colin Lucas, `Nation, Region and Revolution in France', 206-227, in Michael Hurst (ed), *States, Countries, Provinces* (Buckinghamshire, 1986). For a relatively recent discourse on early modern Scotland, albeit permeated by anglocentricism, see Michael Hurst, `Scottish Identity and Identities under Crown and Legislative Unions', in Hurst (ed), *States, Countries, Provinces*, 91-121. See also Craig Beveridge and Ronald Turnbull, *Scotland after Enlightenment: Image and Tradition in Modern Scottish Culture*

(Edinburgh, 1997). For a recent contribution on the legal profession, see John W. Cairns, `Scottish law, Scottish lawyers and the status of the Union', in John Robertson (ed), *A Union for Empire. Political Thought and the British Union of 1707* (Cambridge, 1995), 243-268. For a discussion of political identities in the early modern period in an European context, see Mark Greengrass, `Conquest and Coalescence', in Mark Greengrass (ed), *Conquest and Coalescence. The Shaping of the State in Early Modern Europe* (London, 1991), vii, 19-20. National identity `myths' were also employed in early modern Europe. For a Swedish example see John Robertson, `Empire and union: two concepts of the early modern European political order', in Robertson (ed), *A Union For Empire*, 17-19

[2]. See, for example, J.G. Kellas, *Modern Scotland* (second edition, London, 1980); John Osmund, *The Divided Kingdom* (London, 1988), 21-22, 78-79.

[3]. Greengrass, `Conquest and Coalescence', vii, 4; Mark Goldie, `Divergence and Union: Scotland and England, 1660-1707', in Bradshaw and Morrill (eds), *The British Problem*, 220-221. In terms of the creation of an Anglo-British identity in historiographical terms, it has been noted that the Scottish Parliament, Scots Law and the Scottish nobility `remained three secular institutions capable of contributing some contemporary inspiration and recognisable structure to the revitalisation of a patriotic historiography' [Colin Kidd, *Subverting Scotland's Past. Scottish Whig Historians And The Creation of An Anglo-British Identity 1689-c.1830* (Cambridge, 1993), 129]. Scottish parliamentary heritage tended to be neglected by eighteenth century commentators, who were more interested in combatting the threat of Jacobitism (*ibid*, 129-132). It could also be argued that such a Whig interpretation of history was necessary to *justify* (my emphasis) the loss of Scotland's Parliament through an incorporating union.

[4]. W. Ferguson, `Introduction', in C. Jones (ed), *The Scots and Parliament, Parliamentary History* Special Volume, (Edinburgh, 1996), 1.

[5]. *Ibid*, 3.

[6]. R. Bonney, *The European Dynastic States 1494-1660* (Oxford, 1991), 316. The Kirk, the Privy Council and the structures of the legal profession must also be incorporated within Scotland's institutional identity. This paper, however, is restricted to that of Parliament. For a recent contribution on the law, see John W. Cairns, `Scottish Law, Scottish lawyers and the status of the Union', in John Robertson (ed), *A Union For Empire. Political Thought and the British Union of 1707* (Cambridge, 1995), 243-268.

[7]. Ferguson, `Introduction', in Jones (ed), *The Scots and Parliament*, 1.

[8]. The two main areas of Scottish parliamentary history which require particular attention are the Restoration Parliaments post-1661 and the Parliaments of 1689-1707. For the field as a whole, a major contribution has recently appeared in the form of M.D. Young (ed), *The Parliaments of Scotland: Burgh and Shire Commissioners*, two volumes (Edinburgh, 1992-1993). The two standard works, C.S. Terry's *The Parliament of Scotland: Its Constitution and Procedure* (Glasgow, 1905) and R.S. Rait's *The Parliaments of Scotland* (Glasgow, 1924), now require

substantial revision. Two examples of most recent contributions are John R. Young, *The Scottish Parliament 1639-1661: A Political and Constitutional Analysis* (Edinburgh, 1996) and Jones (ed), *The Scots and Parliament*.

[9]. D. Stevenson, `The Century of the Three Kingdoms', in J. Wormald (ed), *Scotland Revisited*, (London, 1991), 107-118.

[10]. B.P. Levack, *The Formation of the British State. England, Scotland, and the Union 1603-1707* (Oxford, 1987), 2.

[11]. James F. Larkin and Paul L. Hughes (eds), *Stuart Royal Proclamations. Volume I: Royal Proclamations of King James I 1603-1625* (Oxford, 1973), 94-98.

[12]. Levack, *The Formation of the British State*, 1.

[13]. *Acts of the Parliaments of Scotland*, T. Thomson & C. Innes (eds), (Edinburgh, 1814-72), IV (1593-1624), 263-264; Alan G.R. Smith, *The Emergence of A Nation State: The Commonwealth of England 1529-1660* (London, 1984), 394-395.

[14]. Brian P. Levack, `The Proposed Union of English Law and Scots Law in the Seventeenth Century', *Juridical Review*, (1975), 97-115; Brian P. Levack, `Law, Sovereignty and the Union', in Roger A. Mason (ed), *Scots and Britons: Scottish Political Thought and the Union of 1603* (Cambridge, 1994), 213-237.

[15]. Smith, *The Emergence of A Nation State*, 395.

[16]. *Ibid*, 393-394; J.P. Kenyon (ed), *The Stuart Constitution 1603-1688: Documents and Commentary*, Second Edition, (Cambridge, 1986), 25-26, 29-35; W. Notestein, *The House of Commons 1604-1610* (New Haven & London, 1971).

[17]. For detailed studies of the attempts to establish a perfect union see, for example, Bruce Galloway, *The Union of England and Scotland 1603-1608* (Edinburgh, 1986) and Bruce R. Galloway and Brian P. Levack (eds), *The Jacobean Union: Six Tracts of 1604* (Scottish History Society, Edinburgh, 1985), J.H. Burns, *The True Law of Kingship: Concepts of Monarchy in Early Modern Scotland* (Oxford, 1996), 255-281; Jenny Wormald, `The Union of 1603', in Mason (ed), *Scots and Britons*, 17-40; Jenny Wormald, `One king, two kingdoms', in A. Grant and Keith J. Stringer (eds), *Uniting The Kingdom ? The Making of British History* (London, 1995), 123-132; Jenny Wormald, `James VI, James I and the Identity of Britain', in Brendan Bradshaw and John Morrill (eds), *The British Problem c. 1534-1707: State Formation in the Atlantic Archipelago* (London, 1996), 148-171; John Robertson, `Empire and Union: Two Concepts of the Early Modern European Political Order', in John Robertson (ed), *A Union for Empire. Political Thought and the British Union of 1707*, (Cambridge, 1995), 13-16. For an analysis of the Anglo-Scottish dynastic union of 1603 as an *imperfect* union (my emphasis), see Conrad Russell, `Composite monarchies in early modern Europe: The British and Irish example', in Grant and Stringer (eds), *Uniting the Kingdom ?*, 133-146.

[18]. A.I. MacInnes, *Charles I and the Making of the Covenanting Movement 1625-1641* (Edinburgh, 1991), 22.

[19]. For the retention of Scottish influence in the new Bedchamber of James VI and I, see Neil Cuddy, `The revival of the entourage: the Bedchamber of James I, 1603-

1625', in David Starkey *et al*, *The English Court from the Wars of the Roses to the Civil War* (London, 1987), 173-225.

[20]. K.M. Brown, 'The Scottish Aristocracy, Anglicization and the Court, 1603-38', *The Historical Journal*, 36, 3, (1993), 543-576; Keith M. Brown, 'The Origins of a British aristocracy: integration and its limitations before the Treaty of Union', in Steven G. Ellis and Sarah Barber (eds), *Conquest & Union: Fashioning a British State 1485-1725* (London, 1995), 222-249.

[21]. Levack, *The Formation of the British State*, 36-38.

[22]. *The Parliaments of Scotland. Burgh and Shire Commissioners*, M.D. Young (ed), two volumes (Edinburgh, 1992-93), volume two, 753-755. Conventions of Estates were employed to consider specific purposes such as temporary legislation or, more usually, taxation (Rait, *The Parliaments of Scotland*, 151-164).

[23]. J.M. Goodare, 'Parliament and Society in Scotland, 1560-1603', (University of Edinburgh, PhD thesis, 1989), 7.

[24]. Levack, *The Formation of the British State*, 219.

[25]. See Macinnes, *Charles I and the Making of the Covenanting Movement*.

[26]. Ronald Hutton, 'The Triple-crowned Islands', in Lionel K.J. Glassey (ed), *The Reigns of Charles II and James VII & II* (London, 1997), 74.

[27]. Julian Goodare, 'The Scottish Parliament of 1621', *The Historical Journal*, 38, 1, (1995), 29-51.

[28]. Sir James Balfour, *Historical Works*, four volumes, J. Haig (ed), (Edinburgh, 1824-25), II, 200.

[29]. Young, *The Scottish Parliament 1639-1661: A Political and Constitutional Analysis*; John R. Young, 'The Scottish Parliament and the Covenanting Revolution: The Emergence of a Scottish Commons', in John R. Young (ed), *Celtic Dimensions of the British Civil Wars* (Edinburgh, 1997), 164-184. For case studies of the committee structure at work, also see D. Stevenson (ed), *The Government of Scotland Under the Covenanters 1637-1651*, (Scottish History Society, Edinburgh, 1982).

[30]. Stevenson (ed), *Government Under the Covenanters*, xlvii.

[31]. For example, D. Stevenson, 'The Early Covenanters and the Federal Union of Britain', in R.A. Mason (ed), *Scotland and England 1286-1815* (Edinburgh, 1987), 163-181.

[32]. *APS*, VI, i, (1643-1647), 150-151.

[33]. W. Notestein, 'The Establishment of the Committee of Both Kingdoms', *American Historical Review*, 17, (1912), 477-478; L. Mulligan, 'The Scottish Alliance and the Committee of Both Kingdoms, 1644-46', *Historical Studies Australia and New Zealand*, 14, (1970), 173.

[34]. *The Letters and Journals of Robert Baillie, 1637-62*, D. Laing (ed), three volumes, (Bannatyne Club, Edinburgh, 1841-42), II, 90.

[35]. A.I. Macinnes, 'The Scottish Constitution, 1638-51: The Rise and Fall of Oligarchic Centralism', in J. Morrill (ed), *The Scottish National Covenant in its British Context 1638-51* (Edinburgh, 1990), 123-124; Glasgow University Library,

Special Collections Unit, James Dean Ogilvie Collection, Ogilvie 259, *A Declaration of The Reasons for assisting the Parliament of England, Against the Papists and Prelaticall Army. By the General Assembly of the Kirke of Scotland* (London, 1643); Glasgow University Library, Special Collections Unit, Ogilvie 398, Richard Ward, *The Analysis, Explication and Application, of the Sacred and Solemne League and Covenant, For the Reformation, and Defence of Religion, the Honour and Happinesse of the King, and the Peace and Safety of the three Kingdomes of England, Scotland, and Ireland* (London, 1643).

[36]. *Some Papers Given in by the Commissioners of the Parliament of Scotland, To the Honourable Houses of the Parliament of England. In Answer to their Votes of the 24 of September 1646. Concerning The disposing of His Majesties PERSON. To which is added, THE SPEECHES OF THE LORD CHANCELLOUR OF SCOTLAND* (EDINBURGH, 1646); *Severall Speeches Spoken by the Right Honourable The Earle of Loudoun, Lord high Chancellour of the Kingdome of Scotland: At a Conference with a Committee of the Honourable Houses in the Painted Chamber, October 1646* (Edinburgh, 1646), both in Glasgow University Library, Special Collections Unit, Tracts Mu 44-d.1.

[37]. National Library of Scotland, Edinburgh, Adv. 22.1.15, Transactions at Edinburgh of affairs between the Parliament and Committee of Estates, 1647; *Calendar of State Papers Venetian, 1643-1647*, A.B. Hinds (ed), (London, 1926), 128-129, 292, 295, 296. The view that the Scots had sold their king was also commented on by Giovanni Battista Nani, the Venatian Ambassador, in 1649. According to Nani, this had been an `abominable example' and the Scots had sold Charles I `to the English for a few pounds sterling' [*Calendar of State Papers Venetian, 1647-1652*, A.B. Hinds (ed), (London, 1927), 87].

[38]. *Calendar of State Papers Venetian, 1643-1647*, 299.

[39]. *The Records of the Commissions of the General Assemblies of the Church of Scotland Holden in Edinburgh in the years 1646 and 1647*, A.F. Mitchell and J. Christie (eds), Scottish History Society, 1st series, 11, (Edinburgh, 1892), 520-526, 530-531.

[40]. Edinburgh University Library, Special Collections Unit, Dc.5.44, `Memoirs of Scots Affairs from the Death of King Charles the 1st to the Restoration By Alexander Hamilton of Kinkell Esqr', folio 12.

[41]. See John R. Young, `Scottish Covenanting Radicalism, the Commission of the Kirk and the Establishment of the Parliamentary Radical Regime of 1648-49', *Records of the Scottish Church History Society*, VOL. XXV Part 3, (1995), 342-375.

[42]. British Library, London, Egerton MS (Nicholas Papers), folio 1.

[43]. Glasgow University Library, Special Collections Unit, James Dean Ogilvie Collection, Ogilvie 137, *The Lord Marques of Argyle's Speech to A Grand Committee of Both Houses of Parliament, The 25th of this instant June, 1646* (London, 27th June 1646), folio (5).

[44]. See, for example, A.L. Rowse, *The Regicides* (London, 1994).

[45]. British Library, Egerton MS (Nicholas Papers), folio 1.

[46]. Edinburgh University Library, Special Collections Unit, Dc.5.44, Alexander Hamilton of Kinkell, 'Memoirs of Scots Affairs', folio 27.

[47]. For the role of the Commission of the Kirk in the purging of the Scottish armed forces, see, for example, *The Records of the Commissions of the General Assemblies of the Church of Scotland Holden in Edinburgh the Years 1648 and 1649*, A.F. Mitchell and J. Christie (eds), Scottish History Society, First Series, 25, (Edinburgh, 1896), 348, 355-356, 361, 364-365, *The Records of the Commissions of the General Assemblies of the Church of Scotland Holden in Edinburgh in 1650, in St Andrews and Dundee in 1651 and in Edinburgh in 1652*, J. Christie (ed), Scottish History Society, First Series, 58, (Edinburgh, 1909), 8, 15-17.

[48]. Glasgow University Library, Special Collections Unit, James Dean Ogilvie Collection, Ogilvie 731, *A Declaration of the Army of England, Upon their march into Scotland* (London, 1650).

[49]. Sir James Balfour, *Historical Works*, D. Laing (ed), four volumes (Edinburgh, 1824-25), IV, 123.

[50]. British Library, London, Egerton MS (Nicholas Papers), folio 58.

[51]. *Ibid*, 129-130, 131, 160.

[52]. John Nicholl, *A Diary of Public Transactions and Other Occurences, Chiefly in Scotland, from January 1650 to June 1667* (Bannatyne Club, Edinburgh, 1836), 32-33.

[53]. *RCGA*, 1650-1652, 131.

[54]. P.J. Pickney, 'The Scottish representation in the Cromwellian Parliament of 1656', *SHR*, 46, (1967); J.A. Casada, 'The Scottish Representatives in Richard Cromwell's Parliament', *SHR*, 51, (1972); H.N. Mukerjee, 'Scottish Members of Richard Cromwell's Parliament', *Notes and Queries*, clxvi, (1934); D.L. Smith, 'The Struggle for New Constitutional and Institutional Forms', in J. Morrill (ed), *Revolution and Restoration. England in the 1650s* (London, 1992).

[55]. See R. Lee, 'Retreat from Revolution: The Scottish Parliament and the Restored Monarchy, 1661-1663', in John R. Young (ed), *Celtic Dimensions of the British Civil Wars* (Edinburgh, 1997), 185-204.

[56]. National Library of Scotland, Edinburgh, MS 3423, Lauderdale Correspondence, 1656-1662, ff 52-53.

[57]. Scottish Records Office, Edinburgh, Dalhousie Muniments, GD 45/14/110/(2).

[58]. M. Lee Jr (ed), *Autobiography, 1626-1670, of John Hay, 2nd Earl of Tweeddale*, Scottish History Society, Fifth Series, Volume 7, Miscellany XII, (Edinburgh, 1994), 89.

[59]. National Library of Scotland, MS 3423, Lauderdale Correspondence, folio 53.

[60]. *Ibid*, folio 124.

[61]. *Calendar of State Papers Venetian 1659-1661*, volume xxxii, A.B. Hinds (ed), (London, 1931), 249.

[62]. *APS*, VII, 3-526, Appendix 1-105.

63. Scottish Records Office, The Transcripts of Cosmo Innes, volume II, RH 2/2/14, 'The Method and Maner of choyseing the Lords of ye Articles as the sams is setled in June 1663'; British Library, Add. MSS. 6308, Ceremonials Presented by Lady Banks [Collections from Printed Works chiefly relating to English Ceremonials in the reigns of King Charles I and King Charles II with a few Articles relating to Foreign Ceremonials at the End], ff 9-12.

64. Airy (ed), *Lauderdale Papers*, I, 210-212, 225, 272-273; Rait, *The Parliaments of Scotland*, 79.

65. Airy (ed), *Lauderdale Papers*, II, xx, 169, 241-244, 245-247, III, i, vi, 2-4, 5, 16-17; J. Buckroyd, *Church and State in Scotland 1660-1681* (Edinburgh, 1980), 106-108, 117, 122-124, 128; Rait, *The Parliaments of Scotland*, 81, 84; Geoffrey Holmes, *The Making of a Great Power: Late Stuart and Early Georgian Britain* (London, 1993), 32; Scottish Records Office, Hamilton Papers GD 406/1/2785; John Patrick, 'The Origins of the opposition to Lauderdale in the Scottish Parliament of 1673', *SHR*, LIII, (1974), 1-21. For Hamilton's opposition role in the 1678 Convention see, for example, Airy (ed), *Lauderdale Papers*, III, 154-159; 'Accompt of the Convention of the Estates in June 1678, with the remarkable occurents that happened therein', in Sir John Lauder of Fountainhall, *Historical Collections*, volume I, 1680-1686 (Bannatyne Club, Edinburgh, 1847), Appendix, 264-279; R. Lee, 'Expectations of Central Government in Restoration Scotland: The Case of the Opposition in the 1670s', E.A. Cameron and F. Watson (eds), *The Government or Mis-Government of Scotland*, (The Association of Scottish Historical Studies, 1996), 24-32.

66. G. Donaldson, *Scotland. James V-James VII* (Fifth edition, Edinburgh, 1987), 376.

67. Hutton, 'The Triple-crowned Islands', 77-78.

68. Ferguson, *Scotland's Relations with England*, 152.

69. Glasgow University Library, Special Collections Unit, Bf 72-c.2, *An Accompt of Scotlands Grievances By reason of the D. Lauderdales Ministrie, Humbly tendred to His Sacred Majesty* (Sir James Stewart, 1872), (1). See also, Daniel Szechi and David Hayton, 'John Bull's Other Kingdoms: The English Government of Scotland and Ireland', in Clyve Jones (ed), *Britain in the First Age of Party 1680-1750. Essays Presented to Geoffrey Holmes* (London, 1987), 246-247, for fears that Scotland was a laboratory for the imposition of Stuart absolutism in England; Goldie, 'Divergence and Union', 224-226.

70. Airy (ed), *Lauderdale Papers*, II, 133-134.

71. Ferguson, *Scotland's Relations with England*, 154-156; Airy (ed), *Lauderdale Papers*, II, 141, 143-145, 154, 155-158; Holmes, *The Making of A Great Power*, 89-90, 95, 434; Hutton, 'The Triple-crowned Islands', 76; J.D. Davies, 'International Relations, War and the Armed Forces', in Glassey (ed), *The Reigns of Charles II and James VII & II*, 225-226. For details of the proceedings of the 1670 union negotiations, see 'Papers Relating to the Union Negotiations in 1670', in C.S. Terry (ed), *The Cromwellian Union. Papers Relating to the Negotiations*

for an Incorporating Union between England and Scotland, 1651-1652. With an Appendix of Papers Relating to the Negotiations in 1670 (Scottish History Society, Edinburgh, 1902).

[72]. For a contemporary criticism of Lauderdale's regime, see Scottish Records Office, Shairp of Houston Muniments, GD 30/2126 'Some matters of fact relating to the administration of affairs in Scotland under the Duke of Lauderdaill' (1676). See also Scottish Records Office, Scott of Harden Papers, GD 157/1657.

[73]. Buckroyd, *Church and State in Scotland*, 131-136.

[74]. Donaldson, *James V-James VII*, 379.

[75]. Ferguson, *Scotland's Relations with England*, 160. For the most recent innovative research into Restoration politics in Scotland see R. Lee, 'Government and Politics in Scotland, 1661-1681' (University of Glasgow, PhD thesis, 1995).

[76]. It has recently been argued that the 1681 Parliament was 'used to stage an ideological refutation of the claims of the Whig-dominated English Parliament' (Goldie, 'Divergence and Union', 226). The legality of the Duke of York presiding in Parliament appears to have been in conflict with legislation of 1609 which stated that no Catholic might be a member thereof. This problem also appears to have been discussed in private (Rait, *The Parliaments of Scotland*, 86).

[77]. Ferguson, *Scotland's Relations with England*, 160.

[78]. Rait, *The Parliaments of Scotland*, 89-90; *Memoirs of Sir John Reresby. The Complete Text and A Selection From His Letters*, A. Browning (ed), second edition (London, 1991), 414, 419

[79]. *Memoirs of Sir John Reresby*, 414.

[80]. Colin, Earl of Balcarres, *Memoirs Touching the Revolution in Scotland*, (Bannatyne Club, Edinburgh, 1841), 37;

[81]. Rait, *The Parliaments of Scotland*, 90-93; *Memoirs of Sir John Reresby*, 423, 426, 429. Donaldson states that James VII's policy of religious toleration for Roman Catholics was 'probably the only issue that could bring down his throne' (*James V-James VII*, 381).

[82]. Quoted in Donaldson, *James V-James VII*, 381.

[83]. For a critique of the demise of James VII and II as a result of his employment of the methods of government of Louis XIV and French 'tyranny', as opposed to the success of the Glorious Revolution based on a confessional agenda for the defence of European Protestantism, see Steven Pincus, 'The English debate over universal monarchy', in Robertson (ed), *A Union for Empire*, 52-62. This analysis is based primarily on James II as King of England. Within a Scottish context, Colin Kidd has noted that 'religious ideas also gave rise to different conceptions of Scottish national identity' and that 'in the pre-modern world, national identity was often inextricably linked to confessional identity'. Ultimately, the fear of 'Louis XIV's ambitions to create a Counter-Reformation Catholic empire in western Europe led to a realisation that Union was a strategic necessity for Protestantism as a whole' ('Religious realignment between the Restoration and the Union', in Robertson (ed), *A Union for Empire*, 116).

[84]. Lionel K.J. Glassey, `Introduction', in Lionel K.J. Glassey, *The Reigns of Charles II and James VII & II* (London, 1997), 9.

[85]. In particular, this has been observed by Keith Brown in *Kingdom* or *Province?*, 192.

[86]. John Robertson, `An elusive sovereignty. The course of the Union debate in Scotland 1698-1707', in Robertson (ed), *A Union for Empire*, 198-199. The political language of the Claim of Right and the Articles of Grievances harked back to that of the Scottish Covenanters in 1641 (ibid).

[87]. Ferguson, *Scotland 1689 to the Present*, 5; Brown, *Kingdom or Province ?*, 175; Rait, *The Parliaments of Scotland*, 95-101; Kidd, *Subverting Scotland's Past*, 21; James Moore and Michael Silverstone, `Protestant theologies, limited sovereignties: natural law and conditions of union in the German Empire, the Netherlands and Great Britain', in Robertson (ed), *A Union for Empire*, 191-192.

[88]. Ferguson, *Scotland 1689 to the Present*, 5; Brown, *Kingdom or Province ?*, 175-176; P.H. Scott, *Scotland: An Unwon Cause* (Edinburgh, 1997), 27-28.

[89]. Ferguson, *Scotland 1689 to the Present*, 13.

[90]. Ferguson, *Scotland's Relations with England*, 170, 172, 192; J. Halliday, `The Club and the Revolution in Scotland 1689-90', *SHR*, XLV, (1966), 143-159; Rait, *The Parliaments of Scotland*, 102-103, 105; Allan I. Macinnes, `Early Modern Scotland: The Current State of Play', *SHR*, LXXIII, `Whither Scottish History ?: Proceedings of the 1993 Strathclyde Conference (1994), 42; Goldie, `Divergence and Union', 232-233. Fletcher of Saltoun's `Limitations' also argued for further constitutional reform of Parliament, seemingly modelled on the reforms of the 1640s (Scott, *Scotland: An Unwon Cause*, 41-42; Kidd, *Subverting Scotland's Past*, 24).

[91]. *Memoirs of Sir John Reresby*, 550. Sir John Reresby, an influential Yorkshire gentleman, was informed of this by a `Court lady' who had indeed talked with the `great lord' in question. The comments specifically relate to 1689 and the two Houses of Parliament and the question of the monarchy: `in case the two Houses agreed to make the government vacant, that Scotland would choos for itselfe' (ibid).

[92]. For a detailed analysis see P.W.J. Riley, *King William and the Scottish Politicians* (Edinburgh, 1979) and P.W.J. Riley, *The Union of England and Scotland* (Manchester, 1978).

[93]. *Spencer House Journals*, in H.C. Foxcroft, *The Life and Letters of Sir George Savile, Marquis of Halifax*, two volumes, (1898), volume two, 202; Robertson, `An elusive sovereignty', 199.

[94]. `Sir John Clerk's Observations on the present circumstances of Scotland, 1730', T.C. Smout (ed), Scottish History Society Miscellany, Volume X, (Edinburgh, 1965), 184.

[95]. *Ibid*, 178; Young (ed), *The Parliaments of Scotland: Burgh and Shire Commissioners*, volume one, 124.

[96]. Sir John Clerk of Penicuik, *History of the Union of Scotland and England*, Douglas Duncan (ed), Scottish History Society, Fifth Series, Volume 6, (Edinburgh, 1993), 186-187.

[97]. Ferguson, *Scotland's Relations with England*, 183.

[98]. Levack, *The Formation of the British State*, 220; Roy H. Campbell, 'A Historical Perspective on the Union', in Patrick S. Hodge (ed), *Scotland and the Union*, Hume Papers on Publi Policy: Volume 2 No 2 (Edinburgh, 1994), 67-69; Scott, *Scotland: An Unwon Cause*, 38.

[99]. Robertson, 'Empire and Union', 32-33; Robertson, 'An elusive sovereignty', 200; David Armitage, 'The Scottish vision of empire: intellectual origins of the Darien venture', in Robertson (ed), *A Union for Empire*, 97-118. Armitage has further noted that 'The Darien venture and the Union of 1707 were both intended as solutions to the same structural problems in the relationship between the two British kingdoms' (ibid, 117); Clerk of Penicuik, *History of the Union of Scotland and England*, 184.

[100]. John Morrill, 'The English, the Scots and the British', in Hodge (ed), *Scotland and the Union*, 84. For an elucidation and reasoning of why the crisis was primarily constitutional see W. Ferguson,'Imperial crowns: a neglected facet of the background to the Treaty of Union of 1707', *SHR*, LIII, (1974), 22-44.

[101]. Szechi and Hayton, 'John Bull's Other Kingdoms', 252-253.

[102]. Beatrice Curtis Brown (ed), *The Letters and Diplomatic Instructions of Queen Anne*, second edition, (London, 1968), 72-73, 88-90; Ferguson, *Scotland's Relations with England*, 205-206.

[103]. Levack, *The Formation of the British State*, 197-213, 218; Rait, *The Parliaments of Scotland*, 115-118; Scott, *Scotland: An Unwon Cause*, 42-44; *APS*, XI, 104, 107.

[104]. *Letters of George Lockhart of Carnwath*, Daniel Szechi (ed), Scottish History Society, Fifth Series, Volume 2, (Edinburgh, 1989), 22. A federal union was simply out of the question in terms of English political interests (ibid, 25, 30). Queensberry was instructed by Queen Anne prior to the 1706 session that any moves for a federal union in the Scottish Parliament were to be answered with 'the throwing out thereof'. Anne was 'convinced that nothing can prove a solid and lasting settlement for the Peace and happiness of our Subjects of this Island but that of an entire Union' (*Letters of Queen Anne*, 190-191); R. Lodge, 'The English Standpoint (I)', in P. Hume Brown, *The Union of 1707. A Survey of Events*, Glasgow Herald Volumes on Current Topics (Glasgow, 1907), 167. For the relative importance of the concepts of federalism, confederalism, incorporation and conquest as fundamental components of the contemporary union debate, see Robertson, 'Empire and Union', 20-36; Kidd, 'Religious realignment between the Restoration and the Union', 161-162; Robertson, 'An elusive sovereignty', 206-209, 210-215, 220-221; Penovich, 'From "Revolution Principles" to Union', 232-233, 237.

[105]. *Ibid*, 220; Ferguson, *Scotland 1689 to the Present*, 40-44; Ferguson, *Scotland's Relations with England*, 214-231.

[106]. See Szechi and Hayton, `John Bull's Other Kingdoms', 241-280;. G. Holmes and D. Szechi, *The Age of Oligarchy: Pre-industrial Britain 1722-1783*, (London, 1993) 71; G. Holmes, *The Making of a Great Power: Late Stuart and Early Georgian Britain* (London, 1993), 232, 235; GUL Special Collections, James Dean Ogilvie Collection, Ogilvie Q34, *Reasons for an Union Between the Kingdoms of England and Scotland* (London, 1706), (32)-(39).

[107]. Mar's key role in securing the passage of the Treaty through the Scottish Parliament was clearly recognised by Anne; `The pains you have taken in bringing this affair about deserves more thanks than I am able to express' (*Letters of Queen Anne*, 218-219).

[108]. William Law Mathieson, *Scotland and the Union. A History of Scotland From 1695 to 1747* (Glasgow, 1905), 112-114.

[109]. Ferguson, *Scotland 1689 to the Present*, 46-48; Ferguson, *Scotland's Relations with England*, 232-270; Scott, *Scotland: An Unwon Cause*, 51-53, 61-62.

[110]. Ferguson, *Scotland 1689 to the Present*, 49-53; Ferguson, *Scotland's Relations with England*, 232-270.

[111]. Kidd, `Religious realignment between the Restoration and the Union', 166.

[112]. Ferguson, *Scotland 1689 to the Present*, 49-53; Ferguson, *Scotland's Relations with England*, 232-270.

[113]. For the distribution of the funds, see D. Szechi (ed), `*Scotland's Ruine':
Lockhart of Carnwath's Memoirs of the Union*, The Association For Scottish Literary Studies, Number 25, (Aberdeen, 1995), 252-261.

[114]. Ferguson, *Scotland 1689 to the present*, 51-52; Ferguson, *Scotland's Relations with England*, 247-253; Scott, *Scotland: An Unwon Cause*, 62-66.

[115]. Ibid; R. Renwick (ed), *Extracts from the Records of the Burgh of Glasgow A.D. 1691-1717* (Scottish Burgh Records Society, Glasgow, 1908), 399-401; GUL Special Collections Unit, Mu 29-e.20/41, *An Account of the burning of the Articles of the Union at Dumfries* (1706); GUL Special Collections Unit, in Mu 44-a.17, *Proclamation against tumults and rabbles. Edinburgh, the twenty fourth day of October, 1706* (1706); *A Proclamation discharging unwarrantable and seditious convocations and meetings, Edinburgh, December 27, 1706* (1706); Christopher A. Whatley, `*Bought and Sold for English Gold' ? Explaining the Union of 1707*, Studies in Scottish Economic and Social History, No.4, (Dundee, 1994), 43-44; Clerk of Penicuik, *History of the Union of Scotland and England*, 144.

[116]. `Sir John Clerk's Observations', 192. For Clerk's comments on mob behaviour and antagonism see *History of the Union of Scotland and England*, 97-103.

[117]. SRO PA 7/28/1-22 (shires)/23-48 (burghs)/49-83 (parishes); John Robertson (ed), *Ecclesiastical Records of the Presbytery of Lanark 1623-1709* (Abbotsford Club, Edinburgh, 1889), 140-141; Mathieson, *Scotland and the Union*, 131. For contemporary fears for the safeguarding of Presbyterianism within a British Parliament and its absorption within a `pan-Britannic Episcopalian Church', see Kidd, `Religious realignment between the Restoration and the Union', 145-168.

[118]. Brown, *Kingdom or Province ?*, 190.

[119]. J.R. Jones, *Country and Court. England 1658-1714* (London, 1978), 332.

[120]. Glasgow City Archives, Mitchell Library, Glasgow, Hamilton of Barns Papers, TD 589/1030.

[121]. *Ibid.*

[122]. For a detailed study of Saltoun see Paul H. Scott, *Andrew Fletcher and the Treaty of Union* (Edinburgh, 1992).

[123]. 'Fletcher dreamed of a pan-European federation of small, free and non-expansionary republics' (Goldie, 'Divergence and Union', 240); Armitage, 'The Scottish vision of empire', 114-116; Robertson, 'An elusive sovereignty', 208-210. Fletcher's envisaged programme of constitutional reform, incorporated in his *Limitations*, harked back to the reforms of 1640-41 and were also influenced by the Club's programme of 1689 (Ferguson, *Scotland's Relations with England*, 209; Robertson, 'An elusive sovereignty', 205-206). Ferguson's *Limitations* should be regarded as a fundamental 'demand to renegotiate the terms of the existing union' (Robertson, 'An elusive sovereignty', 206).

[124]. Armitage, 'The Scottish vision of empire', 98.

[125]. See Andrew Fletcher of Saltoun, *United and Separate Parliaments*, P.H. Scott (ed), Saltire Society Pamphlets, Number 3, (Edinburgh, 1982); Andrew Fletcher of Saltoun, *Selected Political Writings and Speeches*, D. Daiches (ed), (Edinburgh, 1979).

[126]. See Robertson, 'An elusive sovereignty', 198-227.

[127]. J.A. Downie, 'The Development of the Political Press', in Jones (ed), *Britain in the First Age of Party*, 111-127.

[128]. Goldie, 'Divergence and Union', 241-242. For the role of Daniel Defoe in the union debates, as well as the wider context of his imperial and commercial thinking, see Laurence Dickey, 'Power, commerce and natural law in Daniel Defoe's political writings 1698-1707', in Robertson (ed), *A Union for Empire*, 63-96, and Katherine R. Penovich, 'From "Revolution principles" to Union: Daniel Defoe's intervention in the Scottish debate', in *ibid*, 228-242.

[129]. Glasgow University Library, Special Collections Unit, Ogilvie 954. See also, for example, Glasgow University Library, Special Collections Unit, Ogilvie Q34, *Reasons For An Union Between the Kingdoms of England and Scotland* (London, 1706).

[130]. John Robertson, 'Preface', in Robertson (ed), *A Union for Empire*, xiii-xiv.

[131]. A.I. Macinnes, 'Studying the Scottish Estates and the Treaty of Union', *History Microcomputer Review* (Fall, 1990); Christopher A. Whatley, 'Burns and the Union of 1707', in K. Simpson (ed), *Love and Liberty. Robert Burns: A Bicentenary Celebration* (Edinburgh, 1997), 186-187; Goldie, 'Divergence and Union', 231. See also John Robertson, 'An Elusive Sovereignty. The Course of the Union Debate in Scotland 1698-1707', in Robertson (ed), *A Union for Empire*, 198-227. For a contemporary justification and pragmatic reasoning behind the incorporating union see Clerk of Penicuik's 'Testamentary Memorial concerning The Union of the Two Kingdoms of Scotland & England in 1707 with a short

account of the share Ihad in the settlement of the present Government of Great Britain', written in 1744, in his *History of the Union of Scotland and England*, 182-208.

[132]. Smout, *A History of the Scottish People*, 200.

[133]. *United and Separate Parliaments*, 23.

[134]. *Ibid.*

[135]. *United and Separate Parliaments*, 24.

[136]. Daiches (ed), *Andrew Fletcher of Saltoun. Selected Political Writings and Speeches*, 78.

[137]. *House of Lords Manuscripts*, volume VII (New Series). *The Manuscripts of the House of Lords*, 1706-1708 (London, 1921), 19.

[138]. Kidd, *Subverting Scotland's Past*, 129.

[139]. Robertson, `Empire and Union', 35.

[140]. Ronald M. Sunter, *Patronage and Politics in Scotland 1707-1832* (Edinburgh, 1986); Alexander Murdoch, *The People Above: Politics and Administration in Mid-Eighteenth Century Scotland* (Edinburgh, 1980); Daniel Szechi, `The Hanoverians and Scotland', in Greengrass (ed), *Conquest and Coalescence*, 117; Szechi and Hayton, `John Bull's Other Kingdoms', 241, 248, 253-259.

[141]. Indeed, as Colin Kidd duly notes, the Scottish Parliament had *survived* (my emphasis) `unlike many of the medieval estates of Europe, in the era of rising absolute monarchies (Kidd, *Subverting Scotland's Past*, 129). A federal union in 1707 would clearly have involved further constitutional reform and a strengthening of the Scottish Parliament.

[142]. John Miller, `Britain', in John Miller (ed), *Absolutism in Seventeenth-Century Europe* (London, 1990), 220-221; Michael J. Braddick, *The Nerves of State. Taxation and the financing of the English State, 1558-1714* (Manchester, 1996).

[143]. Archie Duncan and Allan Macinnes, `Scotland's Parliament', *The Sunday Mail Story of Scotland*, 7, (1988), 196.

[144]. John Patrick, `A Union Broken ? Restoration Politics in Scotland', in Jenny Wormald (ed), *Scotland Revisited* (London, 1991), 128.

[145]. Robert Sutherland, `Aspects of the Scottish Constitution prior to 1707', John P. Grant (ed), *Independence and Devolution: The Legal Implications for Scotland* (Edinburgh, 1976), 33.

CHAPTER SEVEN

Caledonia or North Britain?
Scottish Identity in the Eighteenth Century

Richard J. Finlay

The 'long' eighteenth century (c. 1700-c.1830) was a crucial period in the development of Scottish national identity. Three key factors were critical in influencing the ways in which the Scots perceived themselves as a national entity. Firstly, the Scots had to accommodate their national identity to the changed political circumstances following the Treaty of Union in 1707 when the Scottish parliament voted itself out of existence and Scotland ceased to be an independent nation state. From now on Scottish national identity would have to be formulated within the parameters of the emerging British state. Secondly, this was a period which witnessed the gradual emergence of democracy as a political force. Although the age of universal suffrage was some way off in the future, the fact remains that more and more Scots, drawn from different backgrounds, were increasingly influencing the shape of Scottish identity. A third, and closely related, factor was that Scottish national identity was subject to a barrage of changes associated with development of an increasingly commercial and urban society. The forces unleashed by modernization would increasingly gravitate power towards the expanding cities and the wealth accumulated by commercial enterprise. Few periods in Scottish history witnessed such rapidity of change and the Scotland of 1807 was a very different place from the Scotland of 1707. Given that there were such profound cultural, social, economic and political transformations during this period, it should come as no surprise to find that Scottish national identity did not escape unaltered. Yet, in many ways, it is much easier for the historian to chart these impersonal forces of historical change. Few would quibble that Scotland moved from an agrarian to an industrial and commercial economy, that it became increasingly urbanized, that the forces of democracy were increasingly challenging the status quo and that the fundamentalism of seventeenth century religion gave way to the rationalism of the Enlightenment. On this there is little disagreement and little confusion.[1]

Regarding Scottish national identity, however, the picture is not so clear cut. Indeed, the period is characterized by cultural confusion and the historian has a great many varieties of Scottishness and Britishness to choose from. For some, the residue of Scottish identity is deposited in the ideology of

Jacobitism, for others the period is marked by the 'forging' of a British identity based on a common Protestantism, the empire and the fear of invasion from Catholic, continental Europe, and for some there is cultural schizophrenia which oscillates between North Britishness and Caledonianism.[2] Given the myriad of varieties of Scottishness, it is necessary to pause briefly and consider some of the difficulties facing the historian of Scottish national identity in this period. Firstly, it is a period of transition. Somewhere in the eighteenth century, the prerogative of national identity passes from being the narrow preserve of the political elite into a form of common 'national' property. This is not to deny that there had been variants of popular Scottish nationalism before this. It is simply to say that it marks the beginning of a fundamental shift away from identity as confined to a few aristocrats and their intellectual puppets to one which was more popular and embraced more people. As has been remarked earlier in this volume, it is dangerous to throw back our own contemporary definitions of national identity on the past. To expect modern notions of national identity in eighteenth century Scotland is anachronistic. Scotland during this period did not have a modern communications infrastructure, it did not have a centralized system of government and facets of regional and religious identity were probably more significant in the everyday lives of most Scots than the abstract notion of national identity. While many intellectuals did ponder such questions and spilled a great deal of ink in argument, it is questionable to what extent they impacted outside a very narrow circle of the elite and governing classes.[3] While this was undoubtedly significant, it does not by any means provide the justification to claim that such ideas and values were those of the nation as a whole. A second related difficulty is the nature of language. While we all would claim to know what is meant by the expression of 'North Britain', it is not the case that our definition would be the same as the contemporaries who first coined it. In our times the term is politically loaded and has Unionist connotations, but for contemporaries, it was part of a wider experiment to construct a new genuine British identity which would be formed from the two nations of Scotland and England. That it became a by word for Anglicization was not necessarily apparent to the intelligentsia of the Enlightenment, nor would they have recognised it as a problem as many admired the progress and prosperity achieved by English constitutionalism. Finally, we have to rid ourselves of the modern notion that national identity is by its nature a homogenous entity. The fact that there were a plethora of Scottish identities in the eighteenth century is simply a reflection of the complexities of the nature of profound change that was experienced by Scottish society at this time. While the temptation is to look for winners and losers, we must accept that multiple identities are part and parcel of most societies and that the lack of a clear direction in the eighteenth century is normal. Not only was there an increasing British dimension in Scottish identity, there were also many (often competing) varieties of Scottish identity.

The Union and Scottish Identity

In many ways the Union was an inescapable facet of Scottish identity after 1707. Yet, we must be careful of ascribing too much influence to it. Far from being an omni-present feature of Scottish life, the Union barely impinged on the ordinary Scot. Indeed, in the first half of the eighteenth century there were only three major pieces of legislation which had a major impact on Scottish society.[4] The truth of the matter is that life went on much the same as it had always done. The people who governed Scotland were the same, the legal system was the same and the Church maintained its pervasive role in Scottish society. The fact that the term North Britain only comes into common currency in the mid century illustrates that there was a belated need to address the new political realities. The fact that its appearance was several decades after the Union demonstrates that there was no sea change in national perception immediately after 1707. Furthermore, that North Britain had to be constructed by intellectuals again suggests that the notion of Britishness was not one that took root naturally in Scottish society after 1707.

For many historians, economics has dominated the debate as to why the Scots surrendered their political independence. Briefly, it has been claimed that the Scots were bankrupt after the famine of the 1690s and the failure of the Darien scheme and had no alternative to Union in order to survive economically. The Union was a trade off. While the economic determinist argument has been blown out of the water by a generation of political historians who have researched the archives, some persistent hankering after the economic model of union still persists. Yet, the facts speak for themselves. The Union did not witness any dramatic up turn in Scottish economic fortunes in the first half of the eighteenth century, which again shows the minimal impact that the Union had on Scottish society. Furthermore, when the Scottish economy does begin to flourish, the key factors in expansion are due to Scottish initiative and enterprise. In short, the Scottish economy boomed because the Scots made it boom. Also, the economic analysis of the Union is lop sided and only takes account of the Scottish perspective. It does not deal with the one overwhelming fact of the Union in 1707; it happened because the English wanted it to happen. Without English involvement it would never have taken place. Furthermore, given English power and determination, it was not a bargain of equals nor was it in any true sense of the word a negotiated settlement.[5]

Where the Union did have a dramatic and profound impact on Scottish society in the first half of the eighteenth century was in the field of politics and military intervention. The same reasons which had propelled the Union settlement in 1707, namely English security and the Hanovarian succession, were the same factors at work in the British state's response to the Jacobite threat. Whereas the Union had little dramatic impact on Scottish society in the fields of economy, society and culture, it did dramatically exert itself in the British state's response to the threat of Jacobite insurrection. Without doubt, the post Culloden policies for the 'civilization' of the Highlands were the most dramatic and profound expression of the changed political realities induced by the Union in the first half century of the eighteenth century.[6] Whereas the Union may have been little more than a piece of paper in the immediate years after its inception, by 1746 it had evidenced itself as military might. Jacobitism was not a form of Scottish national identity that was acceptable to the British state and steps were taken ruthlessly to remove it from the agenda. In many ways, it is perhaps more appropriate to date the beginning of the Anglo-Scottish Union as a tangible entity from 1746, rather than 1707.

North Britain

The construction of a new British identity was one that was pursued with vigor by Scottish intellectuals, more so than their English colleagues. The reason for this state of affairs is quite simple. Whereas the Union did not represent a fundamental break with the continuity of English history, the same could not be said of Scotland.[7] In short, it was impossible for Scots intellectuals to pretend that things were the same as before. Much debate has been generated as to the origins of the Scottish Enlightenment. While some have endeavoured to explain it as a belated consequence of the Union, most scholars would stress the pre-Union development of the Scottish intellectual tradition as being of paramount importance.[8] While it may be argued that the intellectual frenzy of Enlightenment Scotland was a patriotic response to the loss of nationhood and parliament, it must never be forgotten that the climate in which the intelligentsia operated was determined by the need to defend the political status quo and the aristocratic patronage upon which most intellectuals depended for their livelihood.[9] Although the Enlightenment intelligentsia fomented intellectual revolution, they did not promote political change. Indeed, it was quite the contrary and did much to provide an intellectual vindication of the status quo. If anything, the Scottish aristocracy consolidated their position in Scottish society and perfected an absolute system of management.[10] Through patronage in the universities and the Church, they were able to determine and ensure that the intellectual development of Scotland did not challenge their dominant position. Secondly, patronage was used to ensure the smooth and effective running of the political machine. The collapse of the Scottish parliament meant that power was much more readily concentrated in the hands of the magnates who had access to the Westminster gravy train.[11] Finally, the Scottish aristocracy did not display any conservatism when it came to harnessing the power of economic growth. Indeed, it was this ability to modernize economically which was instrumental in maintaining their pivotal role in Scottish society.[12] Whereas many of the thinkers of the Scottish Enlightenment congratulated the Scots for the progress and liberty which had been attained by Scotland joining the Union, the reality was that eighteenth century Scotland was not a liberal society by any stretch of the imagination, as Whig intellectuals were only too keen to point out in the early nineteenth century. The Enlightenment in Scotland rested on the most unenlightened foundation of a corrupt system of patronage which permeated the whole of society.

All of this leads to the question; what were the Scottish intelligentsia trying to achieve by the creation of a North British identity? With hindsight, it is too easy to assume that it was nothing more than Anglicization. Endeavours to create a genuine Whig, Scoto-British identity were hampered by an intellectual civil war in which Whig and Jacobite historians in Scotland decimated each others arguments.[13] It would appear that Jacobite military weakness was not reflected in its intellectual endeavours. Father Thomas Innes ruthlessly destroyed the Whig version of Scottish history which claimed that constitutionalism was an inherent part of the nation's past. Increasingly, Whigs in Scotland called upon the reinforcements of English historical experience to bolster their claims and in doing so constructed an inferiorist vision of Scottish history which offered little example to posterity. In future, economic growth, modernity, and constitutional propriety were best served by following an English model and many Scottish intellectual disowned the nation's past. The collapse of the distinctive Scottish debate on political ideology by the latter part of the eighteenth century may have been a factor in explaining the apparent ease with which political management asserted its influence over the Scottish political system. Few could claim that eighteenth century Scottish politicians were ideological animals who were motivated by principle.[14]

There was a head long rush to divest the nation of its previous 'barbarisms'. The Highlands were an embarrassment to any civilized nation and efforts were made to Presbyterians and modernize those who had ungratefully rejected the benefits of British constitutionalism in 1745.[15] Polite society endeavoured to rid itself of Scots barbarisms in language.[16] Fanatical Presbyterianism was held at arms length and Scottish intellectuals, with some degree of success it must be said, endeavoured to project themselves to the centre of a London oriented culture.[17] Yet, British uniformity remained elusive as ever. Some, such as MacPherson, attempted to mold the residues of Gaelic culture into the heroic epic which might appeal to a gentile audience.[18] Indigenous Scottish culture still held a fascination for many and was not rejected.[19] Finally, the real stumbling block faced by the Scots intelligentsia was that they could not overturn centuries of ingrained anti-Scottishness which was endemic in English society.

Many commentators have noted that in spite of their best efforts, Scots suffered great prejudice in England with some furious outbursts of Scottophobia in the mid-eighteenth century.[20] It was a source of great regret and painful consternation that this rejection of the North British ideal should be so public. More than anything, the failure of the North Britain was due to English reluctance to part with their national identity. Linda Colley has explained the savage anti-Scottish outbursts of the radical John Wilkes and his followers as evidence of the growing success of the British nation. After all, it is argued, Scots were prominent in public life and had made great commercial inroads into the burgeoning empire and many held important state office. Popular English reaction was little more than base prejudice, flamed by rabble rousers and spiced with a hint of jealousy. In short, it was little more than minor teething problems associated with the expansion of the British state.[21] While the claims of Wilkes and his followers may seem a little over the top from today's perspective, there was more than an element of truth in their claims. The Scots were denounced as being either tyrants or servile lackeys and as such were a danger to English liberty. Yet, the English experience would appear to bear this out. After all, the Jacobite threat was explained as originating in a land in which the despotic leaders could command their clansmen to follow them into battle. Much of this propaganda and the explanation of Jacobite support in Scotland, it has to be remembered, was put about by the Scots themselves who claimed that the ignorant heathen Highlanders did not know any better.[22] The nuances of the Highland Lowland divide did not percolate down to the London mob, but the one which did was the savage Highlander who became representative of the Scots as a whole. After all, in the panic stricken days of the '45, they were the one who mattered most because they were the ones who invaded England to depose the English of their liberties.[23] The behaviour of Scottish politicians and MPs after the rebellion did nothing to enhance the reputation of the Scots. The notion that the Scots were servile creatures who followed autocrats was borne out by the experience of Scottish politics in Westminster where MPs fell over themselves in order to curry favour from the Scotch managers who invariably managed to ingratiate themselves with the government. In short, they were not a good advert in defence of traditional English liberty.

The Scots could not remove such stigmas. There was outrage at the refusal to allow a Scottish militia. It was feared that to do so would arm Scots whose loyalty was questionable. This offended many in the Scottish establishment who argued that a militia was one way of guaranteeing a virtuous society. Although the Scottish intelligentsia may have ditched their history, the English governing classes had not forgotten the lessons served by it.[24] It was a very public slap in the face to the notion that the Scots were equal citizens in the new British experiment.

Given the indifference, if not open hostility, of many English to the North British project, it should come as no surprise to find that many Scots tended towards cultural schizophrenia. Side by side with handbooks on how to avoid Scottisicims and a craze for elocution lessons, there were frequent outbursts of Scottish patriotism. Collections of Scottish historical documents, poetry and other cultural artifacts reinforced notions of Caledonianism. The vernacular poetry of Ramsay, Ferguson and Burns had great appeal and even when contributing to the North British experiment, Scottish intellects appear to have been conscious of the peculiarities of their own nation's endeavours.[25] While this feature of Scottish cultural life has a long pedigree and has been noted by many commentators as an inherent weakness within the Scottish psyche, others have been less judgmental. Chris Smout, for example, argues that this is not so much evidence of cultural schizophrenia, but rather symptomatic of the dual loyalties held by many Scots. The notion of concentric loyalty, that is that the Scots could be loyal to both Scotland and Britain without any sense of contradiction and conflict, does have a great deal to recommend it. After all, while Scots could be fiercely patriotic to their history, culture and community, they could also be loyal to the British monarchy, the British constitution and the British Empire without any sense of contradiction.[26]

Yet, some difficulties remain. Firstly, there is the problem of hindsight. The fact that concentric loyalties developed in Scotland does not mean to say that this was by design. Indeed, the ideas concerning North Britain tend towards the creation of a British identity which was not compartmentalized into its Scottish and English components. Also, the principal determinant of making Scottishness appear was English rejection. This duality most clearly exposed itself when there was a conflict of Scottishness and Britishness. As Boswell put it in 1762 when the London mob hissed two Scots soldiers: 'I hated the English; I wished from my soul that the Union was broke and that we might give them another Bannockburn.' [27] In short Scottish identity surfaced when British identity or English identity is denied. Finally, the fact that the Scots took advantage of British institutions does not necessarily imply a strong commitment to a British identity. The opportunities of the British Empire, for example, simply enabled the Scots to get on and make money. Britishness, if anything was conditioned more by pragmatic reasons, rather than notions of national sentiment. Indeed, the clannishness of Scots in the Empire tends to suggest that their Scottishness was of paramount importance.[28]

Britons?

Before considering this question, it is necessary to remember that the North British experiment was a failure. Scotland was not subsumed into a uniform British identity and the Scots emerged in the nineteenth century attached to a whole range of symbolic representations of Scotland, most of which belonged to the Highlands. It short, Highlandized Scotland was almost as different as it was possible to be from England. Yet, for many, the period from 1707 to 1837 when Queen Victoria acceded to the throne was the crucible in which Britain as a nation with a national identity was forged. The principal proponent of this view is Linda Colley who argues that a shared monarchy, economy, wars and Protestantism welded Britons together in opposition to the 'other' of continental, Catholic Europe.[29] Throughout the eighteenth century, it is argued, the Scots, English and Welsh (the Irish are curiously missed out of the equation), increasingly became wedded to the notion of Britain as a nation. Scots businessmen flourished within the confines of the British state and empire, Scottish politicians acted on the British political stage, intellectuals and writers targeted their endeavours to a British audience, Scottish soldiers and generals fought for Britain and the British populace came increasingly to identify with British symbols and institutions through public demonstrations of loyalty.

   Yet, we must be careful. Firstly, was this British identity a national identity or was it an identity confined to the upper reaches of society? In short, was it an elite identity as opposed to a national identity? It is all very well to talk of a process of Britification, but how far down did it go? This is essential given that the function of national identity is one that must by its very nature and definition encompass a significant proportion of the people. True, businessmen, imperial administrators, generals, politicians and intellectuals may have identified with British identity, but does that constitute a national identity? It is somewhat akin to saying that a European national identity exists today because the upper echelons of Scottish society have an intellectual affinity to the concept of a unified Europe. Furthermore, although such groups may have used the auspices and opportunities of the British state its does not necessarily imply a commitment to Britain as an national entity. Again, we can draw parallels with the European experience of our own times. Does the fact that politicians, businessmen and others take advantage of the opportunities of Europe mean that they are committed to Europe as a national entity? While many Scots were keen to take advantage of the opportunities of the British state it does not mean that they had to compromise their essence of national identity to do so, nor did they need to construct a new identity as part and parcel of the development of the British state.

What evidence exists, suggest that there was a marked ambiguity lower down the social scale when it comes to British identity. Furthermore, the key proponents of British identity in Scotland were more intent on persuading each other of their North British identity that their fellow Scots lower down the social scale. Popular literature was focused mainly on Scottish issues.[30] The survival of the Scots language, the vibrancy of the Scottish Church and popular Presbyterianism, together with popular culture and the minimal impact of the British state on the lives of most Scots suggests that there was an alternative vision of Scottish and more importantly regional identity which largely remained untouched by high flying notions of Britain.[31]

Religion is central to the argument of a common sense of British identity, yet, the Scottish experience tends to fly in the face of this assertion. While the period is characterized by a top down imposition of moderatism on the Church of Scotland, the issue of patronage remained a running sore which would ultimately culminate in the Disruption of 1843.[32] Evangelicalism within the Church of Scotland, the growth of dissent and the persistence of patronage disputes all show that, far from a common sense of Protestantism developing in Britain, it was a major source of division.[33] Furthermore, those campaigning against patronage, both from within and without the Church of Scotland, tended to be drawn from the new commercial middle-class which was the group most likely to benefit from the growth of commerce in the shared British economy.[34] Also, the fact that it was the elites which attempted to introduce Catholic toleration in the 1780s tends to fly in the face of anti-Catholicism being a unifying force in British society.[35] Indeed, the widespread rioting in Scotland which accompanied the attempted introduction tends to suggest that religious differences permeated relationships between the upper and lower orders.[36] For many Scots, Catholic toleration was a betrayal of their *national* religious inheritance. Also, the Napoleonic Wars, which were arguably the greatest spur to British unity, was not against a Catholic 'other', but a Godless tyranny.[37]

Perhaps the most popular and enduring argument which is used to explain the success of the Union is the economic benefits which accrued to Scotland. As we have seen, the Scottish economy remained relatively stagnant in the first half of the eighteenth century. Also, the key determinant of Scottish economic success thereafter was not due to any intrinsic feature of the Union. As Tom Devine has pointed out, the Union had both opportunities and risks and it was by no means certain that the opportunities would automatically flow on tap. The example of Ireland provides a warning to a simple deterministic interpretation of the benefits of Union. Rather, the key factor in Scottish economic success was the response of Scots to those opportunities and the fact that there was entrepreneurial dynamism on the ground.[38] As has been mentioned earlier, even within the empire, which was surely the most British of institutions, the tendency was for the Scots to group together in a clannish fashion.

The notion that war bonded the Scots to the British state and empire is also likewise problematic. As we have seen, the Militia campaign of the mid-eighteenth century revealed that the Scots were at this juncture denied access to notions of British military prowess. Furthermore, given the strongly local flavour of military recruitment, not only in Scotland, but elsewhere in the British Isles, factors of regional identity probably weighed more heavily. This is especially the case in the Highlands where coercion was used as a key feature in recruitment.[39] In any case, militarism in Scotland drew heavily upon perceived Scottish martial traditions, especially with regard to the Highland soldier.[40] If anything, British wars in the eighteenth century reinforced the distinctiveness of the Scottish military caste. The same can be said for monarchism. The crown was absent from Scottish society until 1822 and when George IV appeared, it was as the tartan clad 'chief of chiefs'.[41] Popular demonstrations were also supposed to be a vehicle of British identity, but the most enduring occasion in Scotland was the King's Birthday, which resembled more of a riot rather than a celebration.[42] Finally, the centenary of the Union in 1807 passed off without comment. Surely, if Britishness was firmly entrenched in Scotland, then this should have been an occasion of great celebration and rejoicing.

The Collapse of North Britain and the Reinvention of Scotland
At the end of the day, the idea of North Britain proved little more than an academic exercise and a point often lost on many historians is that it failed to produce a homogenous sense of British identity. Instead, Britain was a

composite of its English, Scottish, Irish and Welsh elements. By the early nineteenth century Scottish national identity increasingly focused on an exclusive set of Scottish symbols. The Highlandization of Scottish culture and the celebration of rural values was largely a middle-class response to the demand for nostalgia in an increasingly urbanized and industrialized society. The key components of British identity in Scotland had a distinctive tartan complexion. Monarchism was associated with the tartan clad George IV or the Balmoralized Queen Victoria. The army in Scotland became more and more Highlandized, the Empire became a vehicle for the expression of Scottish values, culture revolved around the romantic depiction of Scotland in the past, politics had a vital Scottish dimension and although religion was a source of division, it was characterized by competing claims that each faction represented the true 'national' Scottish church. In view of this, it should come as no surprise that in the mid-nineteenth century when, in response to the evils of urbanization and modernization, the National Association for the Vindication of Scottish Rights appeared it proclaimed its fears for the future of Scottish identity which it argued was in danger of erosion. The National Association was like other anti-modernist groups which sprang up in Europe in response to the growth of urbanization and industrialization and the fact that it appeared in Scotland promoting the defence of Scottish identity is perhaps the best illustration that the roots of British identity at this time were very shallow indeed.[43]

NOTES

[1] See T .M. Devine and R. Mitchison (eds), *People and Society, 1750-1830* (Edinburgh, 1988); T. M. Devine, *The Transformation of Rural Scotland* (Edinburgh, 1994); T. M. Devine (ed), *Conflict and Stability, 1700-1850*, (Edinburgh, 1990); E. Macfarland, *Scotland and Ireland in the Age of Revolution*, (Edinburgh, 1995); T.M. Devine and J. R. Young (eds), *New Perspectives on Eighteenth Century Scotland* (forthcoming).
[2] See M. Pittock, *The Invention of Scotland: Stuart Myth and Scottish Identity, 1638 to the Present* (London, 1991); L. Colley, *Britons: Forging the Nation, 1707-1837* (Yale, 1992); T. C. Smout, 'Problems of Nationalism, Identity and Improvement in late Eighteenth Century Scotland' in T.M. Devine, *Improvement and Enlightenment* (Edinburgh, 1989) 1-22; K. Simpson, *The Protean Scot: The Crisis of Identity in Eighteenth Century Scottish Literature*, (Aberdeen 1988); D. Daiches, *The Paradox of Scottish Culture: The Eighteenth Century Experience*, (Oxford, 1964); J.A. Smith, 'Some Eighteenth Century Ideas of Scotland' in N. Philipson and R. Mitchison (eds), *Scotland in the Age of Improvement*, (Edinburgh, 1970), 107-25.

[3] On the ideas of the Scottish intellectual community in the eighteenth century see C. Kidd, *Subverting Scotland's Past: Scottish Whig Historians and the Creation of an Anglo British Identity, 1698-c. 1830*, (Cambridge 1993); J. Robertson, *The Scottish Enlightenment and the Militia Issue*, (Edinburgh, 1985); J. Dwyer, *Virtuous Discourse: Sensibility and Community in Eighteenth Century Scotland*, (Edinburgh, 1987); R. Sher, *Church and University in the Scottish Enlightenment: The Moderate Literati of Edinburgh*, (Edinburgh, 1985); D. Allan, *Virtue, Learning and the Scottish Enlightenment*, (Edinburgh, 1993); N.T. Phillipson, 'Politics, Politeness and the Anglisisation of Early Eighteenth Century Scottish Culture', in R. A. Mason (ed), *Scotland and England, 1286-1815*, (Edinburgh, 1987) 226-46; N. T. Phillipson, ''The Scottish Enlightenment', in R. Porter & M. Teich (eds), *The Enlightenment in its National Context*, (Cambridge, 1981), 19-40; J. Dwyer and R. Sher (eds), *Sociability and Society in Eighteenth Century Scotland*, (Edinburgh, 1993).

[4] See T. M. Devine, 'The Union of 1707 and Scottish Development', *Scottish Economic and Social History*, 5 (1985).

[5] *ibid.;* J. R. Young, 'The Union of 1707' in Devine and Young (eds), *New Perspectives.*

[6] See A. I. Macinnes, *Clanship, Commerce and the House of Stuart, 1607-1788* (East Linton, 1996), 188-247; R. Clyde, *From Rebel to Hero:The Image of the Highlander, 1745-1830*, (East Linton, 1995), 49-97.

[7] See Kidd, *Subverting Scotland's Past*, 73.

[8] See David Allen, *Virtue and Learning.*

[9] See N. T. Philipson, 'Public Opinion and the Union in the Age of Association' in Phillipson and Mitchison (eds), *Scotland in the Age of* Improvement, 125-48; and Sher, *The Church and University*, 93-120.

[10] See J. Shaw, *The Management of Scottish Society, 1707-64*, (Edinburgh, 1983), A. Murdoch, *The People Above: Politics and Administration in Mid-Eighteenth Century Scotland*, (Edinburgh, 1980); R. Sunter, *Patronage and Politics in Scotland, 1707-1832*, (Edinburgh, 1986); William Feguson, 'Dingwall Burgh Politics and the Parliamentary Franchise in the Eighteenth Century', *Scottish Historical Review*, 38 (1959), and M. Fry, *The Dundas Despotism*, (Edinburgh, 1992).

[11] See J.Simpson, 'Who Steered the Gravy Train, 1707-1766?' in Philipson and Mitchison (eds), *Scotland in the Age of Improvement*, 47-73.

[12] See Devine, *Transformation of Rural Scotland.*

[13] See Kidd, *Subvering Scotland's Past*, 101-65.

[14] See Sunter, *Patronage and Politics.*

[15] Clyde, *From Rebel to Hero*, 49-97.

[16] Diaches, *Paradox of Scottish Culture*, 20-1.

[17] Mary Jane Scott, 'James Thomson and the Anglo Scots', in A. Hook (ed), *The History of Scottish Literature, Volume 2, 1660-1800*, (Aberdeen, 1987), 81-101; Simpson, *Protean Scot*, 70-97.

[18] See H. Gaskill (ed), *Ossian Revisited* (Edinburgh, 1991).

[19] See K. Simpson, *Protean Scot,* esp. 185-219; Iain G. Brown, 'Modern Rome and Ancient Caledonia: The Union and the Politics of Scottish Culture', and A. M. Kinghorn and A. Law, 'Allan Ramsay and Literary Life in the First Half of the Eighteenth Century' in Hook (ed), *History of Scottish Literature.*

[20] See L. Colley, *Britons,* 105-117, J. Brewer, 'The Misfortunes of Lord Bute', *Historical Journal,* 16 (1973) and P. Womack, *Improvement and Romance: Constructing the Myth of the Highlands,* (London, 1989).

[21] Colley, *Britons,* 125.

[22] Clyde, *Rebel to Hero,* 1-20.

[23] R. Harris, 'England's Provincial Newspapers and the Jacobite Rebellion 1745-6', *History,* 80 (1995), 5-21.

[24] Robertson, *The Scottish Enlightenment and the Militia Issue;* Smout, 'Problems of Nationalism', Sher, *Church and University,* 215-36.

[25] Sher, *Church and University,* 214.

[26] Smout, ' Problems of Nationalism'.

[27] See Smith, 'Eighteenth Century Ideas of Scotland' and Simpson. *Protean Scot,* 1-14, for examples.

[28] See Fry, *Dundas Despotism,* 99-155.

[29] Colley, *Britons,* .

[30] M. Pittock, *Inventing and Resisting Britain: Cultural Identities in Britain and Ireland, 1685-1789,* (London, 1996); J. Brims, 'The Scottish Jacobins, Scottish Nationalism and the British Union', in R. Mason, *Scotland and England, 1286-1815,* (Edinburgh, 1987), 254.

[31] See R. J. Finlay, 'Keeping the Covenant: Scottish National Identity in the Eighteenth Century', in Devine and Young (ed), *New Perspectives.*

[32] See A.L. Drummond and J. Bulloch, *The Scottish Church 1688-1843,* (Edinburgh, 1973), 59-61, 138-40, 223-39; R.B. Sher, 'Moderates, Managers and Popular politics in Mid-Eighteenth century Edinburgh: The Drysdale 'Bustle' of the 1760s', in J. Dwyer, R. Mason & A. Murdoch (eds), *New Perspectives on the Politics and Culture of Early Modern Scotland,* (Edinburgh, n.d.) 179-210; Callum G. Brown, 'Protest in the Pews. Interpreting Presbyterianism and Society in Fracture During the Scottish Economic Revolution', in Devine (ed), *Conflict and Stability,* 83-106.

[33] C. Brown, *A Social History of Religion in Scotland Since 1730,* (London, 1987), 22-57.

[34] *ibid,* 57-89.

[35] I am grateful to Colin Kidd for this point. See his 'Sentiment, race and revival: Scottish identities in the aftermath of Enlightenment' in Laurence Brockliss and David Eastwood (eds), *A Union of multiple Identities: The British Isles c. 1750-1850,* (Manchester, 1997), 110-126.

[36] Finlay, 'Keeping the Covenant'; Sher, *Church and University in the Scottish Enlightenment,* 277-97.

[37] H. T. Dickinson, 'The Impact on Britain of the French Revolution and the French Wars, 1789-1815' in H. T. Dickinson (ed), *Britain and the French Revolution, 1789-1815*, (London, 1989), 17-19.

[38] Devine, 'The Union of 1707 and Scottish Development'; Fry, *Dundas Despotism*.

[39] I am grateful to A. MacKillop for this point. See his 1996 Glasgow University PhD, 'Military Recruiting in the Scottish Highlands, 1739-1815: The Political, Social and Economic Context'.

[40] Clyde, *Rebel to Hero*, 150-81.

[41] J. Prebble, *The King's Jaunt: George IV in Scotland*, (London, 1988).

[42] C. Whatley, 'Royal Day, People's Day: The Monarch's Birthday in Scotland, *c.*1660-1860' in R. Mason & N. Macdougall (eds), *People and Power in Scotland: Essays in Honour of T.C. Smout*, (Edinburgh, 1993).

[43] See R. J. Finlay, *A Partnership for Good? Scottish Politics and the Union Since 1880*, (Edinburgh, 1997), 15-25.

CHAPTER EIGHT

What if?: The Significance of Scotland's Missing Nationalism in the Nineteenth Century

Graeme Morton

What if national identity in nineteenth century Scotland was not a problem? What if it was the *real thing* that fitted neatly into the category of a *Risorgimento* or matched other bourgeois nationalisms more usually found lurking in the shadows of the Dark Gods of Europe? It need not be ideal, but what if Scotland's nationalism actually fitted? Would this chapter and indeed this book need to be written at all? Could it have been replaced by any one of the many standard textbooks or Readers on nationalism and would we then find Scottish nationalism receiving its fair share of index citations?

But this is mere wishing for a quiet life! Scotland's nationalism has been a problem because it has been 'missing' and citations on this stateless nation are rare and without doubt this topic (and so this book) remains worthy of attention. So, if there is no immediate solace, does this mean that the problem is insurmountable and Scotland's failure is complete and *that* is its pigeon-hole? Or does it mean something else? Could it be that Scotland had a national identity and a nationalism of a sort that only now an analysis has been found to do justice to the historical evidence? What if Scottish nationalism in the nineteenth century is more important than a plea to fulfil the usual criteria? What if Scottish nationalism was an early example of what has come to be called 'civic' nationalism? What if the only nationalism missing in Scotland was of an 'ethnic' variety and so Scotland, rather than being late for the party, is from its nineteenth century history an early example of the future of nationalism? What if...?

What if it is time for historians to propose a new sobriquet for the nineteenth century? How *do* you place a handle it? Eric Hobsbawm is one who has offered a range of *Ages*[1], but what Britain did not have, and Scotland in particular, was the 'age of nationalism'. Scotland in this period, and Scotland's national identity, has also gained a not insignificant reputation - one that maintains a strong resonance in the twentieth century. Scotland somewhat disappoints domestically, certainly as far as nationalists are concerned. Scots are good at emigrating and doing well when they get there. They had always been successful throughout the empire and governing the United Kingdom through the Imperial Parliament was never beyond reach.

Yet, there is a perception that somehow Scotland became less Scottish at home. The term North Britain smacked of Anglicisation and of belittling by its larger neighbour. Today it is the Union of 1707 which is blamed for the encouragement of Anglicisation by 'bribing the Scots to eschew nationalism...'[2] But this is a reflection where the nineteenth century is the mirror: the age of equipoise, of Balmoral, of kailyard of cultural but not political nationalism.

In many ways the student of nationalism in Scotland is not helped by the tools available to do the job. The search for a universal theory has proved increasingly fruitless, and the discipline remains fragmented into communicative, elitist, modernist and ethnic theories (to name but a few).[3] This is despite a convergence between those who regard the nation-state and nationalism as inherently modern - an invention of the late eighteenth century - and those who stress the ethnic sentiment which all 'nation-states' use to legitimate their existence. Yet Scotland's pre-modern identity (with the Declaration of Arbroath in 1320 at its pinnacle) has not become the 'blood and belonging' of ethnic cleansing or genocide or xenophobia or emancipation characteristic of modern nationalisms.[4] The problem has been that Scottish nationalism 'did nothing at the right time'.[5] Right in part, Steve Bruce argues that 'if Scotland's intellectuals in the 19th century had wanted to promote Scottish nationalism, they would have been unable to do so. The real world prevented them.' But then he falls for the orthodoxy of purity, a condition quite unachievable. He argues that this was the result of the 'absence of pre-existing community, imagined in ethnic, religious or linguistic terms, or the absence of economic, political or material pressure sufficient to overcome internal divisions...' necessary to create a nation.[6] But this is too dismissive and too tight a stricture: there are many other versions of nationalism which are not products of, or claimants of, an ethnically and politically homogeneous nation-state.

The political Union between Scotland and England was not imposed at knife point despite the acknowledged bribery and corruption. The best summary of the process comes from Whatley who concludes that it was no *diktat* but an example of early modern *realpolitik*.[7] It was an incorporating Union and it was relatively early in the history of nation-making in Europe. The Union created Great Britain before this new state-nation faced the revolutions of 1776, 1789 and the 1840s, and this timing has proved to be remarkably significant. As Halévy comments on the Chartist uprisings of 1848, 'although the Committee appointed by the House of Commons to inquire into the causes of the crisis sat from January till June, not a single allusion to the European revolution can be found in its proceedings.'[8] No matter how resolute the efforts by commentators, there is immense difficulty incorporating Scotland into the general models of nationalism because of the lack of congruence between nation and state immediately prior to and subsequent to these historical ages. That is, theorists find it difficult to deal with nationalist rhetoric or symbolism that does not have a clear enemy or have an unambiguous notion of the singular state to be.

Nor had Scottish nationalism in the nineteenth century much of a parliamentary or state focus, certainly not in comparison with the centuries which bounded it. The eighteenth century had its anti-Union riots, most notably at Edinburgh under the gaze of Daniel Defoe and in Glasgow and Dumfries.[9] It had abortive Jacobite uprisings in 1708 and 1719 as well as the two main events of 1715 and 1745. The benefits of Union were never likely to be immediate, with more costs than gains in the first half of the century. In 1715 Scotland's loss of power to change its affairs was mourned: 'If the English had a mind to dissolve the Union, they can command their own Times and Seasons; but the Scotch must labour this Point, through many Difficulties from Abroad.'[10] The two full-blooded Jacobite uprisings and Charles Edward Stuart's defeat at Culloden in 1746 and the subsequent disarming legislation caused the Scots' national psyche to shudder then and since. In the first half of the eighteenth century Hanoverian Britain 'teetered on the brink of potentially lethal violence at least once every decade'.[11] The end of the nineteenth century was also more active - it saw political nationalism of a sort that had appeared in Ireland, and even to a certain extent in Wales, fifty years earlier: but at last Scottish nationalists seemed to have found their political voice. National identity had become proper national*ism*, the -ism of course meaning politically active. Home Rule for Ireland was the political scheme which rekindled national sentiment as a motivating force in politics, but in Scotland it lacked the bite of recent supporting action - of recent pre-history - to give it the necessary legitimacy for its own parliament to be a demand or a progression.

Despite a weakness of party political machinery to mobilise this nationalism, there is enough evidence of national sentiment in the nineteenth century which demonstrates that the Scots were not unaware of the question 'who are we?'. Nor has it been ignored by historians, but they remain uneasy with it. Part of the problem has been a heuristic one: between unionist and nationalist. Whose parameters should hold? Debates have raged, especially over the economic benefits of Union, to the extent that it is now a 'largely artificial exercise which is ultimately subjective rather than scientific.'[12] Yet this range of evidence is represented as something that if not culturally infirm, it is assumed to be the acceptance of Britishness or the coexistence of

Scottishness and Britishness as equals of 'noisy inaction' or 'romantic radicalism'.[13]   Thus John Brown pandering to Victoria's creation of Balmoralism in memory of Albert, or Patrick Geddes shaping the infrastructure of the British empire are the two sides to this coin. Yet still the view persists here: are these arguments really no more than manifestations of a Scottish national identity rather than its explanation?

Perhaps Scotland was in fact expressing a form of nationalism *before* its time? What if the Scots maintained their Scottishness through civil society in the age of modernity a century and more before (Eastern) Europe discovered it in the late twentieth century? What if Scotland's nationalism had embraced the types of national identity which are taken as the norm in the late twentieth century? Something that has come to be called 'civic nationalism' and is linked to prescriptive associations and charitable bodies set up in recent decades and whose aim is to spread 'democracy'?[14] Nationalism need not be particularistic or exclusivist, but it is an idea at the heart of which is the nation.[15] If the nation, then, is an imagination, can we expect the same of its 'government' (its 'state')? What if Scots in the nineteenth century located both in their civil society? What if...?

These questions are not just idle speculations from the vantage point of historical reflection. They can be posed in the firm knowledge that Scotland was forced to re-invent its national identity again and again. Earlier than probably all comparable nations, Scotland was forced to protect what had been relatively unproblematic and to sustain it throughout the European ages of nationalism without its own state to foster and to direct it. This is unlike England which could turn the 'sceptr'd isle' of Shakespeare into the patriotism of inter-state warfare[16], particularly in the nineteenth century.[17] England/Britain and Scotland/Britain were state formations: the patriotism of everyday loyalty to the monarch and her armed forces, the church and the Imperial Parliament. But as we look back on recent events in the 'liberated' nations of Czechoslovakia and Georgia we note that they have achieved what Scotland (as a singular identity) has had to do since 1707: exploit mechanisms other than the state to maintain national identity; these mechanisms have been embodied in that catch-all phrase 'civil society'. It is the gap between state and civil society, identified so importantly by Tom Nairn, which is the key to this creation.[18] By leaving Scotland effectively to propose its own solutions, the British state was importantly distant from Scottish life. This 'gap' legitimated Scottish civil society and empowered it in a way many new nationalisms in the late twentieth century have literally died for. It created a dual identity of Scottishness and Britishness which sat astride notions of multiple identity (from family, to kin, to supranational organisations for example.)[19] Often observed by commentators, this duality has allowed great intricacy and complexity in the Scottish identity.[20] Its power, perhaps to injure fatally a recently popular term, is in the 'banality of duality': the 'gap' allowed Scottish civil society to maintain a national identity in the institutions of everyday life of Scottishness *and* Britishness in a way believed only to exist in ('singular') core state-nations such as England/Britain and the United States of America.[21] But stateless nations have banal nationalism too; it tends to be found in civil society.

Scotland, more than most nations, can lay claim to the origins of civil society - at least in terms of its development in intellectual thought. Adam Ferguson's *An Essay on the History of Civil Society* published in 1767 explored the liberties secured by law and regular and legitimate government, but also the dangers from the injustices it can cause.[22] An understanding of civil society has changed dramatically over time. The main transformation has been from an institution coterminous with the state as a 'political society' of Locke's 'Civil Government' to a nineteenth century sense of civil society existing outwith the state and indeed acting as both a legitimating balance to it and a means of avoiding despotism and tyranny.[23] The sustaining social structure of civil society is popular civic consciousness and civic virtue, and much of this is built around Tocqueville's notion of 'the art of association' maintaining a 'political society' independent from the state for its direction.[24] In his observations the cultivation of the value of citizenship through the process of local and associational democracy allows society to 'counteract the centrifugal impetus of democratic centralism.'[25]

This contemporary observation is the guide which insists that the idea of civil society is an important one and one in need of close empirical study; but such detail is often absent, although its assumed importance is without doubt. One recent commentator restates the outcome of 1707 thus: "The Scots negotiators were less concerned with keeping their weak parliament, which had never attained the status of its English counterpart, than with retaining their institutions of civil society'.[26] Or the injustice to McCrone's sociological understanding of running Scotland as a civil society too readily reduced to meaning 'its own legal, religious and educational systems' by commentators whose primary concern is elsewhere.[27] Chanting the mantra which is the 'holy trinity' of kirk, law and education is not enough.[28] It is a short-hand certainly for pointing out that Scotland was not conquered, that both sides lost their Parliaments, and that Scottish society was not simply abolished by edict. For commentators the role of this rhetoric has been to construct the nation and to maintain the nation as the natural division of society.[29] But it is a different exercise in social construction to make the (next) step to imagining the nation-state. To many observers civil society appears to have given Scotland its head, but not its head of state. We then find Scotland was not England, *because of its civil society* (not defined). It had a different sense of national identity because ... Is it therefore so very strange that its nationalism failed? No, that is because ...

At its most straightforward, civil society is the social structure which exists between the household and the state and it is an arena where extensive and intricate association can take place without personal obligation.[30] What obligation there is, comes from a sense of civic virtue. It was the double separateness of Scottish civil society from the British state and the formal institutions of Scottish administration which gives it its importance to our study. It is at that point that a dual national identity is sustained. This then leads to the question, what if there really was nationalism that developed out of this duality? What is the evidence and is it really mere political acquiescence or cultural infirmity? What are we to make of the manifestations of Scottish national identity?

The first is the widely touted argument that Scotland expressed its national identity through its vigorous role in the economic opportunities of the British empire. The 'insidiousness' of the language of imperialism can be found in all important events and ceremonies in Scotland's civic and cultural life at this time.[31] The skilled working class were at the forefront of this self-promotion.[32] Linda Colley has set up the warring and the trading of empire as a fundamental plank in the forging of the Britons within a Protestant calling.[33] Without doubt these arguments are important manifestations of Scottishness in this 'missing' century, although the empire was of course an identity of the British state and the British monarchy. Thus Peter Scott has argued that the Empire as a plank of nationalism stems only from 1707 and is therefore embedded deeper into Great Britain, than it is in Scotland, Wales and England.[34]

There was no alternative for Scots than to regale themselves in Britishness when focusing their identity through Empire. A Scottish accent to this symbolism was appropriate and indeed uplifting, as David Livingstone more than any other projected to his home nation: 'inescapably a working class Scot, who energised Englishmen and impacted on British governments.'[35] In popular consciousness Scots made the empire flourish.[36] 'Even within the Commonwealth itself the best ambassador for England has always been the Scot. For Scotland, an outlying part of the same Island, has never been insular in quite the same degree as England.'[37] But this was still without doubt a nationalism of the British state and since Scotland was a part of this unitary state, it remained unequivocally attached. Now, is this Scottish nationalism? It was high politics, but in a singularly British not a Scottish sense. The answer must be 'yes', because it was there and we know it was there; we can't wish that it was something else, namely the actions of a Scottish state acting on behalf of a Scottish nation within the British empire. Until the end of this period Scots rarely called for their lost Parliament to be recalled or for a new federal structure to be put in place, and this was the case until the issue of Home Rule was ignited by the 'problem' of Ireland in the 1880s.[38]

Culturally, too, there was no little lack of reflection on Scotland throughout this century and a range of examples can be found whenever a toe is dipped somewhat randomly into the archive. To take some examples: in the first decade of the century Sir William Wallace and then Charles Edward Stuart were portrayed as great inspirations to the Scots, but also to the British nation. The poetry celebrating Sir William Wallace which was composed in the first decades of the century concentrated either on Wallace's exploits against the Southern foe or, in the second extract, his and the Stuarts' role in promoting the ultimate success of a Protestant and Hanovarian Britain:

FIRST
"Thou Sword of true valour! tho' dim by thy hue,
And all faded thy flashes of light
yet still my mem'ry thy sight shall renew
The remembrance of WALLACE that night![39]

Tho' thou gleam not around the mountains of stain
As when sternly in battle he stood;
When he strew'd the bold Southern in heaps o'er the plain
And quench'd thy deep radiance in blood!

SECOND
When Neptune gently wafted o'er
King William to Britannia's shore
For him they strove, great hardships bore
With Resolution
No mortals did so much adore
The Revolution

(...)

In the years fifteen and forty-five
With patriotic flame alive
Did they at Stirling, Falkirk strive

Envince their zeal
Before them Charlie's warriors drive
For Britain's weal.[40]

The second extract in particular indicates at a more populist level what has been shown for the intellectual Whigs of the second half of the eighteenth century and into the nineteenth century. Namely, the pervasive influence of notions of essentially English constitutionalism to Scottish national identity.[41] These were historic English traditions but presented as British ones. From this the argument could be sustained by contemporaries that a fresh start was being made and a fresh identity was being created.[42] This was an important part of the explanation for why the doctrine of revolution was not embraced in Scotland at this time, but instead couched within a mixed duality and even multiplicity of identities. George Washington wrote of Wallace that 'The political principles of that patriot were worthy of the purest periods of the British constitution',[43] yet England was the only vehicle for this 'British' creation. Despite the lack of direct protest directed at Westminster in the radicalism around 1820,[44] the Magna Carta was central to the ideology of the radical weavers,[45] as it was to Edinburgh's 1832 reform jubilee which featured a working class still excluded from the franchise.[46]

In the 1840s it was religion which focused the Scottish psyche. Interestingly, the Disruption in the Church of Scotland in 1843 was the only Scottish event worthy of inclusion in Lord Acton's *Growth of Nationalities* in the *Cambridge Modern History* of 1934.[47] It has been argued that that ecclesiastical split and the provisions of the 1845 health reforms - by taking away the role of the church in the relief of the poor in Scotland - buried finally the Reformed vision of Scotland as a godly nation.[48] Yet the Free Church replicated the voluntary and spiritual activity of the kirk in Scotland's civil society. Its immediate effect was to create more, not less, voluntary organisations and associations in the towns and cities, adding to the everyday experience of civil society.[49] Scotland's banality of duality was helped also by the two churches keeping within Protestantism and resisting the Catholicism of the Irish immigrant.[50] It is noted by Michael Fry that during the ten years of agitation which preceded the Disruption there were occasional cries of Wallace and Bruce and 'Scotland for ever!', yet he could not divide the British sense of Protestantism so crucial to Colley's thesis, although one should never underplay the influence of non-conformity.[51] Dissenting was a fine line, in terms of education and politics as well as religion.[52] The Free Church *Witness* newspaper could be stinging in it criticism of its Whiggish rival the *Scotsman* which it chided for sending a Commissioner to enquire after the famine in the Highlands and Islands who could not speak Gaelic ('the ugly and offensive language of Ossian'): 'he insults the whole Celtic race only when he can't understand them - his reports are more generous when he has an interpreter.'[53] Or, in reference to the *Scotsman*'s advocacy of post office deliveries on the Sabbath and of Sabbath trains, it added:

> All the world knows that if there be any one thing more characteristic of Scotsmen, and for which nationality, and ever since the era of the Reformation, they have more honourably distinguished than any other, it is for the due external observance of the "Lord's Day".
> (...)
> A Bombay pirate, who hoists the flag of England the better to effect his unlawful purpose acts not, in my opinion, a part more truculent or base than the person who, bearing the name of a Scotsman, endeavours to write down our Sabbath.[54]

Concurrent with this ecclesiastical constitutionalism, the more legislative variety saw the National Association for the Vindication of Scottish Rights demand that mid-century Britain be saved from the terrors of 'centralisation' and 'functionaryism' which had gripped France, Hungary, Austria, Poland and Italy and plunged them into war.[55] This was 'the centrifugal impetus of democratic centralism' which, as we have seen, Tocquville had warned was an inexorable threat to civil society. Scotland was poised at the sharp end of these developments in state control and so it was the Scottish *ethnie* that was mobilised most visibly in opposition. Only a Union of equals would be the guarantee of national independence in the face of these perceived threats to Scotland's governance.[56] Wallace and Bruce, not Bonnie Prince Charlie were used in this particular version of Scottish history and it is remarkable how invisible Culloden was in pre-1850s Scotland, with little discussion appearing until its centenary in 1846 and even that day was marked by light-hearted celebration rather than the expected elegiac.[57]

But what of ethnic identity? John Wilkes and Samuel Johnson inspired in their different ways stories of the ethnic deficiencies of the Scots and produced the expected rancour in return. A 'Caledonian ancestry was at that time a most serious embarrassment to any public man who desired to make his mark in English politics', remarked the satire of Wilkes.[58] Yet it has been observed that the cult of the Highland hero became powerful in the late eighteenth and the nineteenth centuries, and acceptably so since the incorporation of the Highland regiments into the British army.[59] It was the Irish as Celts who were flagged as 'something other' and 'outcasts'.[60] The racial undertones to this cult drew deeper breath from the 1850s, most notably on the back of Robert Knox's influential *The Races of Men*.[61] This type of language also permeated less prosaic commentators such as the best selling Alexander Smith who wrote that: 'Men are racy of the soil in which they grow, even as grapes are. A Saxon nurtured in fat Kent or Sussex, amid flats of heavy wheat and acorn-dropping oaks, must of necessity be a different creature from the Celt who gathers his sustenance from the bleak sea-board, and who is daily drenched by the rain cloud from Cuchullin.'[62] This notion of strength from adversity and hardship (conditions which castigated the Irish tenant farmer) appeared to fit so well the Highland life-style yet somehow they could inspire Victoria to exclaim in 1868 that 'I think the Highlanders are the finest race in the World.'[63] Calls were made to revise their history 'Now that the "Land of the Heather" is familiar to all, when Britain is proud of her Highland Regiments, - when so many of her Southern sons migrate annually to seek health and recreation in the north, some record of the People of the Highlands, as they *now* are, may claim a national interest, and prove useful to the future historian.'[64] With so little racial downgrading from the core nation, although it was not invisible, it is no surprise that blood ties - as gore - played so little part in Scotland's nationalism at this time. Xenophobia could be contained, even by a Tory chairman of the National Wallace Monument organising committee obliged to make a speech to 800 contributors in 1861. Aware that it 'would have been easy to have wound the audience up to the highest pitch of enthusiasm by praise of the Scotch and abuse of the English, for they were to a man intensely national, and highly excited', he was relieved that order was maintained, that the speeches were reported in full in the English and Scottish press and that 'no unpleasant feelings were expressed.'[65]

Heroes appealed to the young and the impressionable because of the romance of their exploits. That romance also ensured that the gore and human tragedy of their lives could be contained. Wallace was one whose memory was used by all sides of the political and cultural divide as an appropriate role model.[66] As the century turned, children could take an everyday scene in a picture and from it make up stories each evening of the daring deeds of Sir William Wallace before they headed off for bed and still remain free of nightmares.[67] Genealogists and local historians were keen to find links to Highland heroes like Rob Roy[68] - a hero 'promised' to expectant readers of clan history in the 1880s.[69] Indeed the resurrection of the clan societies in that period was essentially for historical artefactual and genealogical reasons, rather than the voluntary imperative of their incarnation in the 1830s and 1840s.[70] There was followed a sense of reclaiming the Highland imagery for the Scots, rejecting the idea that 'only Englishmen wear the kilt' and noting how 'at foreign courts, too, a happy disposition has been manifested of late by gentlemen of Scots nationality and Celtic race to disappoint prejudice and uniformity by appearing, on suitable public occasions, attired in their beautiful national dress.'[71]

This is but a mere sketch which offers no more than a glance at the century, but it gives an impression of the range of self-reflection which was not tied to set-piece anniversaries or 'invented traditions', although neither was absent. This is because it was the nationalism of a stateless nation and located in civil society; it was inevitably rootless. But was this 'Scottishness'? Again the answer is 'yes' because they were the statements addressed primarily to Scots about the Scottish nation. And clearly these statements could not be made without some implicit thoughts about the nature of the Union and the nature of government; in the same why that the *Risorgimento* nationalism of Mazzini or Kossuth would structure the thinking behind their statements supporting emancipation of the Italian and Hungarian nations.[72] Rather than there being a missing nationalism in this period, we have uncovered at least two strands and, undoubtedly, when class and gender and religion are introduced, notions of Scottishness would be seen to be sustained even more widely in everyday life.

How can both these versions of Scottish national identity be explained? This takes us back to the 'What if...?' at the crux of this chapter. What if Scotland was an early example of a very modern form of nationalism (if not a post-modern form of nationalism)? One that was sustained primarily within civil society and was therefore highly undirected precisely because it was not state created. It was a civil society whose strength lay in the 'gap' between it and its (shared) state. In this sense civil society really did manage its everyday affairs to a remarkable extent. This is one of the central conceptual reasons why no demand for a Scottish parliament was made. Such a means of government was regarded by contemporaries as a contributor to 'centralisation' and that was deemed an unacceptable betrayal of the personal freedoms that had been negotiated at the time of Union.[73] That future was neatly summed up in an attempt in 1709 to unite the two Protestant variants around this new Union-made British parliament: 'The *Pars Imperans*, or Supreme Authority (absolutely so) of this Nation, and so of Scotland, lies not in the King or Queen alone, but in King or Queen, Lords and Commons, in one Corporation or Parliament.'[74] The future's bright, the future's English constitutionalism: the incorporating parliament was a triumph of the negotiation of equals, and the Union was presented as the best guarantor of that equality.[75]

The constitutional theorists of the nineteenth century believed than no rival supreme powers could co-exist in any single legal or political order[76], and the promise made not to change private laws 'except for evident utility of the subjects within Scotland' was generally maintained despite some convergence on matters directly linked to industrialisation.[77]   The highly influential commentator on life and politics in nineteenth century Scotland, Henry Cockburn, declared that the 'regeneration of Scotland is now secured!' and believed the sole purpose of the reforms of 1832 was to 'bring Scotland within the action of the constitution.'[78]   It has been argued persuasively that the Scottish intellectual Whigs could only see Scotland's progress as being locked-in to a British constitutional heritage that was clearly of English pedigree[79] (indeed, it was the defining feature of Englishness[80]).   Looking back for inspiration to his federalist proposals for the whole of the United Kingdom, the geographer C.B. Fawcett wrote in 1919 that the identity and the politics of the nineteenth century 'progressed alike'.   Practical life and political endeavour were thus at one; hence the expansion of England, the centralisation of France, the American war of Union, the unification of Germany, and even of Italy, were now seen as kindred processes.[81]   In his constitutional arrangement, England would co-ordinate rather than be subordinate to the British parliament and devolution was no problem if supported by a federal structure.   The administrative units would be along 'natural geographical divisions'.[82]

By linking the constitutional issues of devolved government with the topography of the country Fawcett offered a means of updating and re-legitimating the British parliament.   Similarly the nationalist demand for federation at the end of this century was a progression in changing notions of governance within the empire.[83]   It is this type of argument, rather than cultural infirmity, which provide more convincing explanations for Scotland in the nineteenth century.   When for instance we re-examine the historiography of the period it is notable for its paucity of material on the Scottish nation post-Union.   The cry of the nationalist Macrae in 1908 was that the ordinary text-book of Scottish history invariably ends with the Treaty of Union in 1707 and text-books of English or British history rarely contain any reference to Scottish affairs after that event, except perhaps a brief account of the Jacobite risings of 1715 and 1745.[84]   In Hume Brown's history of Scotland, first published in the same year, we wait until chapter 83 before we are introduced to the Union of Parliaments, and no more than a dozen chapters are needed to cover the period that follows.[85]   There are just two examples, but clearly the history of Scotland lost its problematic as the Union-created 'freedoms' became ingrained.   Thus the notion of cultural infirmity as embodied in the important thesis of Marinell Ash has come to be revised as too simplistic. Other (dual and constitutional) identities have been stressed as the foundations of a wide and non-ethnic representation of Scottishness.[86]

Cultural nationalism in Scotland is a manifestation of civil society structured by its constitutional development: it is the civic identity which is the determinant. This supports the apparent confusion generated by ideas of Teutonism as a mechanism for allowing the lowlands of Scotland to peg their ethnic identity to that of England.[87] English commentators of the nineteenth century stressed with conviction their Anglo-Saxon stock (although Rowse has claimed the real genetic make-up was Anglo-Celtic).[88] Note also the earlier argument from Kidd which demonstrated the Anglo-British identity of the Whig intellectuals. In each the lowland link to liberalism, economic improvement, free government and democracy were vital to identity formation.[89] And this connects to the Unionist-nationalism inherent in the mobilisation of Wallace and Bruce and Burns as well as the more expected Walter Scott as key nineteenth-century icons. Their promotion as national images produced a range of feelings which were superimposed on one another from the primordial through to the national and to abstract claims to liberty.[90] Taken together, these are the very factors which have been termed civic nationalism as it is sheered off from ethnic identities.

The civic/ethnic duality is most commonly ascribed to Greenfeld and she proposes England to be the earliest (civic) nation because it was the first to solve the conflict between crown and government in favour of the latter and the first where the term 'nation' came to represent the whole people.[91] 'The English nation was born in the Puritan revolution and confirmed in the Glorious Revolution', stated Kohn.[92] Yet it is Scotland that appears as a greater and closer fit to the notion of a civic nation in the age of nationalism. This is not in terms of democratic enfranchisement, which is one important version of this concept, but in a way that is ethnically weak, or 'ethnically-civic', in the construction of lowland identity,[93] and in the way in which its governance was sustained within civil society. This is a civic nationalism where its strength is its seeming unimportance, its banality, or in Scotland's case its 'absence'. It is wide ranging and free-floating. It had no state to make it or capture it as a single identity. What we find in Scotland is the existence of a multiplicity of personal identities, but also one national identity maintained through the institutions and the civic culture of civil society, and another in the unthinking patriotism of the British state.

The significance of Scotland's nationalism in the nineteenth century was this construction of what appears to be a thoroughly modern civic nationalism. It was achieved through the banality of duality, banishing blood and belonging to the pre-modern past. What if Scotland had therefore already shown Europe the complexities of successful civic nationalism? What if the stateless nations of the world start to reclaim nationalism from the nationalists? What if blood need not flow? What if ... ?

NOTES

[1] E.J. Hobsbawm, *The Age of Revolution: Europe, 1789-1848* (London, 1963); *The Age of Capital* (London, 1975); *The Age of Empire* (London, 1987); and for the twentieth century, *The Age of Extremes* (London, 1994).

[2] *The Economist* 26 May 1990, quoted in S.J. Connolly, R.A. Houston and R.J. Morris, 'Identity, conflict and economic changes: themes and issues', in *ibid.* (eds.), *Identity, Conflict and Economic Development: Ireland and Scotland, 1600-1939* (Preston, 1995), 13.

[3] J.A. Hall , 'Nationalisms: classified and explained', *Daedalus*, 122, 3, Summer (1993); J. Hutchinson & A.D. Smith (eds.), *Nationalism* (Oxford, 1994), and *Ethnicity* (Oxford, 1996) provide useful introductions to a range of these viewpoints. Of the four themes highlighted here, see, respectively, K.W. Deutsch *Nationalism and social communication: an inquiry into the foundations of nationality*, 2nd edn. (Cambridge, 1966); M. Hroch, 'Social and Territorial Characteristics in the Composition of the Leading Groups of National Movements', in A. Kappler, F. Adanir, A. O' Day (eds.), *The Formation of National Elites* (Dartmouth, 1992); E. Gellner, *Nations and Nationalism* (Oxford, 1983); A.D. Smith, 'The resurgence of nationalism? Myth and memory in the renewal of nations, *British Journal of Sociology*, 47, 4, December (1996).

[4] The common use of the term 'blood and belonging' to denote what nationalism 'really meant' is seen in Billig's discussion of M. Ignatieff, *Blood and Belonging: journeys into the new nationalism* (London, 1993), in M. Billig, *Banal Nationalism* (London, 1995), 46-8.

[5] S. Bruce, 'A Failure of the Imagination: Ethnicity and nationalism in Scotland's history', *Scotia*, XVII, (1993) 1.

[6] *ibid.*, 11-12, 15.

[7] C.A. Whatley, *'Bought and Sold for English Gold'? Explaining the Union of 1707*, Studies in Economic and Social History No. 4 (1994), 47.

[8] E. Halévy, *History of the English People in the Nineteenth Century, Volume 3. The Triumph of Reform (1830-1841)* (London, 1961), 242.

[9] P.H. Scott, *1707 The Union of Scotland and England* (Edinburgh, 1979), 55.

[10] Scotch-man, *The History of the National Address for Dissolving the Union* (London, 1715), 8.

[11]B. Lenman, 'Union, Jacobitism and Enlightenment', in R. Mitchison (ed.), *Why Scottish History Matters* (The Saltire Society, 1991), 53.

[12] M. Lynch, *Scotland. A New History* (London, 1991), 323. The best attempt at an evaluation is C.H. Lee, *Scotland and the United Kingdom: the economy and the union in the twentieth century* (Manchester, 1995).

[13] N.T. Phillipson, 'Nationalism and Ideology', in J.N. Wolfe (ed.), *Government and Nationalism in Scotland* (Edinburgh, 1969); H.J. Hanham, 'Mid-century Scottish nationalism: romantic and radical', in R. Robson (ed.), *Ideas and Institutions of Victorian Britain* (London, 1967).

[14] See for example *The Foundation for a Civil Society*, founded in 1990, is 'a US - based non-profit, non-governmental organisation committed to fostering the development of democracy, civil society and the rule of law in the Czech and Slovak Republics'. See their *Project on Justice in Times of Transition* begun in 1992.

[15] L. Greenfeld, *Nationalism: five roads to modernity* (Cambridge, Mass, 1993), 3-4, 6. Cf. Gellner's comment that nations are products of the age of nationalism, Gellner, *Nations and Nationalism,* 55.

[16] N. Evans, 'Introduction: identity and integration in the British Isles', in N. Evans (ed.), *National Identity in the British Isles* (Harlech, 1989), 16.

[17] C. Tilly, *European Revolutions, 1492-1992* (Oxford, 1993), 111-2.
'External wars of British states, by century begun, 1492-1991'

1492-1591	11	1792-1891	44
1592-1691	14	1892-1991	31
1692-1791	11		

[18] T. Nairn, *The Break-up of Britain*, 2nd edn. (London, 1981).

[19] T.C. Smout, 'Perspectives on the Scottish Identity', *Scottish Affairs*, No. 6, Winter (1994).

[20] This is explained in D. McCrone, *Understanding Scotland: the sociology of a stateless nation* (London, 1992), 194-5.

[21] Billig, *Banal Nationalism*, 5-9ff.

[22] D. Forbes, 'Introduction', xiv, to A. Ferguson, *An Essay on the History of Civil Society 1767* (Edinburgh, 1966).

[23] K. Kumar, 'Civil Society: an inquiry into the usefulness of an historical term', *British Journal of Sociology*, 44, 3, September (1993); J. Keane (ed.), *Civil Society and the State: New European perspectives* (London, 1988). 'The only way whereby any one divests himself of his Natural Liberty, and *puts on the bonds of Civil Society* is by agreeing with other Men to joyn and united into a Community, for their comfortable, safe, and peaceable living one amongst another, in a secure Employment of their Properties, and a greater Security against any that are not of it', Ch. VIII 'Of the Beginnings of Political Societies' (original emphasis), in J.

Locke, *Two Treatises of Government* (1698), ed. Peter Laslett (Cambridge, 1960, 1990).

[24] Kumar, 'Civil Society', 381.

[25] R.W. Krouse, '"Classical" images of democracy in America: Madison and Tocqueville', in G. Duncan (ed.), *Democratic Theory and Practice* (Cambridge, 1993), 72.

[26] M. Keating, 'Scotland in the UK: a dissolving Union?', *Nationalism and Ethnic Politics*, 2, 2, Summer (1996), 233.

[27] V. Duke & L. Crolley, *Football, Nationality and the State* (Essex, 1996), 17; R. Crawford, 'Dedefining Scotland', in S. Bassnett (ed.), *Studying British Cultures: an introduction* (London, 1997), 83-4.

[28] MacInnes points out that everybody knows this threesome, but there is little evidence of their influence on personal consciousness on a regular basis, J. MacInnes, 'The Press in Scotland', *Scottish Affairs*, No. 1, (Autumn 1992), 137. Similarly, see: W. M. Humes, 'The cultural significance of Scotland's educational system', in *The Scottish Government Yearbook* (1984), 150.

[29] J. Penrose, 'Reification in the name of change: the impact of nationalism on social constructions of nation, people and place in Scotland and the United Kingdom', in P. Jackson & J. Penrose (eds.), *Constructions of Race, Place and Nation* (London, 1993).

[30] E. Gellner, *Conditions of Liberty: Civil society and its rivals* (London, 1994); C.G.A. Bryant, 'Social self-organisation, civility and sociology: a comment on Kumar's 'Civil Society'', *British Journal of Sociology*, 44, 3, September (1993).

[31] R.J. Finlay, 'The rise and fall of popular imperialism in Scotland, 1850-1950', *Scottish Geographical Magazine*, 113, 1 (1997), 16.

[32] W. Knox, 'The Political and Workplace Culture of the Scottish Working Class, 1832-1914', in Fraser, W.H. and Morris, R.J. (eds.), *People and Society in Scotland, Volume II, 1830-1914* (Edinburgh, 1990), 154.

[33] L. Colley, *Britons: forging the nation, 1707-1837* (New Haven, 1992).

[34] P. Scott, *Knowledge and Nation* (Edinburgh, 1990), 169.

[35] J. M. Mackenzie, 'David Livingstone: the construction of the myth', in G. Walker and T. Gallagher (eds.), *Sermons and Battle Hymns: Protestant culture in modern Scotland* (Edinburgh, 1990), 27.

[36] R.J. Morris, 'Victorian Values in Scotland and England', in T.C. Smout (ed.), *Victorian Values* (Oxford, 1992), 44.

[37] R. Law, 'The Individual and the Community', in E. Barker, *The Character of England* (Oxford, 1947), 34.

[38] From the 1870s and 1880s the Glasgow branch of the Home Government Association, then to become the Irish National League, was one of the strongest in Britain; Coatbridge, where 42% of those employed as miners in 1861 were Irish, was also able at this time to provide the greatest contribution to the treasurer of the League, J.M. Bradley 'Integration or Assimilation? Scottish Society, Football and Irish Immigrants', *The International Journal of Sport*, 13, 2, August (1996), 63-4,

P. Panayi, *Immigration, ethnicity and racism in Britain, 1815-1945* (Manchester 1994), 63.

[39] *The Sword of Wallace* in *Wallace or, the vale of Ellerslie with other poems* (Glasgow, 1802).

[40] *The Shade of Wallace. A poem* (Glasgow, 1807), 8.

[41] C. Kidd, *Subverting Scotland's Past: Scottish whig historians and the creation of an Anglo-British identity, 1689-c.1830* (Cambridge, 1993).

[42] The dis-engagement with previous identities, in favour of new versions, is emphasised in Greenfeld, *Nationalism*, 14.

[43] *Copy of Earl of Buchan's letter to General Washington, President of the United States of America, sent enclosed in the box of Wallace's oak, Dryburgh Abbey, June 28, 1791, and reply* (1811), 18-19.

[44] C.A. Whatley, 'An Uninflammable People?', in I. Donnachie and C.A. Whatley (eds.), *The Manufacture of Scottish History* (Edinburgh, 1992), 69.

[45] T. Clarke and T. Dickson, 'The Birth of Class?', in T.M. Devine & R. Mitchison (eds.), *People and Society in Scotland, Volume I 1760-1830* (Edinburgh, 1988), 302.

[46] *The Scotsman*, 6 June 1832. It was estimated that 15,000 took part in the jubilee, W.M. Gilbert (ed.), *Edinburgh in the Nineteenth Century* (Edinburgh, 1901), 96. This is also discussed in G. Morton *Unionist-Nationalism: Governing Urban Scotland, 1830-1860*, (East Linton, forthcoming),ch. 8.

[47] *The Cambridge Modern History. Volume XI The Growth of Nationalities* (Cambridge, 1934), 5ff, 18.

[48] W. Storrar, *Scottish Identity: a Christian Vision* (Edinburgh, 1990), pp 42-4.

[49] Morton, *Unionist-Nationalism*, ch. 4.

[50] K. Robbins, *Nineteenth Century Britain: England, Scotland & Wales, the making of a nation*, (Oxford, 1988).

[51] Michael Fry, 'The Disruption and the Union', in S. J. Brown & M. Fry (eds.), *Scotland in the Age of the Disruption*, (Edinburgh, 1993), 31; Fry cites Thomas Guthrie, in Anon, *Practical Remarks on the Scotch Church Question* (London, 1841), 56. Machin has argued that 'in spite of the distinctiveness of the Scottish church question its outcome was influenced by the general British situation because of the political union', G.I.T. Machin, 'The Disruption and British politics, 1834-43', *The SHR*, 51 (1972), 20.

[52] It is argued that the simple 'Scottish education is different' argument for the mid-century period underestimates the influence of politics and religion to cut across the denominational splits in R.D. Anderson, *Scottish Education Since the Reformation*, Studies in Economic and Social History, No. 5 (1997), 24-5

[53] *The Witness* 10 February 1847.

[54] 'Scotus', letter to *The Witness* 12 February 1847.

[55] J. Grant, 'Scotland for ever!' (n.p., c.1853), 222.

[56] G. Morton, 'Scottish rights and 'centralisation' in the mid-nineteenth century', *Nations and Nationalism*, 2, 2 (1996).

[57] C. McArthur, 'Culloden: a pre-emptive strike', *Scottish Affairs*, No. 9, (Autumn 1994), 106.

[58] H. Bleackley, *Life of John Wilkes* (London, 1917), 72-5.

[59] C.W.J. Withers, 'The Historical Creation of the Scottish Highlands', in Donnachie & Whatley, *The Manufacture*, 149.

[60] C.W.J. Withers, 'Class, culture and migrant identity: Gaelic Highlanders in urban Scotland', in G. Mearns and C.W.J. Withers (eds.), *Urbanising Britain: essays in class and community in the nineteenth century* (Cambridge, 1991), 57. L.P. Curtis, *Anglo-Saxons and Celts: a study of anti-Irish prejudice in Victorian England* (Connecticut, 1968); L.P. Curtis, *Apes and Angels: the Irishman in Victorian Caricature* (Devon, 1971); although Curtis has been accused of overemphasising simple racial prejudice to the detriment of the influence of class and religion; R.F. Foster, *Paddy and Mr Punch: connections in Irish and English History* (London, 1993), 192-3.

[61] R. Knox, *The Races of Men: a philosophical enquiry into the influence of race over the destinies of nations* (London, 1850, 1862) Kidd has commented on Robert Knox that the nationalism in Scotland - such of a mixed nation - would be abhorrent to him: C. Kidd, 'Teutonist Ethnology and Scottish Nationalist Inhibition, 1780-1880', *SHR*, LXXXIV, 1, 197, April (1995). This trend was carried into the twentieth century by Karl Pearson and the measurement of Bruce's skull in comparison with that of Jeremy Bentham, Sir Thomas Browne and the average English skull in the 17th century, K. Pearson, *King Robert the Bruce, 1274-1320, his skull and portraiture* (Cambridge, 1924), 15 Table 1.

[62] A. Smith, *A Summer in Skye* (London, 1865), 233-4.

[63] Royal Archive Add U 32/26 May 1865, Queen Victoria to the Crown Princess, quoted in A. M. MacGregor, *The Highlanders* (1870) reproduced in *The Highlanders of Scotland: the complete watercolours commissioned by Queen Victoria from Kenneth MacLeay of her Scottish retainers and clansmen* (London, 1986). 17. When reminded that both armies at Bannockburn were commanded by her ancestors, Edward II and Robert Bruce, Victoria said: 'It is so; but I am more proud of my Scotch descent than of any other: when I first came to Scotland I felt as if I were going home', A. Alison, *Some Account of my Life and writings, I* (Edinburgh, 1883), 613.

[64] MacGregor, *The Highlanders*, preface.

[65] Alison, *Some Account*, 313-317

[66] E.g. Hodgeson's Juvenile Drama, *Wallace, the Hero of Scotland; a drama, in three Acts*. Adapted to Hodgeson's Theatrical Characters and Scenes in the same (London, 1822); G. Grant, *The Life and Adventures of Sir William Wallace, the Liberator of Scotland* (Dublin, 1840); J.D. Carrick, *Life of Sir William Wallace of Elderslie* (London, 1840); Rev. C.G. Glass, *Stray Leaves from Scotch and English History with the life of Sir William Wallace, Scotland's Patriot, hero, and Political Martyr*, 2nd edn. (Montreal, 1873).

[67] J. Bone, *Edinburgh Revisited* (London, 1911), 158-9.

[68] *Rob Roy, the Celebrated Highland Freebooter; or Memoirs of the Osbaldistone Family* (Glasgow, n.d.).

[69] J.S. Keltie (ed.), *A History of the Scottish Highlands, Highland Clans and Highland Regiments, volume II* (Edinburgh, 1881), 245-250.

[70] Morton, *Unionist-Nationalism*, ch. 4.

[71] The Hon[ble.] Stuart Ruadri Erskine, *The Kilt; and how to wear it* (Inverness, 1901), 1-2.

[72] This is despite Mazzini's famous map of an 'Ideal Europe' in 1857 pointing out that the peripheral nations of the UK lacked the fundamental characteristics of nations (such as language and customs) and a 'historic mission'; P. Alter *Nationalism*, 2nd edn. (London, 1994), 19-23.

[73] Morton, 'Scottish rights', 273.

[74] *A Draught for a National Church Association whereby the Subjects of North and South Britain, however different in their judgements concerning Episcopacy and Presbytery, may yet be united* (Edinburgh, 1709), iv.

[75] Morton, *Unionist-Nationalism*.

[76] N. MacCormick, 'Sovereignty: myth and reality', *Scottish Affairs*, 11, (Spring 1995), 7.

[77] R. Rait & G.S. Pryde, *Scotland*, 2nd edn. (London, 1954), 177.

[78] *Journal of Henry Cockburn, being a continuation of the Memorials of his Time, 1831-1854, Volume 1* (Edinburgh, 1874), 31; M. Fry, 'The Whig interpretation of Scottish History', in Donnachie and Whatley, *The Manufacture*, 81; Alison *Some Account*, 306.

[79] Kidd, *Subverting*.

[80] W. Bagehot, *The English Constitution* (1867) (London, 1963).

[81] C.B. Fawcett, *Provinces of England: a study of some geographical aspects of devolution* (London, 1919), i.

[82] Fawcett, *Provinces*, 23-24.

[83] J. Mackinnon, *The Union of England and Scotland: a study of international history* (London, 1896), 516.

[84] A. Macrae, *Scotland from the Treaty of Union with England to the present time (1707-1907)* (London, 1908), v.

[85] P. Hume Brown, *A Short History of Scotland* (Edinburgh, 1908).

[86] M. Ash, *The Strange Death of Scottish History* (Edinburgh, 1980); K. Iwazumi, 'The Union of 1707 in Scottish Historiography, c. 1800-1914', (unpublished MPhil, University of St Andrews, 1996), 37-59; C. Kidd, '*The Strange Death of Scottish History* revisited: Constructions of the Past in Scotland, c.1790-1914, *SHR* LXXVI, 201, April (1997); Morton, 'Scottish Rights'.

[87] Kidd, 'Teutonist' 50-51.

[88] A. L. Rowse, *The Spirit of English History* (London, 1943), 12.

[89] Kidd, *Subverting*, 279; Kidd, 'Teutonist', 61.

[90] G. Gadoffre, 'French National Images and the Problem of National Stereotypes', *International Social Science Bulletin*, 3, 3 (1951), 582.

[91] Greenfeld, *Nationalism*, introduction and ch. 1.

[92] H. Kohn, *Prophets and Peoples: Studies of Nineteenth Century Nationalism* (London, 1946), 12.

[93] Greenfeld argues that ethnic identities are never unique identities; that they become arbitrary through the constant re-presentation of the material; Greenfeld, *Nationalism*, 13.

CHAPTER NINE

The Vanduaria of Ptolemy: Place and the Past [1]

Catriona M.M. Macdonald

Divided into the 'Five Bob Side' and the 'Half Crown Side', Paisley's High Street at the turn of the twentieth century represented something more than the commercial heart of a provincial cotton town.

> The Five Bob Side was for clerks, shop assistants and those more genteel people: the Half Crown Side was for manual workers - shipyard apprentices, message boys, mill girls, jam works girls. The roadway divided these class strata as sternly as a high wall: if a Half-Crown Side parader was seen on the other pavement we made catcalls, hissed and sneered. Any girl who crossed the roadway was the subject of our vengeance for months. We would have no truck with the swankers.[2]

Social relationships, economic divisions and appreciations of personal identity generated an encoded urban landscape in which the universals of 'nationality' and 'class' had meaning only in so far as they resonated with an inherently *local* social structure and *mentalite*. Whilst in material terms, the High Street existed independently of this conceptual geography which ascribed meanings to its form and the place of people within it (no sign-posts indicated which side different occupations should walk on), it is in the series of associations which generated the conceptual geography of the street that local identity is revealed. This was a contested geography - a geography of power, a geography of boundaries.

Placing the past
Thus far it has been geographers who have taken the lead in 'mapping' the conceptual geographies/ 'places'/ 'spaces' which contextualise (and generate) aspects of local culture and politics, by attacking the sacred national and social shibboleths of the social sciences. Foremost in this field, John Agnew has argued against the 'privileged status' of 'the national' and 'the global' which restricts 'authentic politics' to that taking place within territorial boundaries and 'equates society with the boundaries established by national states'.[3] According to Agnew, local identity has been misinterpreted as a

'residual' of a bygone age or a 'primordial' aspect of a cultural divine in which traits and beliefs are reproduced unwittingly.[4]

Similarly, others - echoing the concerns of historians such as Patrick Joyce - have attacked 'class' as a governing concept.[5] Michael Keith and Steve Pile have cautioned against a 'nostalgia for the simplicity of class war' by claiming its rhetoric to be 'increasingly useless'.[6] David Harvey has stressed the tendency in class-based arguments to 'hide, marginalize, disempower, repress and perhaps even oppress all kinds of 'others''.[7] And, responding to this challenge, Susan Hanson and Geraldine Pratt have stressed the importance of particular historical geographies in shaping localised class and gender practices. 'Geography', they emphasise, 'is inseparable from class formation; classes are not just distributed in space, they are constructed in and through space.'[8]

Such re-assessment has generated a new interest in local identity and local history. Having suffered from its association with contested sociological formulations of the concept of 'community', and tainted with parochialism, romanticism and reaction, the study of localities (regions) has acquired a new credibilty since the 1970s.[9] Yet Marxist condemnation of the spatial contingency of social action as 'fetishization' and 'false consciousness' has been slow to abate.[10] Space, locality and geography have been taken as 'given', inert and immutable - the site, as opposed to the context, of social or historical enactment - and thus unproblematic.[11] In this sense, historians have rightly been criticised for their obsession with the temporal plane to the exclusion of much else.[12]

Increasing appeals within historical texts to regional difference at the subnational level, however, hint at least to an implicit acknowledgement of the importance of 'space' as well as time. Yet, with few exceptions, Scotland's local history has dealt with space as little more than the backdrop for the play of social actors - the necessary material plane upon which things happen, yet from which we gain little more than a site for social structures and the raw materials of life and industry.[13] It is the intention of this essay to problematise 'space' in the context of the conceptual geographies of late Victorian and early twentieth-century Paisley, by following the geographical lead in identifying 'space' as a contested expression of power relations within society. In doing so, it encourages Scottish History to think again about Scotland as both metaphor and material entity.

> For most of its modern history, Scotland has been able to exist with benign multiple identities. Class-consciousness, Britishness and Scottishness have co-existed. But they have coexisted in different ways in different places.[14]

What was I when I left Paisley that night? What was Paisley to me?[15]
The questions which the author Lennox Kerr asked himself when he left
Paisley in 1915, point to the complex nature of the relationship between the
production of conceptual geographies and the making of history. It can be
safely assumed that at this certain point of time (history), Kerr's perception of
Paisley (conceptual geography) would be different to that which would have
dominated his thoughts whilst 'safe' within its bounds. He sets himself outside
Paisley, yet continues to relate his identity to it.

Edward W. Soja has highlighted that:

> The production of spatiality in conjunction with the making of history can...
> be described as both the medium and the outcome, the pre-supposition and
> the embodiement, of social action and relationship, of society itself.[16]

Kerr's Paisley does not exist outwith his history, yet Kerr's identity is also
partly determined by his place within a personal geography. Moving from the
individual to the social, Paisley does not exist outwith the ever-changing
history of its citizens yet the identity of its citizens owes much to how they
understand Paisley as an imaginary or symbolic space evoking memories,
beliefs, social relations, economic ties and emotions.[17] As Pile and Keith have
made clear, 'the symbolic and the literal are in part constitutive of one
another.'[18]

Like 'space' - and emerging from and constitutive of it - local identity
is thus less an historical or social artefact than a process which is in a
perpetual state of 'becoming'.[19] It forms and reforms at the point of
intersection of 'space' and 'time' and in turn influences the transmission and
reception of new social, political and cultural forms through appeals to
precedent and tradition.[20] Partly determined by the contested nature of local
conceptual geographies, it itself is the arena of contests over social,
economic, political and cultural representations - the context of the brokerage
of a multitude of power relations.

Yet, whilst conceptual geographies of Paisley - allied to a keen sense
of change over time - provide one method for analysing expressions of past
ways of seeing and knowing, they tell us little of ways of 'belonging' - that
sense of security of identity which emerges from an attachment to place
through ancestral lineage and geographic rootedness. Importantly, a sense of
belonging assumes a state of not-belonging and thus a sense of 'otherness',
commonly personified by the 'stranger', 'alien', or - to use the parlance current
in Highland popular culture - the 'incomer' or 'white settler'.[21] This process

involved in the definition of identity in relation to its apparent opposite or
'other', posits a discourse operating within the 'time' - 'space' relationship
which breaks the bounds of the local by acknowledging identity as a position
which is ascribed from 'outside' as well as being negotiated 'internally', and
formed as a result of exclusion as well as incorporation.[22]

How 'others' identify Paisley, how Paisley defines itself against
'others' and what is excluded in Paisley's definition of itself are as important
to local identity as that which Paisley believes itself to be. Together such
discourses posit a potential state of being *in* Paisley but not *of* it, or sharing
unequally in the manufacture of local identity. These are the necessary
preconditions which are at the root of the contested nature of local identity.
The local identity of Paisley is thus treated as subject as well as object, as an
active force as much as the outcome of action elsewhere, as society as well as
geography. It is this complex appreciation of local identity which is
considered in what follows.

Passeleth, Pasgel-laith, Bas-leac, Paisley, Suburb

The interplay of 'time' and 'space' in moulding and remoulding the local
identity of Paisley is evident in its change of name from the Vanduaria of the
reign of Ptolemy, recalled by Victorian antiquarians and said to originate
from the *wen dur* or *white water* of the Cart river; through numerous Gaelic
and 'ancient British' versions; to Paisley - the 'lea of Peace' or the more
organic 'lea of Peas', depending on etymological preference.[23] Yet, beyond
such antiquarian interest, 'time' and 'space' had a more profound impact on
the expression and language of local identity.

It is self-evident, but worth highlighting, that different areas -
regions, towns, neighbourhoods, etc - have different relationships with the
national state which, in turn, influence their culture and identity.[24] On a more
mundane level, popular stereotypes of individual localities inevitably shape
local identity, either through absorption - when the stereotype is
complimentary or acknowledged to be representative - or through defensive
rejection - when the caricature is seen as offensive or misrepresentative. In
Paisley's relationship with Glasgow, we see clear evidence of such tension
between the accommodation and rejection of identities ascribed by a powerful
'other'.

In the 1950s, the authors of Paisley's contribution to the *Third
Statistical Account* stressed how 'A less vital township so near to Glasgow
would have lost its individuality long ago'.[25] Yet, whilst admitting that in
terms of commerce and popular entertainment Paisley had been 'absorbed into

the great 'conurbation' of Glasgow', they stressed that 'Paisley ha(d) quite sufficient of the old inbred qualities to remain a large village'.[26]

Paisley's struggle to avoid 'suburb' status in the early twentieth century highlighted a conflict between its self-image and an inferior identity ascribed from 'outside'. Examples abound: in an article attacking Paisley's record on health, the *Glasgow Herald* referred to Paisley as a 'suburb' in 1888; seven years later, the *Paisley and Renfrewshire Gazette* attacked Glasgow's adoption of 'superior airs', in response to a Glasgow newspaper which suggested the 'Eu-de-cologning' of the Cart River, now that the Clyde was to be purified. [27] In 1904, the *Gazette* again felt compelled to defend Paisley's reputation after criticisms from the Glasgow press of the unfashionable dress of the Paisley mill girls; yet undaunted, Glasgow Provosts throughout the Edwardian period made frequent references to 'annexing' Paisley into a greater Glasgow.[28]

Glasgow's mission seemed to have been achieved when, in August 1923, Glasgow Corporation acquired the Paisley District Tramways. Glasgow's Provost Paton declared that this would be the beginning of the end of Paisley as a separate municipality.[29] The tramways themselves, however, represented far more than an emblem of Glaswegian aggrandisement. They were part of a complex conceptual geography in Paisley, the history of which reflected conflicting interpretations and concepts of Paisley's civic identity in relation to that of her more powerful neighbour.

Unlike Glasgow, where civic pride was symbolised by efficient municipal tramways, Paisley's tramways were never owned by the municipality and were famous for their poor service and unprofitability.[30] Yet, whilst Glasgow seemed to hold out the only hope of a cheap and effective service in 1898, suggestions that Paisley should allow Glasgow corporation to take over the running of the trams were attacked in Paisley. The *Gazette* feared that the Glasgow scheme would threaten Paisley's independence and relegate the town to humiliating 'suburb' status, complaining that it would 'tag us on to the coat-tails of Glasgow'.[31] Others claimed that, as the 'heart' of Renfrewshire, Paisley's 'natural' connections were with other smaller towns in the county rather than with Glasgow - a city which would undermine Paisley's status.[32] Though there were some voices in support of the scheme, Glasgow had to wait 25 years to take over Paisley's tramways.

In the interim, Paisley's trams were in the hands of a private operator. Negotiations leading to this state of affairs were lengthy and contrived, but interestingly brought to the surface, competing interpretations of the role of municipal government. Whilst the Trades Council fought hard for a local municipal scheme, demanding that no individual had the right to *own* Paisley's streets, a referendum on municipalisation in November 1900 recorded a majority in favour of a private scheme.[33] Glasgow's tramways 'utopia' was thus far from 'portable' without the support of local communities.

Yet, did Paisley's decision reflect a commonsense response to a potentially costly municipal scheme and the threat of a stronger neighbour, or a lack of courage on the part of its council to control the arterial links of its own economic infrastructure? The long-running tramways debate encouraged competing interpretations of Paisley's civic identity which prohibited a truly hegemonic conceptual geography of the town. The association of the 'ownership' of the streets with the ownership of the trams generated debates which were embedded in a sense of place as well as status.

The debates were familiar ones in Paisley and owed their origins to the powerful industrial paternalism of the foremost employers of the town which threatened to substitute patronage for civic pride. Paisley's civic landscape was dominated by industrial patronage. The Fountain Gardens, the Public Library, the Town Hall, the Museum and many other halls and churches were material testament to the extent to which Paisley's civic identity had been generated by a public vision from above rather than below - a fact to which Glasgow frequently drew its neighbour's attention.

In 1889, proposals for a municipal garden in the 'Open Space' in front of the Clark Town Hall were rejected at a meeting of Paisley ratepayers. The *Glasgow Evening News* responded:

> There is hardly a town in Scotland where the people have had so many gratuitous benefits conferred upon them as Paisley; and now, when they are asked to give a farthing per pound to maintain a blessing vital to themselves alone, they meet in their thousands and shreik out No![34]

In 1891 Paisley's new MP, William Dunn, seemed to confirm Paisley's dependency on elite 'gifts' when he bought the land for the town, stipulating that it was to display statues of local industrial employers. It was an impression further enhanced the following year when further municipal plans to develop the site were opposed as they would have neccesitated 1/2d. increase on the rates. The *Gazette* despaired:

> An old story this in Paisley, which has received so many costly gifts from liberal-handed sons that it really does not feel inclined to do anything for itself in the way of improving the amenities and increasing the attractions of the town... It is not through a spirit of this kind that Glasgow has been so

much improved and its citizens provided with ample facilities for recreation...[35]

The feeling that Paisley's civic identity had been something 'given' rather than earned contrasted starkly with the Glasgow experience and made key emblems of local identity in Paisley simultaneously symbols of an 'inferior' civic ethos - symbols which could not easily be adopted as direct expressions of a public will.

The 'outside' view of Paisley thus had important consequences for how citizens considered the material world in which they lived. The tramways and 'Open Space' debates highlight that this was something more than fanciful rivalry over reputations - it could determine the lived and conceptual geographies of Paisley's citizens and generate tensions over the meaning of local identity.

Threadopolis: Manufacturing Conflicting Realities

in the robustious hurly burly of late-Victorian enterprise, the Burgh played a strenuous part that stamped the physical face of the town with the grimy irregular lineaments we know so well today.

John A. McGregor, *Paisley Pattern: A Preview* (Paisley, 1947)

Edward Soja has emphasised how 'social existence is made concrete in geography and history' and how, in a landcape 'scarred' by capitalism, space is an arena of important power-relations which disrupt the smooth translation of economic and/or social dominance into spatial dominance.[36] He writes:

The production of capitalist spatiality... is no once-and-for-all event. The spatial matrix must constantly be reinforced and, when necessary, restructured - that is, spatiality must be socially reproduced, and this reproduction process is a continuing source of conflict and crisis.[37]

The social relations which generated and were thereafter dependent upon the employment provided by the thread mills in Paisley were significant determinants of the conceptual geographies and local identity of Paisley. As Lennox Kerr made clear in his autobiography:

To J.P. Coats and Company, Paisley is a place where the climate is damp enough for the spinning of cotton threads. Because of what Paisley is to J.P. Coats, a town of one hundred and thirty thousand people has emerged from a small, hand-loom weaving town - a town with a large percentage of women, because women are the mill workers.[38]

Yet Soja cautions us that 'Capital is never alone in shaping the historical geography of the landscape and is certainly not the only author or authority.'[39] It is as foolish to assume a uni-directional and united voice on the side of capital as it is to assume a unity among *all* workers. Furthermore, whilst the industrial impulse may originate in capitalistic endeavour, its purpose and expression are influenced by a multitude of competing interests. These twin considerations will influence the following analysis of Paisley's industrial identity.

By necessity, pressures of space restrict what follows to illustrative examples of far wider trends and artificially ignores the role of chaos as well as order in spatial relations - the 'happenstance juxtapositions, the accidental separations, the often paradoxical nature of spatial arrangements'.[40] Yet, in appreciating how the divided voice of capital and the competing voices of labour determined conflicting conceptual geographies, it is hoped that something of the 'paradoxical' consequences of industrial development for local identity will be appreciated.

Discussions over the improvement of the Cart River in the late 1880s and 1890s highlighted divisions in the apparently monolithic power of capitalism in Paisley by identifying contradictory visions of Paisley's future among the industrial elite. The divisions could, on one level, be explained in accordance with the conflicting economic interests of - on the one hand - the shipbuilders, who supported the improvement of the river, and - on the other - the starch manufacturers who saw little benefit for their industry in a scheme for a river which already suited their purposes and which would increase local taxation. However, beyond this, in the debates surrounding the scheme to improve the river, the position of the Cart in contrasting conceptual geographies of Paisley was critical. How the Cart was envisioned shaped the conflicting discourses which came to light and reflected competing definitions of local identity and local history.[41]

Let us consider the case for the defence. In its defence of the scheme to make the Cart navigable for larger vessels, the *Paisley Daily Express* saw the Cart improvement scheme as part of a new Paisley:

> The Paisley of today is not the Paisley of that by-gone time; we have fairly stepped out, determined to march in step with our fellow cities and towns that are moving along in the path of progress...[42]

Opposition was defined as generational:

there is such a thing as superfluous interference on the part of old men with the more youthful and ardent spirits, whose life is *before* and not *behind* them.[43]

Opposition was also unrepresentative. The opponents were a minority of the population, representing:

not one tenth of the valuation (of the burgh) and only a five hundred and sixty fifth part in point of householding population. This is the deadweight that is hanging like a millstone round the neck of our river...[44]

Opposition was, moreover, a legacy of the past - a past which had seen the town bankrupted in the 1840s - which made many cautious. Yet, the *Express* encouraged: 'Let us shake our feet clear of the dust of ages - forget the ancient, sleepy days of bankruptcies and bunglings, and decline to repeat history..'.[45]

The Cart Bill was eventually passed in July 1885 and the first sod was cut by contractors in 1887. However, far from the rival to the Clyde which was envisioned at the scheme's inception, even in the 1950s, it could be said that the Cart had 'never fulfilled the aspirations of the inhabitants'.[46]

In the late nineteenth century, however, the Cart brought together discourses concerning industry, history, and democracy - issues which were not easily divided into simple economic arguments. As a feature of a contested conceptual geography, the Cart highlights how 'space' and 'time' moulded competing definitions of local identity and symbolised the failure of capital to give ultimate shape and meaning to local geography.

Division within capital, however, was also paralleled in divisions *between* labour and capital and divisions *within* labour itself, making industrial geographies - apparently made in the image of capital - 'spaces' open to the reappropriation of conflicting labour interests.[47] This applies both in a conceptual and material sense: the factory, for instance, is both the site and symbol of power and resistance. As Anderson and Gale have made clear, 'our landscapes are valuable documents on the power plays from which social life is constructed, both materially and rhetorically.'[48]

The thread mills of the Coats syndicate were, perhaps, the most powerful symbols of capital in Paisley, but imposed different constraints and fulfilled contrasting purposes in the different conceptual geographies of the employers, the female workers and the local Labour movement. Whilst each vision was important in material and symbolic terms, each shared unequally in the 'manufacture' of industrial 'space'. To deny this hierarchy would be to deny the power-relations which, in a primary sense, determine the differences between the discourses. But such power relations changed over time, altering the balance in the hierarchy and the relative importance of each vision in determining local identity.

For the employers, the mills were pre-eminently the site of capitalist industrial production and the focus of their wider economic, social and political dominance in the town. Control over production generated power both within and beyond the mill gates - power which was expressed in civic buildings and political leadership.[49] Yet the mills themselves were also identified as cultural symbols - symbols of industrial success grounded in technological innovation and paternalistic management which encouraged an association of interests between the employer and the employed. In 1893 a Factory Inspectorate report highlighted 'very good relations ... between the firm and the workers', and recorded that: 'Every attention is paid to the comfort of workers while engaged at their work'.[50] Four years later, the local press emphasised that the Paisley mills were 'far and away the most comfortable factories in the kingdom, and the wages which the girls can earn are exceptionally high.' The result, according to the *Gazette*, was to be seen in the:

> higher morale of the Paisley mill-girl; she is better fed, better dressed, better looking and brisker and livelier than her poor sisters in less fortunate places. Our young women are a credit to the town a finer ornament than all our Town halls, kirks and open spaces, and grand buildings, and the Coats family have a just cause for pride in the reflection that they have helped to make them so.[51]

The inter-relationship between mill, worker and local identity is evident in the *Gazette*'s remarcks as is the debt each owed to the paternalism of the mill owners. Yet even at this time there was mounting evidence that not all shared this vision. When the *Gazette* article appeared, Paisley mill girls were on strike.

In the thread mills, the gender division of labour acquired spatial expression. Dominated by female labour, the role of the mills in shaping local and class identity was therefore far from gender neutral and competing definitions of the work-place in a wider conceptual geography of the town were influenced by the gender relations which developed in the mills. Geography was thus inseperable from local identity and emerging class relations.[52]

The female experience of work was thus clearly different to that of many male workers. At a meeting of the Paisley Trades Council in 1893, Mr Martin, the plumber's delegate, reflected that:

> they as men could have little idea of what girls had to put up with. He had been informed that it was quite a common thing, when a girl had become proficient and able to earn a fair wage at a certain class of work for the foreman, without any reason whatever, to put her to work at which, from her inexperience, she could not earn as much as would keep body and soul together. Situated as they were at present, girls could do nothing but submit...[53]

Through the male figure of the foreman and the patriarchy exercised by the management, industrial concerns at once became gender concerns as authority was viewed by an overwhelmingly female workforce as gendered as well as 'classed'. Women's interpretation of their interests was therefore different to that of their male counterparts in other industries - a reality which was evident in their mode of protest against capital.

In the 1890s and early Edwardian period, the 'Paisley mill girls' expressed a competing conceptual geography of the work-place through spontaneous strike action, in which the divisions into 'skills' and 'processes' and work areas dictated by capital were overwhelmed by a unity determined by gender. On various occassions, windows of mill buildings, once decorated to celebrate the 'rites of passage' of the mill owners' families were smashed and thousands of women flooded the streets around the mills, filling the air with cries of defiance.

Yet such protests were never entirely accommodated within a 'class' or specifically 'Labour' analysis of industrial capital.[54] Labour identified a need to 'control' such spontaneity, but attempts to unionise the workers repeatedly failed and female involvement in labour organs never reflected their influence in the local economy. Whilst acknowledging the potential in mobilising their 'sisters' in the mills, the Trades Council and the ILP failed to express an inclusive class agenda which took sufficient account of the specific dynamics of the local labour market. According to the Trades Council in 1894, the mill workers 'did not treat the proposal for organisation seriously. They regarded it rather in the light of a burlesque and a joke. They did not understand it properly.'[55]

Whilst this may be interpreted as a tactical failure rooted in the male-dominated Radicalism which defined labour organisation in these years,[56] it was also a consequence of the dominance which industrial paternalism maintained in defining the 'best interests' of the community. In this way, throughout the strikes of 1906 and 1907, union organisers were symbolised as *'outsiders'*, *'unconnected'*, *'from elsewhere'*. Councillor R.D. Brown addressed a 'large crowd' in May 1906 and emphasised to his audience that he spoke *'in the interests of the town in general'* and warned the girls not to let 'an agitator *into* the town'[57]. In the *Gazette*, a statement from the spoolers opposed the *'outside* interference in connection with the union movement'[58] and Sir Thomas Glen Coats emphasised that the building of a new mill had been cancelled 'due to interference with their workpeople *from outside'*.[59]

The strikes were more than industrial disputes in Paisley: they challenged a dominant image of local identity. The powerful imagery of the conceptual geography which placed activists 'outside' Paisley, however, also prohibited women workers from sharing equally in the processes which shaped the dominant identity of the town. In turn, the failure of the Labour movement to accomodate this marginalised discourse highlights the limitations of 'class' in defining the interests of a locality and its people.

'The Political Capital of Scotland':[60] *a 'sense of place'*
So far, component elements of the material geography of Paisley - the tramways, the Cart, the mills - have driven the discussion of local identity yet, as has been illustrated, the identity of a 'place' is far more than the sum of its physical parts. A 'sense' or 'spirit' of place can persist 'in spite of profound changes in the basic components of identity.'[61] So it was that Paisley *as a Radical burgh*, dominated popular thinking of its collective conscious despite changes in industrial and municipal relations. Treating Paisley as *subject,* as well as the 'product' of conflicting component discourses, in this way allows for an analysis of local identity as an active social phenomenon - something which, though 'subtle and nebulous', 'contentious and disputed', nevertheless is very real.[62]

Identity in this sense, does not evolve directly from any particular documented incident or experience, making it difficult to analyse in any empirical sense. Rather, it exists in the ways in which Paisley presents images of itself, to itself and to the outside world and how such images are expressed through language.[63] There is no Paisley, in this sense, without Paisley imagined.[64]

Throughout the late nineteenth century, platform orators and the local Liberal press drew on Paisley's Radical and Chartist past as the origins of a local Radical identity and styled it as a property of the place. Examples abound. Commentators pointed to 'the sturdy old Radicalism of Paisley', the 'robust Liberalism of this good town' and in 1885, the editor of the *Paisley*

Chronicle emphasised that 'Paisley is Liberal, and Liberal to the very heart' - the organic imagery emphasising the 'natural' association of politics and place.[65]

Furthermore, an intrinsic part of Paisley's self-image as the guardian of the heritage of the weaver Radicals, was the translation of this political tradition into ballad-style poetry - much of it exploitative of familiar verses by Motherwell, Tannahill and Burns. Consider the following extract from *Radical Lyric* by the Liberal Donald Cameron from 1891:

> O Paisley! never let thy sons
> Their Liberal sires disgrace;
> As an MP for thee, O let
> No Tory show his face!
> Thy sons make heroes of the free
> Them properly array;
> Upon the mighty battlefield
> Place round their brows the bay.
>
> One hour of Patrick Brewster grant!
> The slogan to upraise;
> The radicals to triumph lead
> And Tory ranks abase,
> One hour of Patrick Brewster give!
> With Paisley's Grand Old Man,
> To fill the Radicals with fire
> In their prevailing van.[66]

Written during a by-election, the poem metaphorically links local personalities of the Chartist era (Rev. Patrick Brewster) with national figures ('the Grand Old Man') to manufacture potent symbols of a Radical continuum to endorse the party's new local Liberal champion. Commitment to the cause is perceived as a duty, an act of loyalty to an heroic 'familial' ancestry elemented by the fathers ('sires') of the current generation ('sons'). Imagery of liberation and servitude, of justice and tyranny are dramatically juxtaposed, echoing the rhetoric of an older Radicalism in the interests of evoking an image of Paisley as a Liberal constituency - simultaneously the battle-ground and the prize of the electoral contest.

If, as I and others have suggested, such imaginings of a place have their own weight, as Patrick Joyce makes clear, 'we can no longer understand (the operation of democracy) solely ...in terms of sources of power lying behind it and controlling it (classes, interests, parties and so on).'[67] Similarly, we cannot understand local politics in terms of the universal monoliths of nationality and class without recourse to the historical and spatial evolution of individual constituencies.

John Agnew has emphasised that:

> political expression in Scotland is *intrinsically* geographical. It is not merely the by-product of an uneven development or population composition that draws Scotland away from the British 'norm'. Rather, it is the product of political behaviour structured by the historically constituted social contexts in which people live their lives: in a word, places.[68]

The local identity of 'places' is frequently - though seldom straightforwardly - expressed in their politics. Paisley's unbroken Liberal representation from 1832 to 1923 expressed and was contingent on the perpetuation of a version of Radical local identity which in turn drew support from shared class interests and the strength of industrial paternalism. Yet after 1886, the equation of Radical sentiment with Liberal party politics was challenged in Paisley by competing interpretations of the Radical inheritance from both Left and Right. The identity of Radical Paisley was shown to be malleable, accomodating the agendas of competing political parties.[69]

Rosslyn Mitchell's victory for Labour in 1924, however, was less the expression of the triumphal inevitability of class politics, following national trends in securing urban constituencies for Labour, than the failure of the Liberal and Unionist parties in appreciating that what was possible politically was defined in local terms by local traditions and contemporary social relations which had very little to do with class in any universal sense.[70] Labour succeeded by offering a vision of Paisley which coincided with the shared symbols, beliefs and expectations which composed local identity.

Amongst other factors, the pact which Asquith established with local Unionists seemed to indicate to Paisley voters in 1924 that Liberalism had abandoned Paisley's inherited politics.[71] In contrast, Hugh Roberton noted at Mitchell's opening demonstration:

> The Labour Party was not a new party, and it carried on the old traditions of the Chartists, the Radicals and the Land Leaguers, and was the lineal descendant of the Paisley weavers of 100 years ago. (Cheers.) Radicalism kept Liberalism alive, the old passionate desire for progress, but Liberalism was not only dead today, but was going to be buried in the bowels of Conservatism...[72]

Mitchell's victory was therefore far from a victory for something 'new', but the affirmation of the claim which had been mooted since the 1890s: that Labour now more accurately articulated the popular radical agenda. Measured against the constants of basic Radical principles, Liberalism - in its post-war mutation as a party of the Establishment - had lost its claim on the Radical continuum. The complex interplay of party and principle, tradition and identity, therefore determined the chronology and character of Paisley's contribution to Scottish politics rather than the operation of blind national or universal social trends.

Conclusion

Local identity is far from the simple articulation of the popular voice of a group of spatially located individuals or the reputation which a particular place enjoys either in the eyes of a nation or neighbouring communities. Rather, it is at the point of intersection in 'space' and 'time' of the externally ascribed and internally generated images of a locality that local identity is formed. Identity is thus never static, never resting and always contested. Conflicting discourses generate a web of contrasting claims to represent the identity of a place and its people - claims which, whilst they may be ascendant at certain moments in an area's history, never hold that position indefinitely or without struggle. Such discourses are, furthermore, both generated by the phyisical features of a place - both natural and manufactured - and reliant on associated conceptual geographies which ascribe meaning to these physical 'spaces'.

Yet, beyond such a contested territory, there is identified a 'sense of place' which - being open to competing interpretations - has the power to withstand changes in the material properties of a locality whilst still retaining meaning for the inhabitants. Again 'ownership' of this 'sense of place' is contested and prone to change over time, yet in competing expressions of it we encounter the processes through which individuals and communities make sense of the places in which they live - places at once less and more than the nation.

NOTES

[1] The surgeon, William Kerr, collaborated with local ministers in presenting the etymology of the word Paisley in the *New Statistical Account of Scotland* of 1845 where it is noted that: 'At Paisley, the Romans had a station or town, which antiquarians regard as the Vanduaria of Ptolemy.' Vol. VII, (Edinburgh, 1845), 136.

Lennox Kerr, *The Eager Years: An Autobiography,* (London, 1940), pp. 15-16.

[2] John A. Agnew, 'Representing Space: Space, scale and culture in social science',

3 James Duncan and David Ley (eds) *Place/ Culture/ Representation,* (London, 1993), 252, 253, 254.

[4] John A. Agnew, 'Place and Politics in Post-War Italy: A cultural geography of local identity in the provinces of Lucca and Distoia', Kay Anderson and Fay Gale, *Inventing Places: Studies in Cultural Geography,* (London, 1992), p. 53.

[5] Patrick Joyce, *Visions of the People: Industrial England and the question of class, 1848-1914,* (Cambridge, 1991); *Democratic Subjects: The self and the social in nineteenth century England,* (Cambridge, 1994).

[6] Michael Keith and Steve Pile, 'Introduction Part 1: The Politics of Place...', Keith and Pile (eds) *Place and the Politics of Identity,* (London, 1993), 3.

[7] David Harvey, 'Class Relations, Social Justice and the Politics of Difference', Keith and Pile (eds), *Place and the Politics of Identity,* 52-3.

[8] Susan Hanson and Geraldine Pratt, *Gender, Work and Space,* (London, 1995), 186-7

[9] John A. Agnew, 'Representing Space', 261; 'The Devaluation of Place in Social Science', J. A. Agnew and J.S. Duncan, *The Power of Place: Bringing Together Geographical and Sociological Imaginations,* (London, 1989), p. 16; Keith and Pile, 'Introduction Part 1', 16; George Revill, 'Reading Rose Hill, Community, identity and inner-city Derby', Keith and Pile (eds), *Place and the Politics of Identity,* pp. 119-20; E. Relph, *Place and Placelessness,* (London, 1976), 56.

[10] Edward W. Soja, *Postmodern Geographies: The Reassertion of Space in Critical Social Theory,* (London, 1989), 126.

[11] *ibid.,* 126.

[12] Soja has called for the 'stranglehold of a still addictive historicism' to be 'loosened'. *ibid.,* 11.

[13] Among the best of recent local histories has been Robert Duncan's *Wishaw: Life and Labour in a Lanarkshire Industrial Community, 1790-1914,* (Motherwell, 1986) and *Steelopolis: The Making of Motherwell, 1750-1939,* (Motherwell, 1991). However, even here no consideration is given to the contested nature and meaning of local geographies.

[14] John A. Agnew, *Place and Politics: The Geographical Mediation of State and Society,* (Boston, 1987), 160.

[15] Kerr, *The Eager Years,*13.

[16] Soja, *Postmodern Geographies,* 126.

[17] Michael Keith and Steve Pile, 'Introduction Part 2: The Place of Politics', Keith and Pile (eds) *Place and the Politics of Identity,* 31-35.

[18] *ibid.,* 23.

[19] See *ibid.,*27-30. See also Relph, *Place and Placelessness,* 3, 45; Soja, *Postmodern Geographies,* 122.

[20] See Catriona M.M. Macdonald, *The Radical Thread: Political Change in Scotland, Paisley Politics, 1885-1924,* (East Linton, Forthcoming 1998)

[21] See Charles Jedrej and Mark Nuttall, *White Settlers: The Impact of Rural Repopulation in Scotland*, (1996).

[22] Kay Anderson and Fay Gale, 'Introduction', Anderson and Gale (eds) *Inventing Places*, 5.

[23] *New Statistical Account*, Vol. VII, 138-9.

[24] John A. Agnew, 'Place and Politics', 58.

[25] *Third Statistical Account: Counties of Renfrewshire and Bute*, (Glasgow, 1962), 322.

[26] *Ibid.*, 324.

[27] P[aisley] D[aily] E[xpress], 20 Nov. 1888; P[aisley and] R[enfrewshire] G[azette], 19 Oct. 1895

[28] See, for example, *PDE*, 23 Nov. 1912.

[29] Reference taken from the *County and Municipal Record* , as quoted in *PDE*, 21 Aug. 1923.

[30] *Forward*, 1 July 1923.

[31] *PRG*, 24 Sept. 1898.

[32] *ibid.*, 15 Oct. 1898.

[33] *PDE*, 11 May 1900, 5 Nov. 1900.

[34] *ibid.,*, 1 Aug. 1889.

[35] *PRG*, 22 Oct. 1892.

[36] Soja, *Postmodern Geographies*, pp. 127, 128.

[37] *ibid.*, p. 129.

[38] Kerr, *The Eager Years*, 13.

[39] Soja, *Postmodern Geographies*, 158.

[40] Doreen Massey, 'Politics and Space/Time', Keith and Pile, *Place and the Politics of Identity*, 156.

[41] 'the identity of a place varies with the intentions, personalities, and circumstances of those who are experiencing it.': Relph, *Place and Placelessness*, 57.

[42] *PDE*, 7 March 1885.

[43] *ibid.*, 9 March 1885.

[44] *ibid.*, 13 March 1885.

[45] *ibid.*, 14 March 1885.

[46] *Third Statistical Account*, 289.

[47] Keith and Pile, 'Introduction Part Two', 25.

[48] Anderson and Gale, 'Introduction', p. 8.

[49] See Macdonald, *The Radical Thread;* W.W. Knox, *Hanging by a Thread: The Scottish Cotton Industry, c. 1850-1914* (Preston, 1995)

[50] *PDE*, 4 Dec. 1893.

[51] *PRG*, 6 Nov. 1897.

[52] Hanson and Pratt, *Gender, Work and Space*, 186.

[53] *PDE*, 29 March 1893.

[54] See Catriona Macdonald, 'Weak Roots and Branches: class, gender and the geography of industrial protest', Unpublished Seminar Paper, February 1997. Cf. W.W. Knox and H. Corr, '"Striking Women": Cotton Workers and Industrial Unrest, c.1907-1914', W. Kenefick and A. McIvor, *Roots of Red Clydeside?* (Edinburgh, 1996), 107, 123, 125.

[55] *PDE*, 5 March 1894.

[56] See J. W. Scott, 'On Language, Gender and Working-class History', L. R. Berlanstein (ed), *The Industrial Revolution and Work in Nineteenth Century Europe* (London, 1992), 172-3; S. Alexander, 'Women, Class and Sexual Difference in the 1830s and 1840s: Some Reflections on the Writing of Feminist History', *History Workshop* (1983),146.

[57] *PRG*, 12 May 1906. (My italics.)

[58] *ibid.*, . (My italics.)

[59] *ibid.*, 19 May 1906. (My italics.)

[60] Asquith speaking of Paisley in a speech in St Andrews Halls. *PRG*, 24 April 1909.

[61] Relph, *Place and Placelessness*,48.

[62] See Relph, *Place and Placelessness*, 48-9; Simon Charsley, '"Glasgow's Miles Better": the symbolism of community and identity in the city', Anthony Cohen (ed), *Symbolising Boundaries: Identity and Diversity in British Cultures* (Manchester, 1986), 183.

[63] Charsley, '"Glasgow's Miles Better"', 183.

[64] Here I follow Patrick Joyce in adapting the words of Benedict Anderson, who maintains that there is no nation without the nation imagined. Benedict Anderson, *Imagined Communities: Reflections on the origins and Spread of Nationalism* (1991).

[65] *PDE*, 13 Nov. 1885, 3 May 1886; *Paisley Chronicle*, 21 Nov. 1885.

[66] *ibid.*, 25 May 1891.

[67] Joyce, *Democratic Subjects*, 20. See also Catriona M.M. Macdonald, "Speaking in Tongues': Poetry, Politics and Paisley's Radical Tradition, 1885-1895', Conference Paper delivered to the Scottish Economic and Social History Society, St Andrews Conference, April 1997.

[68] Agnew, *Place and Politics*, 108.

[69] See Catriona M.M. Macdonald, 'Locality, Tradition and Language in the Evolution of Scottish Unionism: A Case Study, Paisley 1886-1910', Catriona M.M. Macdonald (ed), *Unionist Scotland 1800-1997* (Edinburgh, forthcoming 1998).

[70] Relph, *Place and Placelessness*, p. 60; Agnew, 'Place and Politics in Post-war Italy', 58.

[71] For a fuller discussion of the 1924 General Election in Paisley see Macdonald, *The Radical Thread*, Ch. 5.

[72] *PDE*, 17 Oct. 1924.

CHAPTER TEN

Embracing the Past: The Highlands in Nineteenth Century Scotland

Ewen A. Cameron.[1]

Introduction

It is a paradox of recent Scottish national identity that many of its most potent symbols have come from the Scottish Highlands. For much of Scottish history, the Highlands were viewed as separate and different from the rest of the nation and the adoption of the kilt, tartan and bagpipes by lowlanders has often been presented as one example of the synthetic nature of national identity.[2] This essay does not attempt to go over this ground anew, but rather to concentrate on a series of historical events which can be cited to demonstrate that a vein of assertiveness can be detected in Highland history in the nineteenth century. Assertiveness can be seen in attempts to draw attention to the vitality of such indigenous features as the Gaelic language, traditional folklore and valued systems of land tenure. Furthermore, there was an apparent tendency to challenge the status quo, in the Disruption of the Church of Scotland in 1843, or the Crofters' Wars of the 1880s, for example. It will be argued here that the apparently forceful nature of these challenges was compromised, not only by a deep seated introspection, but also by a profound attachment to an idealised view of the past. The status quo may have been challenged, but only in an attempt to embrace an idealised vision of the past.

While the eighteenth century creation, or recreation, of the Highlander took place largely from without, the nineteenth century assertion of identity came from within. Nevertheless, one should not exaggerate Highland distinctiveness. The forces which shaped Highland history were the same ones which shaped wider Scottish History; the fluctuations of the industrial economy, demographic change, imperialism, evangelicalism, the development of state education and the rise and fall of laissez-faire Liberalism.

Any discussion of Highland history must recognise the changing perceptions of the Highlands within Scotland. Prior to 1300 there was no contemporary perception of a line dividing Scotland into Highland and Lowland regions. Prior to this date, Gaelic was not a retreating regional language, although a linguistic divide had emerged in Scotland by the middle of the fourteenth century.[3] The long process of the integration of the Highlands into the Kingdom of Scotland, and then into the United Kingdom of Great Britain after 1707, took place alongside the development of a perception of the

Highlands as a separate and distinct region. The early seventeenth century saw a more concerted effort by central government to deal with what they perceived as a 'Highland problem'. This presaged a period from the mid-seventeenth to the mid-eighteenth century when the Highlands became the location for a series of rebellions which helped to define the region as lawless and threatening.[4] This perception ultimately became an important factor in precipitating its transformation.[5]

The intellectual exercise of trying to divide Scotland into Highlands and Lowlands is complicated by the range of factors involved.[6] Language is not a straightforward determinant given the contraction of Gaelic speaking areas.[7] The existence of cultural perceptions which do not easily translate into geographical terms further complicate the matter.[8] Physical conditions can provide a static frontier, but not a straightforward one. The existence of 'Lowland' conditions on the East coast, north of Inverness complicates the matter.[9] Internal diversity is as important a consideration as distinctions between the Highlands and the Lowlands.[10] Government intervention to draw a Highland line was evident in both the 1820s, in an attempt to regulate whisky distillation, and the 1880s, in an effort to confine crofter tenure.[11]

This is an indication, perhaps, that the modern Highlands have been perceived in important ways by outsiders. This was especially so in the eighteenth and early nineteenth centuries. During the course of the nineteenth century, culminating in the 1880s, indigenous perceptions began to challenge this position. This is an important aspect of the increasing assertiveness of Highlanders which can be detected in this period. Of course, this is not say that external perceptions did not remain influential. Representations of the Highlands in art and photography, and the direct engagement of outsiders with the Highlands, in the form of commercialised sport or tourism, created an image of the region which was at odds with the reality of the indigenous perception.[12]

A considerable body of historiography exists on the subject of the appropriation of Highland symbols for Scottish national identity. Most writers have concentrated on the interesting change in the perception of the Highlander from bloodthirsty rebel and deadly enemy of the Hanoverian state in 1746, to staunch and heroic defender of the British empire by 1815.[13] Highland symbols moved from a state of proscription in the late 1740s to a position of eminence by 1822, the year in which Sir Walter Scott, not content with romanticising the Highlander in the pages of his historical novels, welcomed a tartan clad George IV to a Highlandised Edinburgh.[14]

Of course, alongside this story of changing images and perceptions there is a less than romantic historical experience. Over the course of the eighteenth century Highland society underwent a vast economic and social transformation. This experience was not confined to the Highlands. Scotland as a whole experienced a social and economic revolution which was remarkably concentrated in time and space. In many ways, events in the Highlands were direct results of these wider changes.[15] The most obvious example of this was the process of clearance which involved the creation of crofting communities, the rationale for which was profit maximisation, whether through kelp gathering, fishing, or military recruitment.[16] It is ironic that these processes have been denigrated while the communities created by them have been celebrated in literature and confirmed by legislation.[17]

Relocation and Expulsion
The period from 1815 to 1886 saw a number of important developments in Highland history. The process of clearance was transformed from an exercise in relocation, driven by the labour requirements of Highland landowners, to one of expulsion motivated by increasing landowning insecurity about the 'vulnerable society' which they had created in the first phase of clearance.[18] This came to a head with the almost complete failure of the potato crop in the Highlands, in common with many other areas in Northern Europe, in the late 1840s and 1850s. The ensuing famine unleashed a concentrated cycle of clearance and emigration in the 1850s. The famine years also saw the growth of a new kind of literature about the Highlands. Polemical social critiques of conditions in the Highlands began to appear in the 1840s and 1850s in greater numbers than before. Robert Somers toured the Highlands in 1847 and his journal, published the following year, with its graphic accounts of the suffering of famine stricken Highlanders, did much to bring the famine to wider attention. More polemical still were Thomas Mulock, editor of the *Inverness Advertiser*, and Donald Ross, whose strident denunciations of laissez-faire shibboleths and landlord actions set the tone for a radical literature which would reach its peak in the 1880s.[19]

A Presbyterian Identity?
The 1840s saw another seminal event in Highland history, the Disruption in the Church of Scotland. The result of a long conflict between Church and State over the issue of spiritual independence, the Disruption led to the creation of the Free Church of Scotland, an institution which became central to the identity of the crofting community but much maligned for its suspicion of vital elements of Gaelic culture. 1843 was also the first of a series of schisms in the Presbyterian Church which had a particular impact in the Highlands. It was followed in 1893 with the creation of the Free Presbyterian

Church of Scotland, and in 1900 a small number of Highland congregations declined to enter the United Free Church of Scotland and pursued their claim to the property of the Free Church in the House of Lords. This increasingly narrow and desperate sectarianism must be contrasted to the broad movement away from the Established Church in 1843.[20]

It has been argued that the Disruption was the central event in the process which created the identity of the crofting community in the nineteenth century. The early decades of the nineteenth century saw a series of evangelical revivals sweep through the Highlands. It has been argued that these 'eventually carried the greater part of the people into the Free Church' and that Highlanders were especially receptive to the evangelical message because of the 'social and psychological consequences of the collapse of the old order'.[21] The same author has argued that the 'indigenous evangelical movement' was exploited by the evangelical wing of the increasingly fractured Established Church of Scotland, and fortuitously complemented existing divisions in Highland society: 'the Disruption was not just an ecclesiastical dispute. It was a class conflict. Its battle line was the line of class demarcation, the line between the small tenantry on the one hand and sheep farmers, factors and proprietors on the other.'[22]

This view has not gone unchallenged. It is possible to stress the 'religious causes of Hebridean revival movements' by pointing to the influence of the Gaelic School Society teachers, the distribution of the Gaelic bible and the rise of an evangelical ministry prior to the Disruption. The latter development was especially noticeable in Lewis where the patrons presented evangelical ministers.[23] The Disruption did not have a uniform impact across the Highlands. In Argyll, and especially in Mull, a substantial proportion of the clergy, even those who could be classed as evangelical, remained with the Established Church. Indeed, until 1855 there was only one Free Church minister on the Island of Mull. At the other end of the spectrum was Ross-shire, and especially Easter Ross, where substantial proportions of the Ministry, and almost the entire Evangelical party, left to join the Free Church. Indeed, the Disruption had a greater impact here than in any other part of Scotland. In Lewis the picture was similar, but in the Presbyteries of Skye and Uist the position was very different, with a majority of the clergy remaining in the Established Church.[24] These were the areas which corresponded most closely to the popular picture of the Disruption in the Highlands; where a moderate ministry was deserted by an evangelical population. There were two notable exceptions to this process; Roderick Macleod and Norman Macleod. The Rev Roderick Macleod (Maighster Ruaraidh) had been a contumacious Church of Scotland minister in Bracadale and Snizort and subsequently became Free Church minister in Snizort. He became known as the 'Bishop of Skye' during the course of a long ministry.[25] Norman Macleod was the minister of the *quoad sacra* parish of Trumisgarry and was the only minister in the Presbytery of North Uist to join the Free Church.[26] The picture in Sutherland was different once again, especially in the west of the county where four out of the five ministers in the Presbytery of Tongue joined the Free Church. This was the area which had been most strongly influenced by the charismatic and subversive activities of the group of lay evangelicals known as *Na Daoine* (The Men).[27] Given these, and many other, complexities regarding the Disruption in the Highlands one should be wary of sweeping statements which do not take sufficient account of the diversity of experience across the Highlands. This does not tell us whether those ministers who remained in the establishment, whether from principle, loyalty to their patron or unwillingness to make the necessary material sacrifices, were preaching to empty churches after May 1843.

An important part of the identity of the Free Church in the Highlands was the way in which the Church exploited the 'Site Controversy'.[28] By assiduous use of their efficient propaganda machine they presented a picture of wholesale refusal by landlords to grant sites for new Free Church buildings in the aftermath of the Disruption. Hugh Miller's Free Church newspaper, *The Witness* was at the forefront of this campaign, lambasting proprietors who had refused sites and concentrating its fire on Cameron of Lochiel and the Duke of Sutherland, who, to compound a range of miscellaneous sins, were Episcopalians.[29] In 1847 a Select Committee of the House of Commons was appointed to look into the matter. By 1847 the outstanding cases of refusal were limited to 35, of which 18 were in the Highlands. The landowners involved included Sir James Riddell of Ardnamurchan (whose refusal led to his tenants worshipping on a craft moored in Loch Sunart), Lord MacDonald, Lady Dunmore of Harris, and Balfour of Whittinghame in Strathconan.[30] The 'Site Controversy' has been the subject of a debate which is reliant on the Report of the Select Committee.[31] This has been used both to exaggerate the extent of the controversy and to attempt to play it down. Mere counting of the instances of refusal underestimates the immediate impact of the issue; many landowners, such as the Duke of Sutherland, granted sites extremely reluctantly.[32] Others who refused, such as Riddell, had invested heavily in the Established Church in the years prior to the Disruption. The Site Controversy reveals a great deal about the attitudes of the Free Church seeking to establish itself in the 1840s and about the mindset of landowners, many of whom were genuinely shocked that their tenants should leave the National Church, to say nothing about the consequent deprivation of a useful means of social control.[33]

Not all landowners took this attitude, the Marquis of Breadalbane was a noted supporter of the Free Church.[34] He not only provided sites for Free Churches, accommodated ministers in spare mansions, provided a yacht to supply preachers to inaccessible areas of the Highlands and purchased driftwood to build a Free Church in Lewis, but he was also behind an attempt to establish a Free Church Teacher Training College in Oban.[35]

The Free Church established itself, in its early years at least, as a stout defender of Highland people. Its massive fund raising efforts were directed not only to the provision of Churches and schools, but also to famine relief. The Free Church Destitution Committee was the first famine relief organisation to respond to the failure of the potato crop in 1846. It played a critical role in bringing the famine to the attention of the country.[36] The role of the Church in the later part of the century is more controversial. It has been argued that the initial period of anti-aristocratic fervour, evident in publications such as *The Witness*, was dissipated in the period from the 1850s to the 1880s, and not rediscovered until the Crofters Wars of the 1880s.[37] On the other hand, it has been argued that as the Free Church underwent a process of liberalisation, the traditional Highland form of religion came to be seen as anachronistic. This, the argument goes, became the basis for a Highland-Lowland divide in the Free Church which culminated in the Free Presbyterian Disruption of 1892.[38] The responses of the Presbyterian Churches to the major events of nineteenth century Highland history have not been fully studied.[39] The tendency in the historiography has been to assume that the Highlands were monolithically Presbyterian. This does a grave disservice to the pockets of Roman Catholicism in Western Inverness-shire, Barra and South Uist and the evangelical Baptist and Congregationalist traditions of Tiree and the fishing communities of the Black Isle. It has been argued that these denominations provided an alternative strand of evangelicalism in the early nineteenth century. As the century wore on, however, this was not sustained.[40]

Education

The relationship between the Scottish education system and the Highlands is a complex one. For present purposes two themes can be highlighted; provision and perception. The notion that educational provision in the Highlands was limited has had a long shelf life.[41] Clearly, the Disruption had a positive impact here as the Free Church applied its redoubtable zeal to the provision of education. This energy was expended partly in the interests of the educational needs of Highland school children and partly in the interests of demonstrating to the Established Church that the newly founded Free Church could match it in every area of activity. A recent examination of the period immediately prior to the Disruption has attempted to revise upwards the scale of educational provision in the Highlands.[42] This is not to argue that there were not particular problems in Highland educational provision. Problems of poverty, geographical remoteness and rugged terrain were expressed in the *New Statistical Account*.[43] They remained pertinent a generation later when Sheriff Alexander Nicolson surveyed the Highland educational scene as part of the Argyll Commission on Scottish education.[44]

There were also problems with perceptions; the late eighteenth and early nineteenth centuries saw not only the continuing marginalisation of Gaelic, but also the creation of the crofting communities with their necessity for temporary migration to maintain living standards. This was especially noticeable after 1815 when local opportunities for wage earning collapsed. There is much evidence in the *Statistical Accounts* concerning the deleterious influence of temporary migration on Gaelic. Contact with the Lowlands deepened the perception that Gaelic was inimical to economic progress; the growing demand for English in Highland schools, and the use of Gaelic as an elementary teaching tool in order to facilitate it, was the end result. The influence of educational agencies since the early eighteenth century has been perceived to be inimical to the Gaelic language. Agencies such as the Society in Scotland for the Propagation of Christian Knowledge (SSPCK) saw their role as one to transform the Highlander by a combined process of education and evangelicalism.[45] Although initial reluctance to countenance the use of Gaelic to produce the transformation was abandoned from the 1760s and the use of Gaelic reading was formalised in 1826, the end remained the same.[46] Gaelic was not seen as the language of progress, commerce and modernity; however, it could be tolerated in the domestic, religious and traditional spheres. The developments in the eighteenth century which destroyed Gaels' perceptions of their own language are central to understanding the seemingly belated assertion of its vitality in the nineteenth century. The fact that the 1872 Education Act could reach the statute book without any real political pressure in the cause of the Gaelic language is as important as the fact that the omissions from the act stung Gaelic activists into action. This is not to argue that there had been no activity on behalf of Gaelic in the period before 1872. The activities of the General Assembly (of the Church of Scotland) Educational Committee, and the Edinburgh Gaelic Schools Society helped to establish the credibility of Gaelic literacy and education.[47] It must be emphasised, however, that the aim of this kind of activity remained one of anglicisation.[48] This was given a modicum of official backing by Alexander

Nicolson's Report into education in the Highlands, undertaken as part of the Argyll Commission's investigation into Scottish Education in the 1860s. This provided a basis which the more politically active lobbyists of the Gaelic Society of Inverness could exploit. The election of Charles Fraser MacKintosh to parliament in 1874 meant that the Gaelic cause had an activist ideally placed to further the campaign.

Urban Highlanders
Substantial communities of Highlanders in urban Scotland originated with permanent migrants from the southern and eastern Highlands moving to the towns close to the Highland Lowland boundary. Greenock, Paisley, Glasgow, Perth, Stirling, Dundee and Aberdeen all had substantial Highland communities from the mid-eighteenth century. The people who made up these communities were mostly drawn from the Highland hinterland of these towns and not from the crofting communities of the north-west Highlands.[49] With the establishment of the crofting system in the late eighteenth and early nineteenth centuries, the importance of temporary migration in search of income became an increasingly important factor in the life of the North and West.[50] In times of crisis, such as the famines of the mid 1830s and mid 1840s, urban Scotland was an important source of philanthropic aid to the stricken Highlands. Clearly, not all of the money came from urban Gaels, a more important consideration was the willingness of urban Scots to support the natives of the romanticised Highlands, this was despite the fact that the prevalence of dire poverty contradicted the romantic image.[51] As these urban communities of Gaels grew, networks which they were able to exploit also expanded. In the early 1840s, the Rev Norman MacLeod recorded the preference which many households had for employing young Highland women for domestic service.[52] Recent wider comparison of the Irish and the Highlanders in Glasgow in the mid nineteenth century has illuminated the extent to which Highlanders were able to integrate into urban Scotland. They were less distinctive in terms of religion and were able to penetrate skilled employment to a greater extent than the Irish. The process of acceptance is symbolised by the prominence of Highlanders in the Police Forces of Glasgow and other towns in the West of Scotland.[53] Although they were not stigmatised, like the Catholic Irish, they retained an identity as Highlanders. This is evident from their cultural activities, which ranged from the classical to the popular.[54] In the religious sphere, for example, they retained a separate identity around the use of Gaelic for worship. It has been argued, however, that separate Gaelic and English church services was a division of class which cut across cultural groups, rather than a simple statement of cultural identity.[55] As important a defining

feature of the urban Gaels was their sense of place. This is reflected in the way in which, as they developed formal societies and sporting clubs in the 1870s and 1880s, the point of reference was the place of origin in the Highlands.[56] These societies often had charitable as well as social functions. For example in Glasgow these societies included the Skye Association founded in 1865, the Tiree Association, founded in 1870, the Lewis and Harris Association, founded in 1887 as well as societies of natives of Mull and Iona, Islay, Lochaber, Appin, Coll and Ardnamurchan, Morvern and Sunart.[57] Similarly, as Shinty was codified and organised in the same period, teams such as Glasgow Cowal, Glasgow Glenforsa, Glasgow Inveraray, Glasgow Inverness-shire, Glasgow Islay, Glasgow Oban and Lorne, Glasgow Kyles and Glasgow Skye, were formed.[58]

This urban sense of community was neither completely devoted to soirees and sport, nor completely atomised and apolitical. The leadership, organisation and drive of the Crofters' movement of the 1880s came from urban areas. Of the Crofters' MPs, Angus Sutherland was a schoolteacher in Glasgow, Roderick MacDonald was a doctor in London, as was G.B.Clark. Urban areas contributed a great deal to the recovery of Highland assertiveness in the final third of the nineteenth century. Two of the most important organisations in the Crofters' Movement were the Edinburgh and London Highland Land Law Reform Associations.

Post Famine Adjustments

The period from the late 1850s to the early 1880s has been characterised as one of 'unprecedented stability' and 'recovery' which was only shattered by a new economic and social crisis in the early 1880s. A more pessimistic view of these years would stress that, although formal clearances were not evident, landlord coercion continued in the form of the control of subdivision. This had the effect of regulating marriage in the crofting communities by restricting access to land.[59] The end of this period saw a considerable interest in the Highland past in terms of both historical study and the collection of folklore. This is interesting in itself, but is even more significant when the links between late nineteenth century views of Highland history and the development of government policy towards the Highlands in that period are explored. If the 1840s were a period in which the roots of a new and more assertive identity in the Highlands in the nineteenth century took hold, then the 1870s were the decade in which that assertiveness become so multifaceted and deep rooted that it boiled over into direct action in the 1880s and produced a limited response from government. That response, although limited in practical terms, was significant in that it can be seen to be an attempt to recognise the distinctiveness of the historical experience of the Highlands. This assertiveness can be seen in three areas; journalism, politics and the creation of Highland pressure groups. The 1870s have been somewhat overshadowed by the more dramatic events of the 1880s, but they deserve scrutiny in their own right. Brief comments on the decade would seem to indicate agreement amongst historians that they were a decade of growing assertiveness.[60] In the field of journalism we have already noted the significance of *The Witness* in the 1840s and 1850s.[61] There were a number of features of this newspaper and the period in which it was published which detract from its relevance in the rise of Highland awareness. Firstly, it was published in Edinburgh and had as its main focus the ecclesiastical controversies of the period. Its interest in the Highlands was based on the role of the Highlander in that controversy, although Hugh Miller, the editor, did have a long standing interest in the Highlands based on family background which straddled the Highland-Lowland boundary.[62] Secondly, Miller's views were strongly influenced by two important mid-nineteenth century shibboleths; race and laissez-faire. The former influence produced frequent diatribes against the Catholic Irish, who were migrating to Scotland in such numbers in this period. The belief in the moral dangers of government intervention tempered Miller's radicalism, despite his awareness of the injustices of the Highland land system.[63]

An awareness of Miller's position serves to emphasise the originality and distinctiveness of John Murdoch in the 1870s. Murdoch, and his newspaper, *The Highlander*, were sustained and unequivocal champions of the cause of the Highlander. *The Highlander* was published in Inverness between 1873 and 1881, its short life was punctuated by financial crises which threatened its existence.[64] Murdoch was a deeply unconventional figure in late nineteenth century Highland life. After a a formative period on Islay, where he was heavily influenced by John Francis Campbell, and a career in the excise service which exposed him to industrial poverty in the North of England and the beginnings of Fenian Nationalism in Ireland, he retired to Inverness and a career in newspaper publishing and land agitation. He combined a fundamental religiosity with a profound suspicion of organised religion and an extreme protestantism with contempt for anti-Irish feeling.[65] He campaigned openly for the cause of the Highlander in a linguistic, political and social context. There is insufficient space here for detailed study of the contents of *The Highlander* but it is possible to discern a number of recurring themes which emphasise the importance of the paper. Murdoch demanded political and linguistic assertiveness. The former manifested itself in his support for Charles Fraser MacKintosh's challenge to the clique which dominated

Inverness politics and eventually resulted in his election as member for the Inverness district of burghs in 1874.[66] The second was evident in his advocacy of Highland pressure groups to respond to the absence of provisions for Gaelic in the 1872 Education Act. The Gaelic Society of Inverness (formed in 1871) and the Federation of Celtic Societies (1877) both took up this issue with some relish.[67] Murdoch was also a constant critic of the associations of Highlanders which were springing up in urban Scotland; he excoriated them for their concentration on social niceties and demanded that they become the basis of an assertive pressure group to fight on Highland issues.[68] He sought to present the case for extensive land reform, embracing issues such as the game laws and crofter tenure.[69] He also attempted to show the citizens of Inverness that they should take an interest in these issues, as the life of the town was not immune from the impact of rural injustice.[70] In a wider perspective, the most interesting theme to emerge from the pages of *The Highlander* is the attempt to counter the overwhelming anti-Irish prejudice which was current at the time. Murdoch tried to inform his readers about the land issue in Ireland, Ireland's position within the union, and to make connections in both these areas to Scottish questions.[71] Of course, *The Highlander* was not the only title where evidence of a new assertiveness can be found. Duncan Cameron's *Oban Times* was steadily emerging to the position of eminence as an organ for the Crofters movement which it would hold in the 1880s. Alexander MacKenzie, whom Murdoch despised, was also active in the journalistic as well as the historical field. His *Celtic Magazine* and later his *Scottish Highlander* were published in Inverness and took an equally strident, if less original, approach to many of the issues which Murdoch had championed in the 1870s.

There was also a rise in political assertiveness in this period. Although the rise of the Crofters' Party at the general elections of 1885 and 1886 is well known, the political history of the 1870s is not such familiar territory. In this area the scope for assertiveness was limited by the extremely restricted franchise in the Scottish county seats. As a result, the Highland county seats were held by landowners such as Cameron of Lochiel, Matheson of Ardross, the Marquis of Stafford, Sir Tollemache Sinclair and various members of the House of Argyll. Many of these MPs regarded their seats as mere sinecures.[72] The Burgh franchise had been extended to a much greater degree in 1868 and there was scope for activity here. The first signs of such activity came in the Inverness District of Burghs. The seat was held by a minor laird Eneas W. MacKintosh of Raigmore who had been returned unopposed in 1868, succeeding Sir Alexander Matheson, and Murdoch regarded it as vital that he should be opposed at the next general election. An alternative candidate emerged in the shape of Charles Fraser MacKintosh, a well known figure in local politics and cultural circles. He faced the electorate, encouraged by editorial support from *The Highlander* and the *Inverness Advertiser*, with a bold programme and a claim to be free of cliques.[73] His victory in that election was the foundation of a long political career, during which he represented the Inverness Burghs until 1885, when he won the county seat as a Crofter Candidate. Prior to the reforms of 1885 and the advent of the Crofters' Party, he was looked to by the disenfranchised in the counties as their representative. He was a member of the Royal Commission chaired by Lord Napier which investigated the crofting question in 1883. After the division in the Liberal Party over Irish Home Rule in 1886 he was the only one of the Crofters' MPs to adopt a Liberal Unionist position. This aroused much suspicion and he was eventually defeated by another Crofter/Liberal candidate in 1892.[74]

There was also a rise in linguistic assertiveness in this period. The focus for this was the 1872 Education Act. This act made no provision for the teaching of Gaelic and the agitation leading up to it was notable for the lack of any pressure group to campaign for the place of Gaelic in Scottish education. The Gaelic Society of Inverness had been founded in 1871 but did not have time to influence the contents of the Act. With the Act as a focus after 1872, however, and with Fraser MacKintosh in parliament after 1874, the issue could be pursued more vigorously. The Scottish Education Department made minimal concessions in 1875, 1876 and 1878. Major changes did not come until the Education Acts of 1908 and 1918, but a new approach was taken to the issue in the 1870s.[75] Linguistic assertiveness can also be seen in this decade in the campaign led by John Stuart Blackie for the establishment of a Chair of Celtic in the University of Edinburgh. Blackie was an eminent classicist and educational reformer who had held chairs in Aberdeen and Edinburgh. He had discovered the Highlands and the various linguistic and political causes associated with the region, late in life. This late conversion produced a remarkable zeal and energy as well as massive eccentricity. Blackie produced an outpouring of writings in the cause of the Crofter and was an hyper-activist in the Gaelic Society of Inverness, but his most significant achievement was in connection with the Celtic Chair. He took over a moribund campaign in 1874 and by 1882 the necessary £14,000 had been raised.[76] Donald MacKinnon was a somewhat surprise choice as the first occupant of the Chair which many thought would have been awarded to John Francis Campbell of Islay, Alexander Carmichael, or even Dr Thomas MacLauchlan of the Free Church.[77] Although the campaign for the Chair can be placed within this framework of increasing linguistic assertiveness, it should be noted that there were a range of motives present among those involved and it should not be assumed that all were sincere believers in the importance of regenerating the language. The Churches and the University of Edinburgh were notable advocates of a 'utilitarian' interpretation of the value of the Chair.[78] A very broad range of individuals contributed to the fund for the endowment of the Chair.[79] It was part of Blackie's genius as a fundraiser to be able to appeal to such a broad constituency. Nevertheless, the Celtic Chair campaign was a core element of the propaganda of assertiveness furthered by Murdoch.[80] Certainly, few of the 'utilitarians' would have been in favour of MacKinnon's assertive views on the place of Gaelic in Scottish culture.[81]

Increasing assertiveness was mirrored in Gaelic poetry of the period, most notably the work of Uilleam MacDhunleibhe (William Livingstone) and Iain Mac a Ghobhainn (John Smith). The assertiveness of these poets can be contrasted with earlier nineteenth century Gaelic poetry which was, according to one commentator, characterised by 'weakness, thinness and perplexity'. These deficiencies were the result of the demoralisation of the Gaels by the process of clearance.[82] By contrast the poetry of MacDhunleibhe and Mac a Ghobhainn, as well as the work of Mairi Mhor nan Oran (Mary MacPherson) has been hailed as having a 'special individuality, strength and gravitas'.[83] MacDhunleibhe (1808 70) was a self educated tailor from Islay who spent most of his life in Glasgow.[84] His poetry is characterised by Anglophobia, a desire for cultural links between the Gaels of Scotland and Ireland and criticism of the clearances. Mac a Ghobhainn (1848-81) was from Lewis, where he spent most of his life, apart from brief medical studies in Edinburgh. His 'fearless' 'Am Brosnachadh' has been described as 'probably the most considered and the most scathing indictment' of the clearances.[85] Mac a Ghobhainn's targets included most of the key representatives of authority in the late nineteenth Century Highlands such as landowners and the Church. Mairi Mhor is a more famous and a more ambiguous figure. Her compositions in support of the Crofters Movement in the 1880s have to be considered alongside her 'Oran an Diuc Chataich' which is highly complimentary to the 3rd Duke of Sutherland. Recently, attention has been drawn to Donald MacPherson's publication in 1877 of a song by Allan MacDougall, originally composed in the late eighteenth century, entitled 'A Song on the Lowland Shepherds'. It is no coincidence that it was published in this period with an introductory essay by MacPherson in the periodical *An Ghaidheal*.[86] A recent comprehensive anthology of nineteenth century Gaelic poetry on social and political protest hints that the base of assertiveness may have been wider than earlier surveys suggested.[87]

This period also saw a concerted attempt to rescue evidence of the oral culture of the Highlands. The most important figures in this folklore collecting exercise were Alexander Carmichael, whose *Carmina Gadelica* was published in 1900 and John Francis Campbell whose *Popular Tales of the West Highlands* was published between 1860 and 1862. These were serious attempts to rescue something of the reality of Highland tradition and can be contrasted with the earlier attempts by outsiders to foist an invented tradition onto the Highlander. Considerable attention has been paid to the rise in interest in folklore across Europe in the second half of the nineteenth century. Certainly, men like Campbell and Carmichael were influenced by European and English collectors like the Grimm brothers and Henry Dasent.[88] Their work, particularly that of Carmichael, can be brought within the framework of increasing assertiveness. There was an imperative to rescue material which otherwise might have been lost, but also an attempt to present it in a positive manner representing a culture which had an independent vitality and had not merely benefited from integration into the modern world by the British state. There are distinctions to be made here though. Campbell was content to present his material as a 'museum of curious rubbish about to perish' and was also closely associated with the Argyll family.[89] He made his first visit to Islay for thirty one years in the course of supporting the Duke's son, Lord Colin Campbell, in his attempt to be elected as the MP for Argyll-shire in 1878.[90] Carmichael's approach was very different, although he had been one of Campbell's army of collectors of stories in the 1850s.[91] He related the oral culture he was attempting to preserve to the agricultural practices of the crofting community. Further, he was clear about the causes of the decline of Gaelic culture. They were, he argued, '... - principally the Reformation, the rebellions, the evictions, the Disruption, the schools and the spirit of the age'.[92] Thus, Carmichael was a more politically engaged folklorist, explicitly engaged in an attempt to rehabilitate Gaelic culture and the cause of the Highlander. He wrote of his motivations to Father Allan MacDonald of Eriskay, another noted collector, in 1898, 'it might perhaps be the means of conciliating some future politician in favour of our dear Highland people'.[93] Carmichael had also contributed a chapter on grazings and agrestic customs to W.F.Skene's Celtic Scotland, and this material was reprinted in the Report of the Napier Commission in 1884.

This interest in the Highland past displayed by folklorists was mirrored by more conventional historical works. Donald Gregory's unsurpassed *History of the Western Highlands and Isles to 1625* was published in 1836 with a second edition in 1881.[94] The work of the Edinburgh lawyer and antiquarian, William Forbes Skene, included a short and popular two volume study of the origins of Highland clans published in 1856 and a longer study of Celtic Scotland published in three volumes between 1876 and 1880.[95] Alexander MacKenzie was a pioneering historian of the more recent history of the Highlands. His polemical *History of the Highland Clearances* was first published in 1883, drawing heavily on the work of Donald MacLeod and including substantial material relating to the early campaigns in the Crofters' Wars.[96] Neither author was free from close involvement in the political events of the period. Skene's legal firm, Skene, Edwards and Bilton (later Skene Edwards and Garson), acted for many Highland landowners in their disputes with crofters, although Skene had largely retired from legal practice to concentrate on scholarship by this period. Skene had also been heavily involved in the famine relief operation in the 1840s.[97] MacKenzie was in the thick of the Crofters agitation as a newspaper propagandist and as an activist, he toured the crofting districts in advance of the Napier Commission to help the crofting community prepare its evidence. A more strident view of history was beginning to emerge from within the Highlands not only in such formal works as those mentioned above and would be reflected in the evidence given by crofters to the Napier Commission in 1883 and to the Deer Forest Commission in the early 1890s.[98] The columns of *The Highlander* and the pages of the early volumes of the *Transactions of the Gaelic Society of Inverness* are replete with such important evidence of the beginnings of an engagement with the recent and traumatic past. Although most of these accounts present a picture of a wholly contented society being broken up by the clearances, this development should not be underestimated.[99] In many ways the palpable sense of shock experienced by landowners and factors, as well as the Whig political establishment in the Highlands, during the Crofters' War and especially the General Elections of 1885 and 1886, is analogous to that evident after the Disruption in 1843.[100]

These changing perceptions are important in their own right, but they assume an extra importance when one appreciates their impact on public policy. The connection between perception and policy has been well documented in the second half of the eighteenth century, and the link between views of the Highlander as indolent and feckless with famine relief and emigration policy in the 1840s has been remarked upon.[101] The policies of these periods had long lasting impacts, but since sustained government intervention in the Highlands only began in the 1880s, the link between perception and policy in that period is especially important. It is also significant that the increasing assertiveness of the Highlander after the 1840s, and especially in the 1880s, also had an impact on government policy. It was that assertiveness and a growing appreciation in the highest levels of government which produced, in 1886,   the first in a series of statutes peculiarly applicable to the Highlands. After emphasising the longevity of Highland protest, Richards has posed the question: 'Why, in the 1880s, did the disturbances yield such rapid returns?'[102] The roots of this process were not only historicist, but the legislation seemed to be an attempt by government to provide a form of atonement for the wrongs of the past. Gladstone wrote of the 'might' of post 1745 landowners and his view that the 'representatives of the old flesh and blood' still had 'title to some legislative consideration'; his Home Secretary, Sir William Harcourt, was more blunt when he wrote of the way in which 'every acre of ground was subtracted from the crofters' and of the 'greed of gold on the part of the proprietors'.[103] Perhaps a cynic would argue that these historicist arguments were camouflage for a government sensitive to the accusation that it was capitulating to lawlessness. The agitation and its results, however, are oddly symmetrical. If the 1886 Act was conservative and backward looking, then so also were many aspects of the protests of the 1880s, not least the evidence given by crofters to the Napier Commission in 1883. This is evident in any consideration of continuing Highland protest down to the 1920s, the objectives were limited and the protest restrained compared to that occurring contemporaneously in Ireland for example. Indeed, one could argue that many of the forms of assertiveness considered here were compromised in one way or another, and if we regard them as the roots of the agitation of the 1880s, it is not surprising that it was restrained in its tactics and limited in its strategy. The proud evangelicalism of the Disruption disintegrated into narrow sectarianism; strident newspapers such as *The Highlander, The Scottish Highlander* or *The Oban Times,* either had short existences or lost their radical edge; even the new politics which began to stir in the 1870s, and which created the Crofters' Party, had largely fizzled out by the 1890s. Perhaps this provides support for the 'pessimistic' assessment of the years between the Famine and the Crofters' War, in that continuing and ever more sophisticated forms of landlord coercion continued to demoralise the crofting population.[104]

In a number of ways the Crofters' Act takes us back to the considerations which began this essay, not only in its historicism but also in its attempt to define the Highlands. The legislative area which the act applied to, the seven 'crofting counties' of Shetland, Orkney, Caithness, Sutherland, Ross, Inverness and Argyll, has proved to be a most enduring definition of the Highlands. The combination of a particular historical interpretation applied to a particular geographic area has had the most profound consequences for the Highlands in the 20th century.

Conclusion

In this essay the elements which contribute to the identity of the Highlands within nineteenth century Scotland have been traced. Stress has been laid on the relationship between the Highlands and wider Scottish institutions, such as the Churches and the education system, or historical forces which have affected Scotland as a whole, such as urbanisation and industrialisation. Within this framework the distinctiveness of the Highlands in linguistic and cultural terms has been emphasised. An underlying theme has been the differing perceptions of the Highlands provided by Highlanders and by outsiders. In the early part of the century the views of outsiders predominated, as the century progressed Highlanders were able to assert their own views to a greater extent. It is important to emphasise the extent to which this apparent assertiveness in the Highlands was compromised by Presbyterian introversion or by idealistic views of the past. Further, although we have not considered the events of the 1880s in depth, the protest of that decade was compromised by an idealistic historicism which has been identified as arising from a series of developments in the decades preceding the 1880s. The relationship between that process and the undoubted continuation of landlord coercion is a substantial issue. The final point to emphasise is the relationship between the Highlanders' wholehearted embrace of an idealistic view of the past and the creation of the crofting legislation in 1886. The justifications for important elements of that policy were found by policy makers in the history of the Highlands since 1745

NOTES

[1]Versions of this paper have been presented to Conferences in the Universities of Edinburgh and York. I am grateful to colleagues for their comments and suggestions on those occasions. I am also grateful to Tom Devine, William Gillies, Margaret Mackay, Andrew Mackillop, James MacLeod, Donald Meek, Alex Murdoch, Charles Withers and Donald Withrington for reading and commenting on the paper.

[2] A.D.Smith, 'Nationalism and the Historians', in A.D.Smith (ed), *Ethnicity and Nationalism*, (Leiden, 1992), 70; B.Anderson, *Imagined Communities, Reflections on the Origin and Spread of Nationalism*, (revised edition, London, 1991), 90; E.J.Hobsbawm, *Nations and Nationalism: Programme, Myth, Reality*, (second edition, Cambridge, 1992), 41, 9.

[3] G. W. S. Barrow, *The Kingdom of the Scots: Government, Church and Society from the eleventh to the fourteenth century*, (London, 1973), 362-3; D. Murison, 'Linguistic Relationships in Medieval Scotland', in G. W. S. Barrow, (ed), *The*

Scottish Tradition: Essays in Honour of Ronald Gordon Cant, (Edinburgh, 1974), 70-83.

[4] D. Stevenson, *Highland Warrior: Alasdair MacColla and the Civil Wars*, (Edinburgh, 1994 edition), 6-31; A. I. Macinnes, 'Crown, clans and fine: the 'civilising' of Scottish Gaeldom, 1587-1638', *Northern Scotland*, 13, (1993), 31-56; A. I. Macinnes, 'Repression and Conciliation: The Highland Dimension, 1660-1688', *SHR*, 65, (1986), 167-195.

[5] A recent effort to untangle governmental perceptions from developments within Gaeldom can be found in A.I.Macinnes, *Clanship, Commerce and the House of Stuart, 1603-1788*, (East Linton, 1996)

[6] C. W. J. Withers, 'The Scottish Highlands Outlined: cartographic evidence for the position of the Highland Lowland Boundary', *Scottish Geographical Magazine*, 98, (1982), 143-157.

[7] C. W. J. Withers, *Gaelic in Scotland, 1689-1981: The Geographical History of a Language*, (Edinburgh, 1984); V. E. Durkacz, *The Decline of the Celtic Languages: A Study of Linguistic and Cultural Conflict in Scotland, Wales and Ireland from the Reformation to the Twentieth Century*, (Edinburgh, 1983).

[8] J. MacInnes, 'The Gaelic Perception of the Lowlands' in W. Gillies (ed), *Gaelic and Scotland: Alba agus a' Ghàidhlig*, (Edinburgh, 1989), 90.

[9] Studies of such areas which touch on this theme include; I. R. M. Mowat, *Easter Ross 1750-1850: the Double Frontier*, (Edinburgh, 1981), esp 1-4 & 139-41; M. C. Storrie, 'Landholdings and Population in Arran from the Late Eighteenth Century', *Scottish Studies*, 11 (1967), 49-74; I. Carter, *Farmlife in Northeast Scotland, 1840-1914: The Poorman's Country*, (Edinburgh, 1979), 165-75; A. Watson & E. Allan, 'Depopulation by clearances and non enforced emigration in the North East Highlands', *Northern Scotland*, 10 (1990), 31-46.

[10] B.Lenman, *The Jacobite Clans of the Great Glen, 1650-1784*, (London, 1984), 1-5; T. M. Devine, *The Great Highland Famine: Hunger, Emigration and the Scottish Highlands in the Nineteenth Century*, (Ednburgh, 1988), 1; M. Gray, *The Highland Economy, 1750-1850*, (Edinburgh, 1957), 3.

[11] T. M. Devine, 'The rise and fall of illicit whisky-making in northern Scotland, c. 1780-1840', *SHR*, 54, (1975), 155-77; Withers, 'The Scottish Highlands Outlined', 149.

[12] T.Pringle, 'The Privation of History, Landseer, Victoria and the Highland Myth', in D.Cosgrave & S.Daniels (eds) *The Iconography of Landscape*, (Cambridge, 1988) 142-161; C.Withers, 'Picturing Highland Landscapes: George Washington Wilson and the photography of the Scottish Highlands', *Landscape Research*, 19 (1994), 68-79; W.Orr, *Deer Forests, Landlords and Crofters*, (Edinburgh, 1982); T.C.Smout, 'Tours in the Scottish Highlands from the eighteenth to the twentieth centuries', *Northern Scotland*, 5, (1983) 99-121; T.C.Smout, 'The Highlands and the Roots of Green Consciousness, 1750-1900', *Proceedings of the British Academy*, 76 (1990), 237-263; R.W.Butler, 'The Tourist Industry in the Highlands and Islands of Scotland', unpublished PhD thesis, University of Glasgow, 1973, 72;

J.M.MacKenzie, *The Empire of Nature*, (Manchester, 1988) 7-53, esp 19-20; S.Schama, *Landscape and Memory*, (London, 1995), 466-67.

[13] R.D.Clyde, *From Rebel to Hero: The Image of the Highlander, 1745-1830*, (East Linton, 1995); P.Womack, *Improvement and Romance: Constructing the Myth of the Highlands*, (London, 1989); M.Chapman, *The Gaelic Vision in Scottish Culture*, (London, 1978); C.W.J.Withers, 'The Historical Creation of the Scottish Highlands', in I.Donnachie & C.Whatley (eds), *The Manufacture of Scottish History*, (Edinburgh, 1992) 143-156; L.Colley, *Britons: Forging the nation, 1707-1837*, (Yale, 1992), 119-20; H.Trevor-Roper, 'The Invention of Tradition: The Highland Tradition of Scotland', in E.Hobsbawm & T.Ranger, (eds), *The Invention of Tradition*, (Cambridge, 1983), 15-42.

[14] Colonel David Stewart of Garth, *Sketches of the Character, Manners, and Present State of the Highlanders of Scotland; with details of the Military Service of the Highland Regiments*, (Edinburgh, 1822); Clyde, *From Rebel to Hero*, 151-2, 174-5; J. Hunter, *The Making of the Crofting Community*, (Edinburgh, 1976), 96.

[15] A. I. Macinnes, 'Landownership, Land Use and Elite Enterprise in Scottish Gaeldom: from Clanship to Clearance in Argyllshire, 1688-1858', in T. M. Devine, (ed), *Scottish Elites*, (Edinburgh, 1994), 1; A. I. Macinnes, 'Scottish Gaeldom: The First Phase of Clearance', in T. M. Devine & R. Mitchison, (eds), *People and Society in Scotland*, Vol.I, 1760-1830, (Edinburgh, 1988), 70.

[16] A.Mackillop, 'Military Recruiting in the Scottish Highlands, 1739-1815: its social, economic and political context', (unpublished PhD thesis, University of Glasgow, 1995).

[17] Hunter, *Crofting Community*; *Crofters Holdings (Scotland) Act*, 1886.

[18] The phrase is Professor Devine's; see Devine, *Great Highland Famine*, chapter 1.

[19] R.Somers, *Letters from the Highlands*, (London 1848), T. Mulock, *The Western Highlands and Islands Socially Considered*, (Edinburgh, 1850), D.Ross, *The Scottish Highlanders*, (Glasgow, 1852). Note that attention has recently been drawn to the Military Register which campaigned against Patrick Sellar, but it is an early and isolated example of such polemical journalism; see E.Richards, 'The Military Register and the Pursuit of Patrick Sellar', *Scottish Economic and Social History*, 16 (1996) 38-59.

[20] A useful case study of the Union of 1900 in Lewis has been provided by D.B.A.Ansdell, 'The Disruptive Union, 1890-1900, in a Hebridean Presbytery', *Records of the Scottish Church History Society* [*RSCHS*], XXVI (1996), 55-103.

[21] J. Hunter, 'The Emergence of the Crofting Community: The Religious Contribution, 1789-1843', *Scottish Studies*, 18 (1974), 99-100.

[22] Hunter, *Crofting Community*, 104.

[23] R. MacLeod, 'The Progress of Evangelicalism in the Western Isles, 1800-1850' (unpublished PhD thesis, University of Edinburgh, 1977), 190-210; D. B. A. Ansdell, 'The 1843 Disruption of the Church of Scotland in the Isle of Lewis', *RSCHS*, 24, (1990-92), 181-197.

[24] J. M'Cosh, *The Wheat and the Chaff Gathered Into Bundles: A Statistical Contribution towards the History of the Recent Disruption*, (Perth, 1843), 56-60, 93, 97, 99-100, 103.; W.Ewing (ed), *Annals of the Free Church of Scotland* [*Ann FC*], (2 Vols, Edinburgh, 1914), ii, 108-123, 131-132, 199-200, 208-238; H.Scott (ed) *Fasti Ecclessiae Scoticanae[FES]*, (new edition, 8 Vols, Edinburgh, 1928), iv, 1-150, vi, 351-373, 430-83, vii, 1-209; MacLeod, 'Progress of Evangelicalism', 233-294.

[25] R.C. Macleod, 'The Bishop of Skye': the Rev Roderick Macleod', *Transactions of the Gaelic Society of Inverness* [*TGSI*], 53, (1982-84) 174-209; A.Beith, *A Highland Tour: Three Weeks with Dr Candlish*, (Edinburgh, 1874), 115-19.

[26] Scott (ed), *FES*, vii, 185-198; Ewing (ed), *Ann FC*, ii, 235; F.P. Morrison, 'The Protestant Churches in North Uist and the Catholic Church in South Uist, 1830-1860',(unpublished MA dissertation, Univesity of St Andrews, 1993).

[27] Scott (ed) *FES*, vii, 101-112; Ewing, *Ann FC*, ii, 222-23; J.Macinnes, *The Evangelical Movement in the Highlands of Scotland, 1688-1800*, (Aberdeen, 1951), 211-22; J.Macinnes, 'The Origin and Early Development of the 'Men'', *RSCHS*, 8, (1942-1944), 16-41.

[28] Beith, *A Highland Tour*, 181.

[29] *The Witness*, 3 Jun 1843, 19 Aug 1843, 6 Sept 1843, 9 Sept 1843, 23 Sept 1843, 30 Sept 1843, 7 Oct 1843, 27 Nov 1843; the Duke of Sutherland was said to have begun to view the Free Church more positively after attending a service in Lairg in 1845, see, Ewing (ed), *Ann FC*, ii, 222.

[30] *3rd Report from the Select Committee on Sites for Churches (Scotland)*, *Parliamentary Papers* [*PP*],1847, XIII, iii; Evidence of Sheriff Graham Speirs, Qs 91-99; L. A. Ritchie, 'The Floating Church of Loch Sunart, *RSCHS*, 22, (1984-86), 159-73.

[31] Hunter, 'Emergence of Crofting Community', 110-11; A.I.Macinnes, 'Evangelical Protestantism in the nineteenth century Highlands' in G.Walker & T.Gallagher, (eds), *Sermons and Battle Hymns: Protestant Popular Culture in Modern Scotland*, (Edinburgh, 1990), 55-58.

[32] National Library of Scotland [NLS], Dep 313/858, Sutherland Collection, H. M. K. MacKenzie to W. Findlater, 1 Jul 1844; W. Findlater to Duke of Sutherland, 17 Jun 1844.

[33] The Free Church was viewed with great suspicion in its early years, one Tory periodical wrote of its 'appalling spirit of Jacobinism'; 'Secession from the Church of Scotland', *Blackwoods Magazine*, 55 (1844), 240; 'Answer of Lochiel to the Petition of his Tenants for a Site on which to build a 'Free Presbyterian Church'', *The Witness*, 3 Jun 1843; Duke of Sutherland to Rt Hon Fox Maule, 6 Jun 1843, *The Witness*, 19 Aug 1843.

[34] D.W.Bebbington, 'Religion and National Feeling in nineteenth Century Scotland and Wales', in S.Mews (ed), *Religion and National Identity: Studies in Church History*, 18 (1982), 498

[35] Beith, *A Highland Tour*, 27, 34-5; Ewing (ed), *Ann FC*, ii, 118, 119, 131, 132, 236; SRO, Breadalbane Muniments GD 112/51/237/13, Proposals for a Free Church College in Oban, August 1847.

[36] Devine, *Great Highland Famine*, 39; Second Statement of the Destitution Committee of the Free Church, 28 Jan 1847, 3-4, 19.

[37] D.C.Smith, *Passive Obediance and Prophetic Protest: Social Criticism in the Scottish Church, 1830-1945*, (New York, 1987), 313-325.

[38] J.L.MacLeod, 'The Origins of the Free Presbyterian Church of Scotland', (unpublished PhD thesis, University of Edinburgh, 1993), 168-254; J. L. MacLeod, 'The Influence of the Highland-Lowland Divide on the Free Presbyterian Disruption of 1893', *RSCHS*, 25, (1993-1995), 400-425; P. Carnegie Simpson, *The Life of Principal Rainy*, 2 Volumes, (London, 1909), i, 429-469.

[39] Local studies which point out the possibilities are A. B. Mearns, 'The Minister and the Bailiff: A Study of the Presbyterian Clergy in the Northern Highlands During the Clearances', *RSCHS*, 24, (1990-92), 53-75; D. M. M. Paton, Brought to a wilderness: the Rev David MacKenzie of Farr and the Sutherland Clearances', *Northern Scotland*, 13, (1993), 75-102; E.M.MacArthur, *Iona: The Living Memory of a Crofting Community, 1750-1914*, 186-190.

[40] Ewing (ed) *Ann FC*, ii, 213; D.E. Meek, 'The Highlands' in D.W.Bebbington, (ed), *The Baptists in Scotland: A History*, (Glasgow, 1988), 280-308; D.E. Meek, 'The Independent and Baptist Churches of Highland Perthshire and Strathspey', *TGSI*, 56 (1988-90), 269-343; D.E.Meek, 'Baptists and Highland Culture', *Baptist Quarterly*, 33 (1989-90), 155-73; D.E.Meek, 'Evangelical Missionaries in the Early nineteenth Century Highlands', *Scottish Studies*, 28 (1987), 1-34; D.E.Meek, 'Dugald Sinclair: The Life and Work of a Highland Itinerant Missionary', *Scottish Studies*, 30 (1991), 59-91.

[41] D. J. Withrington, 'The S.P.C.K. and Highland Schools in the Mid-Eighteenth Century', *SHR*, 41 (1962), 89-99, was an early attempt to correct this impression.

[42] D. J. Withrington, 'Schooling Literacy and Society' in T.M.Devine & R. Mitchison (eds) *People and Society in Scotland*, Vol. I, 1760-1830, 164-171.

[43] *New Statistical Account*, xiv, Inverness, 50, 62, 77, 114-15 126, 142-3, 180, 196-7, 215-7, 233-4, 218-2, 295, 298-9, 503-4, Ross and Cromarty, 87, 113, 149, 168, 179; xv, Sutherland, 78, 102, 182.

[44] 'Report on the State of Education in the Hebrides', *PP* 1867, XXV.

[45] R. D. Anderson, *Education and the Scottish People, 1750-1918*, (Oxford, 1995), 10-11.

[46] Durkacz, *Decline of the Celtic Languages*, 161.

[47] *ibid.*, 162-4.

[48] Withers, *Gaelic in Scotland*, 135, 146.

[49] C.W.J.Withers, 'Highland Migration to Dundee, Perth and Stirling, 1753-1891', *Journal of Historical Geography*, 11, (1985), 16-27; C.W.J.Withers, 'Highland Migration to Aberdeen, 1649-1891', *Northern Scotland*, 9, (1989), 21-44; C.W.J.Withers, *Highland Communities in Dundee and Perth*, (Dundee, 1986);

R.D.Lobban, 'The Migration of Highlanders into Lowland Scotland (c1750-1890) With Particular Reference to Greenock', unpublished PhD thesis, University of Edinburgh, 2 Volumes, 1970, i, 88-104.

[50] T.M.Devine, 'Highland Migration to Lowland Scotland, 1760-1860, *SHR*, 62, (1983) 137-149; T.M.Devine, 'Temporary Migration and the Scottish Highlands in the Nineteenth Century', *Economic History Review*, 32, (1979), 344-59.

[51] Devine, *Great Highland Famine*, 117-9, 127-8; G.Morton, 'Unionist-Nationalism: The Historical Construction of Scottish National Identity, Edinburgh 1830-1860', unpublished PhD thesis, University of Edinburgh, 1993, 160-2.

[52] *First and Second Reports from the Select Committee on Emigration, Scotland, PP* 1841, VI, 115, Evidence of Rev Norman MacLeod, St Columba's Gaelic Church, Glasgow.

[53] W.Sloan, 'Religious Affiliation and the Immigrant Experience: Catholic Irish and Protestant Highlanders in Glasgow, 1830-1850', in T.M.Devine (ed), *Irish Immigrants and Scottish Society in the Nineteenth and Twentieth Centuries,* (Edinburgh, 1991), 67-90; W.Sloan, 'Employment Opportunities and Migrant Group Assimilation: the Highlanders and Irish in Glasgow, 1840-1860', in A.J.G.Cummings & T.M.Devine, (eds), *Industry, Business and Society in Scotland since 1700*, (Edinburgh, 1993), 197-21; Lobban, 'The Migration of Highlanders into Lowland Scotland ', i, 124-139, 161-175; R.D.Lobban, 'The Irish Community in Greenock in the Nineteenth Century', *Irish Geography*, 6 (1969-73), 270-281.

[54] K.D.MacDonald, 'Glasgow and Gaelic Writing', *TGSI*, 57 (1990-92), 395-428.

[55] C.W.J.Withers, 'Class, culture and migrant identity: Gaelic Highlanders in urban Scotland', in G.Kearns & C.W.J.Withers, (eds), *Urbanising Britain: Essays on class and community in the nineteenth Century*, (Cambridge, 1991), 55-79.

[56] D.MacAulay, 'Canons, myths and cannon fodder', *Scotlands*, 1, (1994), 41-2.

[57] MacPhail, *Crofters' Wars*, (Sornoway, 1989) 9-10.

[58] H.D. Maclennan, *Shinty!* (Nairn, 1993), 336.

[59] Hunter, *Crofting Community*, 107; Devine, *Great Highland Famine*, 273-96.

[60] E. Richards, *A History of the Highland Clearances*, (2 vols, London, 1982-85), i, 75-6; ii, 487; MacPhail, *Crofters' War*, 21; Hunter. *Crofting Community*, 129.

[61] Comments on the importance of *The Witness* from a range of perspectives can be found readily; see, J. C. Williams, 'Edinburgh Politics, 1832-1852', unpublished PhD thesis, University of Edinburgh, 1972, 316-18, 327; G. Rosie, (ed), *Hugh Miller, Outrage and Order: A Biography and Selected Writings*, 59; P. Bayne, *The Life and Letters of Hugh Miller*, (2 Volumes, New York 1871), ii, 163-303; R. M. W. Cowan, *The Newspaper in Scotland; A Study of its First Expansion, 1815-60*, (Glasgow, 1946), 236-53, 261, 366.

[62] M.Shortland (ed), *Hugh Miller's Memoir: From Stonemason to Geologist*, (Edinburgh, 1995), 44-54, 181-3.

[63] *The Witness*, 22 Mar 1851, 30 Apr 1851, 26 Jul 1851; C. Kidd, 'Teutonist Ethnology and Scottish Nationalist Inhibition, 1780-1880', *SHR*, 74, (1995), 63;

Smith, *Passive Obedience and Prophetic Protest*, 315; Devine, *Great Highland Famine*, 176, 249.

[64] J.Noble, *Miscellanea Invernessiana: with a bibliography of Inverness newspapers and periodicals*, (Stirling, 1902), 198-200.

[65] J. Hunter, (ed), *For the People Cause: From the Writings of John Murdoch, Highland and Irish Land Reformer*, (Edinburgh, 1986) 5-40; D.E.Meek, `The Land Question Answered from the Bible', *Scottish Geographical Magazine*, 103, (1987), 84-9; MacPhail, *Crofters' War*, 11-12.

[66] *Highlander*, 24 May 1873, 26 Jul 1873, 23 Aug 1873, 31 Jan 1874, 7 Feb 1874.

[67] *ibid.*, 12 Jul 1873, 24 Jan 1874, 29 May 1875, 3 Jul 1875, 20 Nov 1875, 8 Jan 1876, 15 Jan 1876, 25 Mar 1876, 29 Jul 1876, 4 Aug 1877, 23 Feb 1878, 18 Apr 1879, 9 May 1879, 9 Feb 1880, 28 May 1880.

[68] *ibid.*, 16 May 1873, 9 May 1874, 15 May 1875, 25 Mar 1876, 10 Mar 1877, 24 Mar 1877, 8 Oct 1877, 12 Jan 1878, 23 Mar 1878, 3 Aug 1878, 16 Nov 1878, 14 Feb 1879, 28 May 1880.

[69] *ibid.,*, 14 Jun 1873, 2 Aug 1873, 27 Sept 1873, 4 Oct 1873, 8 Nov 1873, 26 Nov 1874, 14 Aug 1875, 4 Mar 1876, 1 Apr 1876, 6 May 1876, 13 May 1876, 27 Jan 1877, 2 Jun 1877, 30 Jun 1877, 29 Sept 1877, 15 Dec 1877, 5 Jan 1878, 23 Mar 1878, 1 Aug 1879, 14 Nov 1879, 29 Dec 1880, 22 Sept 1880, 9 Mar 1881, 23 Mar 1881.

[70] *ibid.*, 9 Aug 1873, 23 May 1874, 4 Sept 1875.

[71] *ibid.*, 16 May 1873, 11 Oct 1873, 25 Oct 1873, 4 Apr 1874, 27 May 1876, 23 Jun 1877, 6 Apr 1878, 16 Jan 1880, 30 Mar 1881, 13 Apr 1881.

[72] SRO, MacKintosh Muniments, GD 176/2393/3, L.Davidson, to the MacKintosh, 5 Feb 1880.

[73] *Highlander*, 31 Jan 1874; *Inverness Advertiser*, 27 Jan 1874; the Whiggish *Inverness Courier*, on the other hand deplored Fraser MacKintosh's candidature as divisive of the Liberal interest, *Inverness Courier*, 12 Feb 1874.

[74] K.MacDonald, `Life of the Author' in C. Fraser MacKintosh, *Antiquarian Notes*, (2nd edition, Stirling, 1913), xiii-xxxi.

[75] M. K. MacLeod, `The Interaction of Scottish Educational Developments and Socio Economic Factors on Gaelic Education in Gaelic Speaking areas, With Particular Reference to the Period 1872-1918', unpublished PhD thesis, University of Edinburgh, 1981, 170, 181-93, 310-42; Anderson, *Education and the Scottish People*, 215-17.

[76] For general treatments of this episode see A. M. Stoddart, *John Stuart Blackie*, (2 vols, Edinburgh, 1895) ii, 112, 115, 120, 138, 148, 168, 212-217; W. Gillies, `A Century of Gaelic Scholarship' in Gillies (ed) *Gaelic and Scotland*, 4-14.

[77] J.MacKechnie, `John Francis Campbell (Iain Og Ile) and his place in the literary History of the Highlands' in *The Dewar MSS* Volume 1, (Glasgow, 1964), 52-4; *Highlander*, 18 Jun 1880, 30 Jun 1880; for a downbeat assessment of MacKinnon, see; J.MacInnes, `Gaelic Poetry in the Nineteenth Century', in D.Gifford (ed), *The History of Scottish Literature, Volume 3, Nineteenth Century*, (Aberdeen, 1988),

393; however, as early as 1876 Alexander Mackenzie predicted MacKinnon's appointment, *Celtic Magazine*, No XXIII, Vol II, September 1877, 444.

[78] The phrase is Professor Gillies's; Gillies, `A Century of Gaelic Scholarship', 11; see also, NLS, Blackie MSS, MS 2653, f 59, Sheriff Shaw, Lochmaddy to Blackie, 25 Sept 1875; SRO, MacKintosh Muniments, GD 176/2280/11, Chair of Celtic Languages and Literature in the University of Edinburgh: Statement on behalf of the Committee of the General Council.

[79] NLS, MS 2653 contains letters from many of those who contributed to the fund.

[80] *Highlander*, 12 June 1875; 10 July 1875; 2 Oct. 1875; 20 Jan. 1877, 17 Aug. 1878; 18 April 1879; 5 Dec. 1879.

[81] Edinburgh University Library, MacKinnon Collection, B.11, `The Need for a History of the Highland People', 24 Feb 1910; B.14 `The Claim of Celtic Studies upon the Lowland Scot' Address to the Graduates, 4 Jul 1913.

[82] S. MacLean, `The Poetry of the Clearances', *TGSI*, 38, (1937-41), 295.

[83] D.Thomson, *An Introduction to Gaelic Poetry*, (2nd edition, Edinburgh, 1989), 233.

[84] MacDonald, `Glasgow and Gaelic Writing', 402-3.

[85] Thomson, *Gaelic Poetry*, 239.

[86] H. Cheape, `A Song on the Lowland Shepherds: Popular Reaction to the Highland Clearances', *Scottish Economic and Social History*, 15, (1995), 85-100.

[87] D.E.Meek, (ed), *Tuath is Tighearna: Tenants and Landlords*, (Scottish Gaelic Texts Society, vol. 18, Edinburgh, 1995).

[88] R.M.Dorson, *The British Folklorists: A Study*, (London, 1918), 392-403; D.Doris, `Contexts of Ambivalence: The Folklorist Activities of nineteenth Century Scottish Highland Ministers', *Folklore*, 103, (1992), 207-21.

[89] J.F.Campbell, *Popular Tales of the West Highlands Orally Collected*, (Islay Association edition, Paisley, 1890), Introduction, ii - iii; Campbell's collection was dedicated to the Marquis of Lorne; MacKechnie, `John Francis Campbell' in *Dewar MSS* Volume 1, 35

[90] *Highlander*, 24 Aug 1878.

[91] For brief details on Carmichael see, *Companion to Gaelic Scotland*, (Oxford, 1983) 35; *Dictionary of Scottish Church History and Theology*, (Edinburgh, 1993), 138-9; for a fuller debate see, H.Robertson, `Studies in Carmichael's *Carmina Gadelica*', *Scottish Gaelic Studies*, 17 (1976), 220-265; J.L.Campbell, `Notes on Hamish Robertson's `Studies in *Carmina Gadelica*'', *Scottish Gaelic Studies*, 18 (1978) 1-17.

[92] A.Carmichael, *Carmina Gadelica: Hymns and Incantations with Illustrative Notes on Words, Rites, and Customs, Dying and Obselete: Orally collected in the Highlands and Islands of Scotland and Translated into English* (2 Vols, Edinburgh, 1900), Introduction, i, xxi.

[93] J.L. Campbell, `Notes on Hamish Robertson's "Studies in Carmichael's *Carmina Gadelica*"', 1.

[94] D.Gregory, *History of the Western Highlands and Isles to 1625*, (Edinburgh, 1836).

[95] W.F.Skene, *The Highlanders of Scotland, Their Origin, History, and Antiquities*, (London, 1837); W.F.Skene, *Celtic Scotland: A History of Ancient Alban*, (3 Vols, Edinburgh, 1876-1880).

[96] A.MacKenzie, *History of the Highland Clearances Containing a Reprint of Donald MacLeod's 'Gloomy Memories of the Highlands'; Isle of Skye in 1882; and a Verbatim Report of the Trial of the Braes Crofters*, (Inverness, 1882).

[97] This may have been an extra factor in the increasing unpopularity of Skene's views in the 1890s and early 1900s, although his Pictish enthusiasms did not endear him to Gaelic scholars, see, A. MacBain, `Mr Skene versus Dr Skene', *TGSI*, 21 (1896-97), 191, 213-4. I am grateful to Mr W. D. H. Sellar for drawing this article to my attention; see also, Devine, *Great Highland Famine*, 127-8.

[98] C.Dewey, `Celtic Agrarian Legislation and the Celtic Revival: historicist implications of Gladstone's Irish and Scottish Land Acts', *Past and Present*, No 64, (1974), 30-70.

[99] J. Murdoch, `The Clan System', *TGSI*, 1 (1871-72), 84-5; C. Chisolm, `The Clearance of the Highland Glens', *TGSI*, 6, (1876-77), 88; J. MacDonald, `The Social Condition of the Highlands', *TGSI*, 10, (1881-83), 239-245, esp 243; *The Highlander*, 27 Sept 1873, 26 Sept 1874, 4 Mar 1876, 2 Jun 1877, 14 Nov 1879.

[100] E.Richards and Monica Clough, *Cromartie: Highland Life 1650-1914*, (Aberdeen, 1989), Chapter 22, `The Shock of the Crofters' Revolt', brings out this aspect particularly clearly; *Inverness Advertiser*, 11 Dec 1885; *Scotsman*, 14 Jul 1886.

[101] K.Fenyo, `How the Scottish press waged war on the Highland poor', *West Highland Free Press*, 11 Nov 1994.

[102] E.Richards, `How Tame were the Highlanders during the Clearances', *Scottish Studies*, 17, (1973), 46; see also E.Richards, `Patterns of Highland Discontent, 1790-1860', in R.Quinalt & J.Stevenson, (eds), *Popular Protest and Public Order: Six Studies in British History, 1790-1820*, (London, 1974) 75-114; E.Richards, `Problems on the Cromartie Estate, 1851-3', *SHR*, 52, (1973), 149-164.

[103] Public Record Office, CAB 37/14/173-4, W.E. Gladstone to W.H Harcourt, 19 Jan 1885; /170, Harcourt to Gladstone, 17 Jan 1885.

[104] This period is one on which more work is urgently required, an exacting model for Scottish historians to follow has been provided by W.E.Vaughan, *Landlords and Tenants in Mid-Victorian Ireland*, (Oxford, 1994)

CHAPTER ELEVEN

Where is the Lass o' Pairts?: Gender, Identity and Education in Nineteenth Century Scotland

Helen Corr

For many Scots, the supposed egalitarian and democratic tradition of Scottish education is a source of great pride. Conventional wisdom holds that the lad o'pairts had equality of access to an educational ladder from the parish or burgh school to a Scottish university and all that was necessary for the young, ambitious, working-class Scot was talent and intellect. The pantheon of Scottish heroes is replete with well educated men from humble backgrounds.[1] Not only was the Scottish education system meritoratic, it was superior in quality to many others, most especially the English. Scotland had five universities when England had two, it had a national system of education which in theory stretched back to the Reformation, there were high rates of literacy and the curriculum offered a broad range of subjects which eschewed the narrow specialisation to be found in England.[2] For many, the Scottish educational tradition reflects the finest qualities of Scottish national identity and this rather cosy consensus has been one of the most enduring of all Scotland's myths. Yet, such notions are all bound up with men. The exclusion of the 'lass o' pairts' in the glowing testaments to the egalitarian and democratic tradition of Scottish education suggests a deep gender bias in Scottish society which militates against many of its lofty claims. If women were not part of the 'democratic intellect', then what was their role in Scottish education, and what light does this shed on gender relations in Scottish society?[3]

Much work has been done which shatters the cosy vision of Scottish education as egalitarian and democratic by highlighting the importance of social class as the key determinant of educational provision. This essay will contribute further to this debate by focusing on gender inequality. As will be argued below, the Scottish structure of education was more patriarchal and rigid in its treatment of women teachers as an occupational group, both in relation to English women teachers and men teachers in Scotland. Scottish women were even more oppressed than their English colleagues in terms of pay, promotion and professional status. Women in England had greater opportunity for promotion in single sex schools and many became heads of departments in elementary schools. Scottish male teachers, on the other hand, did better than their English counter-parts. Scottish schoolmasters held a superior position in the profession in terms of pay, social status and higher intellectual prestige. The strong connection with Presbyterianism influenced gender relations which according to one critic 'stamped women as second class citizens'.[4]

Before the demise of the parish school system in 1872, the Scottish educational tradition was highly patriarchal. Dominies, derived from the Latin for lord or master, numerically dominated the school teaching profession, in contrast to England where women were increasingly becoming a larger part of the workforce. In Scotland, however, there was a great deal of prejudice among the Presbyterian clergy and heritors towards women teachers. Prior to 1872, women teachers mainly found employment outside the mainstream sector in female industrial schools, charity schools, Society for the Propagation of Christian Knowledge schools and 'dame' schools. The 1872 Act made schooling compulsory for every Scottish child, unlike England, and by 1911, women comprised over seventy per cent of elementary school teachers. The expansion of education in Scotland in this period was made possible through cheap female labour. Also, the 1872 Act marked the end of control by the Presbyterian churches as power shifted to the Scotch Education department [SED].[5]

Under the Act, locally elected school boards were created and they were responsible for the employment of teachers. These were the first local government boards to admit women on equal voting terms as men. It was the period which witnessed a fundamental transformation in the gender composition of the elementary teaching force. By 1881, women made up 8,000 of the 13,000 workforce. Economic necessity was the principal determinant in the feminisation of the teaching workforce. As will be seen below, women were paid less, willing and in plentiful supply. Following the 1872 Act, gender inequalities became more formalised and institutionalised as an integral part of state educational policy than at any time previously. Two distinct pay scales were constructed which maintained women's pay at just under half that for men. Average salaries for certificated male teachers in Scotland were considerably higher than their English colleagues which reflected their higher economic and professional standing north of the border.[6] Yet, this raises a recurring theme concerning the paradoxes inherent in the Scottish education system There was a tension between the twin drives towards meritocracy and elitism. The first was rooted in the social conformity and deep conservatism, so characteristic of Scottish religious and educational institutions; the second was manifested in the search for male advancement and reward in the ability to rise up the social hierarchy.

After the 1872 Act there was a reaffirmation of the elitist tendency within Scottish education as the middle-class reorganised their own separate system which meant a growing number of academies, high schools and 'public' schools. These arose in response to the demand of an expanding anglicized middle-class which wished to save on the expense of sending their children to such schools south of the border.[7]   One traditional method of social advancement, however, was the schoolteaching profession. Yet, by the late nineteenth century, it was widely feared within Presbyterian circles that the influence and prestige of the Dominie was being eroded. This was largely due to the declining number of schoolmasters in an increasingly female profession. One consequence of this, it was believed, would be a decline in the teaching of classics which was a necessary pre-requisite for university education. Scottish schoolmasters were paid higher salaries as a way of defending the professional standing of men and the proud Scottish tradition. From the male perspective of the educationalists who made and influenced policy in the pre-war era, this was further evidence of the superiority of Scottish education. During a period of profound social change, the dominie was maintained as a symbol of Scotland's patriarchal tradition. Indeed, even during the twenties and thirties, policy makers continued to be concerned about the feminisation of the teaching occupation and the recruitment of male teachers.[8]

It was established that teaching should not only be more attractive to men of the right calibre, but that career and salary prospects should also be enhanced. Whereas the scholarship of the Scottish schoolmaster was celebrated and romanticised, the contribution of women teachers was marginalised and denigrated relative to both Scottish men and English women. English women teachers maintained higher salaries and professional status than their Scottish counterparts.[9] This was in spite of the fact that by the outbreak of the First World War Scottish women teachers were more highly qualified that their English colleagues.[10]   Oral evidence indicates that individual Scottish women teachers were both aware and participated in the legacy of the superiority of the Scottish system. According to one women teacher: 'my sister and I gained from being brought in Scotland because if we had been brought in England without the tradition of helping the academic which was part of the Scottish academic tradition, then we would not have gone to university and our lives would have been very different'. Another attributed her success to her women teachers and her mother: 'We were all driven as far as we could go and it was decided that I should go to Hutchesons'. [11]

Scottish women who went to England were rewarded with better employment and promotional opportunities in schools because of their university education. according to one Scottish headmistress in 1884: 'Scotchwomen who have gone through university training are compelled to look almost entirely to England for a worthy professional career'.[12] Another university graduate, Margaret Rose, found that having a degree could be a disadvantage. Signing on at an employment agency, she was told : 'Keep quiet about having a degree. Don't mention the word. Because in England, not everyone has degrees and they think that it is something superior and you will want a superior job. Take whatever you can get.'[13] Middle-class women with a university education participated in the belief of a superior Scottish educational tradition which in turn ensured the social reproduction of myths of meritocracy.[14] In practice however, in the nineteenth century, women teachers had greater occupational upward mobility under the single sex schooling system in England than in the Scottish co-educational system. A very significant difference was that in England, male policy makers actually encouraged a separate career path for women towards achieving educational mobility and promotional opportunities in the single sex schooling system.

Educational policy in England assumed that boys and girls education should be different and regulations clearly stipulated that the principal of a women's college should be a women. Furthermore, the Board of Education was, to some extent, able to pursue a policy of positive discrimination by stipulating that 'the staff of a college at which some of the students are women must include a reasonable proportion of women, and in the case of colleges attended mainly by women students, at least half of the permanent staff other than the principal must be women'.[15] Statistics for the year 1907-8 show that there was a total of 18,086 women headteachers and 13,865 male heads in England. Overall, educational policies facilitated more promotional opportunities and better wages for qualified women teachers in England, whereas in Scotland, the contribution of women teachers was often denigrated both relative to the dominie and to women teachers in England.

Despite women teachers having a numerical superiority in Scotland, headships continued to be monopolised by men in Scottish elementary schools. Public opinion in Scotland did not object to girls being taught by men, and the prestige of the male graduate ensured the monopoly of headships in secondary schools. For example, when the Merchant Company opened its new girls' school in Edinburgh in 1870, the school along with others, had all male heads and male teachers for all the principal subjects; while women teachers taught the younger girls and performed pastoral rather than academic functions, Also, in Glasgow, Hutchison's Grammar School for Girls and the new Girls' High School had male headmasters.[16]

The oppressive nature of the Scottish structure of education relative to England was acknowledged by individuals who had experience of both the single sex and co-educational system: 'The Association of Headmistresses cut little ice in Scotland. The co-educational schools under headmasters were the rule except in large cities. It was impossible to get a hearing for the interests of girls... the prestige of women teachers is lower in Scotland than England.'[17] Presbyterian culture and the patriarchal structure of Scottish education even appears to have inhibited womens' capacity for political action in the struggle for equal pay and promotional opportunities. Women activists in the Educational Institute for Scotland [EIS] and the National Union of Teachers [NUT] pursued very different strategies on equal pay before 1914. In Scotland, the Ladies Committee, which acted as the mouthpiece for women teachers, publicly opposed equal pay and adopted an anti-feminist stance on issues of equality. In England, the NUT supported equal pay from 1900.[18]

In England and Wales, membership in teachers' associations enhanced women teachers' sense of professional identity. For many, the conjunction of the suffrage movement combined with their existing employment concerns helped them to become politicised as active feminists.[19] In Scotland, this did not happen. The EIS female leadership Committee's unwillingness to support equal pay was bound up with an ideology of professionalisation which was masculine and Presbyterian in character. Women teachers perceived themselves as having lower professional status than men which in turn, became a major inhibiting force against organising an equal pay campaign in the pre 1914 era. Evidence for this can be found in the attitudes of the first female president of the EIS, Elizabeth Fish, who was elected to the post in 1913. fish symbolised the official position of the Ladies Committee on the joint issues of equal pay and professional status of school teachers. In her presidential speech she raised the question of equal pay and acknowledged that it was a source of controversy. She explained that she was against equal pay because male teachers' work had a higher economic and social value:

It would be a disastrous thing for our country were the work of education to fall almost entirely into the hands of women. Men teachers are scarce and their service can naturally command a higher price than that of women which is so abundantly offered. If we women ask that the salaries of all teachers be now raised to the level of what men teachers think theirs ought to be we shall alienate the sympathies of the public.[20]

Fish argued that men had a higher professional status than women and that the feminisation of the teaching profession would have a detrimental effect on Scottish society. This was a clear indication of the low self -esteem and deep seated oppression of women in Scottish society. It also shows how retarded the issue of womens' rights were in the Scottish teaching profession compared to England. Such notions of middle-class respectability surfaced in her attitude towards the use of trade union methods to achieve higher pay. This was denounced because it went against the perception of teaching as a profession: 'If teaching is a profession and not a mere trade, it must not resort to trade union methods in its demand for increased remuneration'.[21] Clearly the Scottish Ladies Committee reflected elitist patriarchal values and it formed part of the ideology which stressed the merits of individualism and meritocracy. The history of the EIS before 1914 was marred by political divisions between the male leadership and the rank and file of men teachers over the different meanings of professionalism and political strategy. The leadership sought to achieve higher professional status for men through social conformity and public approval and as such, women teachers remained second class citizens.[22]

The reason why the EIS reflected such attitudes were bound up with male teachers' insecurity about their occupational structure within the social structure of Scottish society. Compared to the professions of law, medicine and the clergy, teaching was regarded by many as inferior. In 1847, the EIS founder members sought to elevate the social and professional standing of Scottish teachers.[23] Yet, there were tensions between the promotion of the professional ethos, favoured by the leadership, and the rank and file who expected increased professionalisation to bring social and economic rewards. Following the 1872 act, resentment was most pronounced among the male certified assistants since the salary and promotional prospects of this group was severely restricted in terms of upward mobility in the male hierarchy. A male assistant could wait several years for promotion due to the small turnover of male headships in Scotland. This was a causal factor in accounting for the declining numbers of men into elementary schools.[24] Many men viewed the civil service as a haven of security. Likewise, there was much disillusionment among the rank and file of women teachers at the failure of the EIS to promote equal pay for equal work. The main forum for women to express their grievances was in the *Educational News* and *The Class Teacher*. Both journals contained a page devoted to 'women's opinions' and 'women's interests' and individual writers voiced their support for equal pay. According to one writer:

We would urge upon our professional sisters to be no longer graciously pleased to accept £30 or £40 a year less than their male contemporaries for the sole reason that they are women. Some will tell us that we may as well cry for the moon as equal pay, irrespective of sex, but not so very long ago there were those who said the same thing of women attempting to storm the peaceful arena of our universities.[25]

Unlike the female EIS leadership, the NUT Ladies Committee saw their election to the National Executive in the early 1900s as a political strategy for economic and social equality. In 1900, Miss Isabel Cleghorn (who was to become the first female president of the NUT in 1911) proposed the motion '.. that women should be eligible for appointment on the staff of junior and senior clerks in this office (NUT) and at the same wages as men.' This motion was overwhelmingly rejected by the male dominated membership on the committee and one male member described the case as 'erroneous' and claimed 'that there were certain duties which could not possibly be performed by women. And was there any need for this proposition at all'.[26] Equal pay was finally granted to female teachers and civil servants in 1961. Before 1914, the NUT Executive Committee did support strike action on issues of pay whereas the EIS leadership was simply not prepared to organise industrial action to protect the material interests of its members and to professionalise the occupation. It is highly significant that the EIS refused to change its name from the Institute into a 'union' of Scottish teachers and, unlike the NUT, it did not openly promote itself as a political organisation.

In conclusion, it can be argued that senior leading educationalists were the product of a dominant cultural tradition which was conservative and elitist. Women such as Elizabeth Fish closely identified with these dominant middle-class values which were essentially Presbyterian and masculine in character and they adopted them as models for themselves. Similarly, some middle-class women university graduates did benefit under the distinctive Scottish system which in turn ensured the social reproduction of myths and the legend of meritocracy. Furthermore, educationalists helped to sustain this myth in the twentieth century. Interviews with policy makers in the post-war era conveyed the dominant belief that they were heirs to 'an actively democratic system of national education serving a society characterised by among other things, 'pride', 'democratic patriotism' and 'freedom from class consciousness'.[27] The argument presented in this essay is that in structural and material terms, the Scottish education system was more oppressive for women teachers than the English structure in terms of salaries, promotions and professional status. But as we can see today, such myths die hard.

NOTES

[1] The best overview of the Scottish education system is R.D. Anderson, *Education and Society in Scotland, 1750-* (Oxford, 1995).

[2] See G.E. Davie, *The Democratic Intellect: Scotland and her Universities in the Nineteenth Century* (Edinburgh, 1964) for a positive view of Scottish educational achievements and R.D. Anderson, *Education and Opportunity in Victorian Scotland* (Oxford, 1983) which takes a more skeptical stance.

[3] For a recent exploration of gender and education in Scotland see F. Paterson & J. Fewell (eds), *Girls in Their Prime: Scottish Education Revisited* (Edinburgh, 1990).

[4] L. Moore, 'Invisible Scholars: Girls learning Mathematics and Latin in the Elementary Schools Before 1972', *History of Education*, 13:2 (1984), 121-37.

[5] For a fuller account of the feminisation of the teaching profession in Scotland see H. Corr 'The Sexual Division of Labour in the Scottish Teaching Profession' in W. Humes & H. Paterson (eds), *Scottish Culture and Scottish Education, 1800-1980* (Edinburgh, 1983), 137-151.

[6] See H. Corr, 'Dominies and Domination: Schoolteachers , Masculinity and Women in 19th Century Scotland', *History Workshop Journal*, 40 (1995), 155.

[7] Humes and Paterson, *Scottish Culture and Scottish Education*, 197-215.

[8] See Fewell's article in Paterson and Fewell, *Girls in Their Prime*.

[9] See Corr, 'Dominies and Domination', 155.

[10] See H. Corr, 'The Gender Division of Labour in the Scottish Teaching profession 1972-1914', unpublished Ph.D. thesis, University of Edinburgh, 1984.

[11] J. Fewell, 'Teachers in inter-war Scotland', unpublished M.A. thesis, University of Edinburgh, 1986.

[12] S. Hamilton, 'Women Graduates at Scottish Universities', unpublished Ph.D. thesis, University of Edinburgh, 1988.

[13] *ibid.*

[14] R. Houston, *Scottish Literacy and Scottish Identity*, (Cambridge, 1985).

[15] *Parliamentary Papers*, Report of Commissioners, 1914, vol. XXV, 36.

[16] Anderson, *Education and Opportunity*.

[17] I owe this information to Alison Oram.

[18] See H. Corr, 'Politics of the Sexes in English and Scottish Teachers' Unions', in H. Corr & L. Jamieson (eds), *The Politics of Everyday Life: Continuity and Change in Work and the Family* (London, 1990).

[19] A. Oram, 'Sex Antagonism in the Teaching Profession', unpublished M.Sc. thesis, University of Bristol, 1984.

[20] *Educational News*, 9 Jan. 1914, 29-30.

[21] *ibid.*

[22] A.J. Belford, *Centenary Handbook of the EIS*, (Edinburgh, 1946).

[23] *ibid.*, 67-8.

[24] For example, see *Educational News*, 10 July 1914, 669-70.

[25] *ibid.,* Feb. 1904, 44.

[26] This issue is dealt with in H.Corr's article in Corr & Jamieson (eds), *The Politics of Everyday Life*, (London, 1990).

[27] A. McPherson, 'An Angle on the Geist: Persistence and Change in the Scottish Educational Tradition' in Humes and Paterson (eds), *Scottish Culture and Scottish Education*.

INDEX